PRACTICAL ENGLISH

A Complete Course

Paul C. Dalmas and Vicki L. Hackett

 J. Weston Walch, Publisher REPRODUCIBLE BOOK

Acknowledgements

Thank you to my family, whose lives are turned upside down when I am working on a project of this magnitude.

A special thank you to my job-sharing partner, Joyce Welch, for her word processing talent and for her advice.

Vicki Hackett

ISBN 0-8251-1195-1

Copyright © 1987

J. Weston Walch, Publisher

P.O. Box 658 • Portland, Maine 04104-0658

Printed in the United States of America

Contents

This overview of the book and its organization stresses the importance of regular writing to teach the practical skill of writing.

PART ONE
Daily Lessons

This section of the book provides the teacher with daily lesson plans and materials for a course in vocational English.

Students learn the basic steps in the writing process (prewriting, planning, writing, revising, and rewriting) by completing a short paper on personal goals.

Students learn to use clear, direct language and avoid wordiness. Specific revision instructions and exercises are included.

Students master a list of frequently misspelled words and learn rules for plurals, prefixes, suffixes and word division. A study guide for learning spelling words is included, and materials are provided to help students learn words they have misspelled in their writing assignments.

Students become proficient in the use of most common language reference books: the dictionary and thesaurus. Exercises on choosing synonyms, using guide words, and determining syllabication are given.

Students become acquainted with a variety of forms: job applications, government employment forms, insurance claims, and more.

PART TWO
Skill Development

This section of the book provides materials for ongoing skill building, (enlarging vocabulary and correcting sentence, punctuation and usage errors). One or two days a week may be set aside for these activities while the units in Part One occupy the remainder of class time.

TOPIC	WORKSHEET NUMBER AND EXERCISE	
Sentence Fragments:	1A & B	Explanation
	2A & B	Exercise
	3	Editing Exercise
	4A & B	Unit Quiz
Run-ons:	5A & B	Explanation
	6	Exercise
	7	Editing Exercise
	8A & B	Unit Quiz
	9	Cumulative Test

Chapter Twelve: *CORRECTING WORD-USAGE ERRORS*   **201**

Students learn to identify and correct 31 common word-usage errors. Adjective and adverb usage is also discussed. Explanation, exercises, quizzes, and tests are provided.

TOPIC   SHEET NUMBER AND EXERCISE

Chapter Thirteen: *CORRECTING PUNCTUATION ERRORS* **237**

Students learn to identify and correct punctuation errors. Explanations, exercises, quizzes, and work tests are provided.

ANSWER KEY **297**

Introduction

English teachers are a philosophical lot. They love to spend long hours debating what they do and why they do it. While the department meetings of teachers in other disciplines tend to focus on the mundane business of curriculum, scheduling, and textbooks, English teachers are likely to undertake such weighty matters as the humanizing effects of literature and the importance of self-discovery through writing. But English teachers also recognize their responsibility for providing students with some of the most important practical skills they will learn in school. The reading and writing skills we teach will serve our students throughout their working lives.

This book is intended as a source of ideas for teaching these practical skills. It includes daily lesson plans and supplemental materials for a course in vocational English, and it provides a systematic approach to instruction in writing used on the job. Because English is a less clearly defined subject than others, there is a special need for such a book. Teachers in other subjects have a set notion of the limits of their responsibility. Geometry teachers walk into the classroom in September knowing pretty much what theorems and proofs constitute a course in geometry. History teachers limit their courses to a given historical period. Science teachers can rely on textbooks to outline their courses. English teachers are not so fortunate, for usually each must individually design the units of study and daily lessons his or her students need. What to include? What to eliminate? The task is difficult, and it can be overwhelming, especially to someone new to the English classroom. English teachers are faced with a seemingly endless stream of days stretching from September to June and with the need to organize that time as profitably as possible for their students. The goal of this book is to provide structure and content that will simplify a teacher's job while maximizing the students' learning.

SOME ASSUMPTIONS ABOUT STUDENTS

Who enrolls in a vocational English course? The typical student is of average or below-average academic ability and will probably end his or her formal education with the close of the senior year of high school. Vocational training may follow graduation, but students in vocational English classes are often already working while attending school and find their lives centered on a job or extracurricular activities rather than on classroom achievement. They want to see practical value in what they are doing in school and are often unaware of how helpful English skills can be in achieving their career goals. For this reason most of the writing assignments in this book are based on work-related experience. Our goal is to help students see that language skills can be as important to a mechanic or a receptionist as they are to an attorney or businessperson. When students attach importance to what we teach, half of our task is accomplished.

AN APPROACH

There is no way to learn writing other than by writing, so our program requires that students write regularly. Classes may spend weeks correcting errors on usage exercises, but if they are not allowed to put what they have learned into practice in their own writing assignments, their time will have been wasted. Moreover, mastery of the rules of usage and punctuation constitutes only a small part of the skill necessary for composing lucid prose. While there is no shortage of editing exercises in this book, these exercises are pointless unless they are part of a comprehensive writing program. Our program involves students in writing based on their actual work experience or situations similar to those they will encounter on the job. Our expectation is that both the quality of their writing and their appreciation of its value will grow as they write.

In addition, students must not merely be given writing assignments; they must learn that writing is a process. It is too easy for teachers to fall into the pattern of assigning, collecting, and grading written work without ever giving writing instruction. The entire procedure can become mechanical, with students having no sense of how and why people outside school really use writing. Each writing assignment we describe follows a process that begins with thought and proceeds through careful planning, drafting, and revision. Several assignments end with students sharing their work with a real audience. They learn that writing is not something that magically flows out of the end of a pen, but is the result of a series of thoughtful steps toward the goal of communicating ideas to a reader. Writing is hard work, but it is work worthy of the effort expended upon it.

ORGANIZATION

This book is divided into two parts. Part One (Chapters One through Nine) provides lessons and materials for a course in vocational English. Each chapter describes one unit in which students master a particular skill or complete a writing assignment. Detailed daily plans are provided, and at the conclusion of each chapter reproducible worksheets for the unit are included. Part Two of the book (Chapters Ten through Thirteen) provides lessons and materials for language development. These skills (enlarging vocabulary and correcting sentence, punctuation, and usage errors) may be taught as a single unit. We suggest, however, that you set aside one or two days a week for these activities while the units in Part One occupy the remainder of class time. In this way, students will see the mastery of these skills as a yearlong commitment and not learn them for a test on one day and forget them the next.

The simplest method for grading the worksheets in Chapters eleven, twelve, and thirteen is to count the number of errors students make and establish a curve with no errors as the highest grade.

PART I

Daily Lessons

Chapter One

THE WRITING PROCESS

This unit has two goals: To introduce students to the writing process which they will use in one form or another throughout the course, and to encourage them to do some serious thinking about their personal and career goals for the years immediately following graduation.

Life goals, the topic on which the students will write, sets a serious and practical tone, yet involves students in writing that matters to them. They begin by discussing their future, then put unorganized thoughts on paper and shape them into a plan for a rough draft. Two fellow students comment on this draft, revision follows, and the paper is finally shared with other members of the class in its final, polished version. This topic has an additional virtue if it is used early in the year; it helps the members of the class and the teacher to become acquainted. Talking and writing about plans for the future is an excellent way to get to know one another.

Although the finished paper may not be terribly long, the unit lasts about two weeks in order to emphasize each step of the writing process and give students time to think about their personal goals. The process of writing the paper is divided into short steps with separate due dates. Each step should receive credit as it is completed so that students understand that they are responsible for the entire writing process and not just the finished product. The lessons include several opportunities to check student progress, but students should save all their work to turn in for final evaluation at the conclusion of the unit.

LESSON I

Begin the unit by telling the class they will learn the basic writing process they will use throughout the year, but that they won't actually start writing their papers for a couple of days. Instead, they will do some preliminary thinking about the topic. Today the class will discuss their goals for work and for life in general. As they participate in the discussion, students should jot down a list of things they want to accomplish in the next few years. This list will be helpful to them as they start their papers.

Use the questions below as a guide for the class discussion, beginning with the subject of work and progressing toward more personal goals. Let the discussion take its own shape, moving from one topic to another, but try to cover as many of the listed areas as possible. Encourage a relaxed attitude of give and take, and don't be hesitant to share some of your own thoughts with the class when appropriate.

Discussion Questions

1. What kinds of jobs have you had? (Keep the definition of "job" broad enough to include baby-sitting, yard work, and responsibilities around home or school so as many students as possible will be able to participate.)

2. What did you like or dislike about:

    a. the work itself?

    b. the hours?

    c. the working conditions?

    d. the people you worked with?

    e. the boss?

3. How did you feel about the "product" you produced, whether it was goods or services?

4. How did you know when you had done a good job?

5. What satisfaction, other than pay, did you receive?

6.   When was it fun? When was it awful?

7.   What disasters occurred?

8.   Why do you work at all?

9.   What would your ideal job be?

10.   What additional training or schooling is necessary to get that ideal job? How will you support yourself while you get it?

11.   What things are important in life besides having a good job?

12.   What kind of a relationship do you hope to have with your parents in five or ten years?

13.   What kinds of relationships do you hope to have with your current friends?

14.   Do you hope to marry? When? Do you expect that both you and your spouse will work?

15.   Do you hope to have children? When? How will you manage if you and your spouse both work?

16.   How do you expect to spend your nonworking hours? What special interests do you think you will have?

17.   What are your financial goals? Do you have any special purchases you hope to make?

18.   In what kind of place do you imagine yourself living?

If discussion is lively enough, you may want to continue the discussion for a second day. Ask each student to come to class next time with a list of five things to accomplish in the first few years after graduation. Some students will be able to use what they have jotted down during class, and others will have a brief homework assignment. The next class will begin with a check for the completed list.

LESSON II

Check to be sure that each student has completed a list of planned accomplishments, but let the students keep their lists for use later.

Pass out Worksheet 1 (Prewriting), and tell the class that today they will be formalizing their goals to prepare for planning their papers. Go over the instructions at the top of the sheet. Next read the questions on personal goals, and spend a few minutes explaining the questions and suggesting some common answers. Remind the class that they may find some useful ideas on their lists of goals. Allow five or ten minutes for the students to write answers for the personal goals questions. Then ask for volunteers to read aloud what they have written. Continue this method for the second, third, and fourth topics, leading the class through the questions, suggesting answers, and having volunteers read aloud. This method may seem tedious, but the questions are extremely general and difficult. As the class works, circulate around the room and help students who seem stymied.

Students should have finished their questions by the end of the period. Check them for completion, but let them keep the work for use later.

LESSON III

Now that the students have a general idea of what they want to say, it is time to introduce the entire process of writing the papers and to start planning the rough drafts. Pass out Worksheet 2 (Assignment), and go over it with the class. Explain again that the process they are using (thinking, planning, writing, revising, rewriting, proofreading, reflecting, and sharing) is the one they will follow throughout the course and the one that any careful writer follows. Provide the dates the planning, rough, and final drafts will be due.

The planning of the paper makes use of the list and worksheet the students have completed and results in a simple outline of the paper. Put the following instructions on the board and go over them with the class:

1.   Using the list of accomplishments and Worksheet 1, decide on three or four major goals. Each of these goals will become a major part of your paper.

2.   Order the goals from most important to least important. This is the order in which you will discuss your goals in your rough draft.

3. Write the goals as complete sentences on a sheet of paper, skipping five or six lines between each goal.

4. On the lines between each goal, jot down the ideas you will use to explain them. You could include:

    a. the reasons your goals are so important to you.

    b. things that have happened to you to make you choose your goals.

    c. people who have influenced you in choosing your goals.

    d. difficulties you will have to overcome to achieve your goals.

Having completed this work, each student will have what amounts to an outline of the body of the paper.

HOMEWORK:

Tonight each student should to write an opening for the paper that states in general terms what his or her goals are. The opening should also make use of detail and description to capture the reader's attention. Both completed plans and opening paragraphs will be checked for completion at the start of the next class.

LESSON IV

Check to be sure students have completed their plans and opening paragraphs.

The primary activity today is for students to hear reactions to their openings and to compare them with the work of others. Emphasize that this is an excellent opportunity to gather ideas for improving the papers. Each student in turn reads the first few sentences of the paper aloud. Allow for comments after each reading, and point out either a good quality or something that needs work for each paper. Ask the class which openings are the most interesting and why. Which use detail or description effectively? Which give the best sense of the direction the paper will take?

When the students have all had a chance to read, they may continue writing their rough drafts if time allows. Many will want to rewrite their openings based on what they have heard. Remind the class of the rough draft due date, and tell them that their drafts must be legible despite changes they make along the way.

LESSON V

At this point it may be a good idea to give the class a day to work on their rough drafts in class. Emphasize again the importance of using detail and description, and circulate around the room giving help as needed.

LESSON VI

Rough drafts are due, so begin by checking for completion. The goal today is for students to get suggestions for improving their papers from two other members of the class. At the end of the period each student should have some specific ideas for revising the paper.

Pass out two copies of Worksheet 3 (Rough Draft Workshop) to each student, and ask the class to divide into work groups of three. Go over the worksheet, and explain that each member of each group should read the papers of the other two members and answer the questions on the sheet. Readers should sign the line marked "Evaluator," but it is the responsibility of the paper's writer to see that there are two worksheets completed on the paper before starting the final draft.

At the end of the period, tell the class that they may now begin the final draft. They should keep the suggestions on the worksheets in mind as they write—especially if similar comments were made by both readers—and save the worksheets and rough drafts to turn in with the completed assignment.

LESSON VII

This is probably another good time to give the class a day to work on their papers in class. Remind them of the due date for the final draft and that they should keep all the work they have done on the paper. Give them the period to work, and be available to help.

LESSON VIII

Final drafts are due today, but not before final proofreading and a chance for writers to reflect on what they have written and learned.

Pass out Worksheet 4 (Comment Sheet), and have the class break into groups of three with different members from the rough draft workshop groups. Each writer should have his final draft proofread by the two other members of his group. The first reader should check for errors in punctuation and spelling. The second should concentrate solely on spelling, reading the paper backwards from the last word to the first, so that each word is checked individually. Each reader signs the Comment Sheet in the appropriate place. The point of this formal proofreading procedure is to place the responsibility for correcting language errors on the student, so that the teacher can concentrate on reading for more important composition matters. Most teachers know how many supposed errors result from simple carelessness.

When proofreading is finished, the writer answers the questions under Writer's Comments. This gives students a chance to think over what they have done and learned. It also gives the teacher insights which can be a point of departure for the general comments made at the bottom of the sheet when grading the paper.

Students turn in their work at the end of the period. They should include:

1.   the final draft

2.   the Comment Sheet

3.   the rough draft

4.   the two Rough Draft Workshop Sheets

5.   the Prewriting Worksheet

6.   the list of goals

7.   a blank sheet of paper to be used later for reader comments

LESSON IX

As a final activity for this unit, students have an opportunity to share their finished papers. As students arrive, the desks should, if possible, be arranged in a single large circle. Pass out the papers, write the following directions on the board, and go over them:

1.   Quietly and carefully read the paper you have been given.

2.   Write a note to the paper's writer on the blank page. Here are some things you might include:

    a.   What did you like best about the paper?

    b.   What did you learn from reading the paper?

    c.   What kind of person does the writer sound like?

    d.   What questions do you have of the writer after reading the paper?

    e.   What about the paper is better than your own paper?

3.   Sign the note, and pass it to the person on your right. Wait to receive a paper from the left.

The teacher's job during the period is to keep papers moving so that each is read several times. Allow time at the end of the period for students to read the comments others have made on their papers, then collect the papers for grading.

FOLLOW-UP ACTIVITIES

1.   Since this unit has taught the students a writing process which they will use throughout the course, the terms introduced should be reemphasized whenever possible. Continue to refer to the stages in the writing process as prewriting, planning, writing, revising, rewriting, proofreading, reflecting, and sharing.

2.   If this assignment is written early in the course, it might be valuable to ask the class to look at their papers at the end of the year and determine if their goals have changed. This second look at the paper could result in a revision or an entirely new paper.

Worksheet 1: PREWRITING

Answer the questions below to gather ideas about what you plan to do in the first years following graduation from high school. Write down anything on the topic that occurs to you during class, whether you think you will use it or not. At this point you are just collecting ideas, not deciding what you will use in the paper you will write, but you should keep yesterday's discussion in mind as you work.

Personal Goals: What expectations do you have for your personal life? For your relationship to your family? For your relationship to your friends? Do you intend to remain single or marry? What reasons do you have for your answers to these questions?

Career Goals: What kind of work would you like to be doing? What would an ideal job for you be like? What kind of rewards, other than financial, would you like to have from your work? What training, if any, will you need beyond high school to begin your career?

Financial Goals: What financial goals do you have for yourself? Do you expect to make any major purchases? What are they? What is a reasonable salary you might expect to make in the career you have in mind? Do you expect to have a working spouse?

Other Goals: What goals do you have for yourself separate from your career? How will you spend your nonworking hours? What special interests do you want to develop?

Worksheet 2: ASSIGNMENT

   Your assignment is to write a paper in which you describe the personal and career goals you have set for yourself for the first years following your graduation from high school. As you write your paper, you will follow a writing process that begins with thinking about what you have to say (you have already done a good deal of this). It continues through planning, writing, revising, rewriting, proofreading, reflecting on what you have written, and sharing it with other members of the class.

Here is the schedule you will follow:

THINKING:	Class discussion on work. Filling out Worksheet on goals. (You have already completed these steps.)	
PLANNING:	Plan your paper.	Due: ————
WRITING:	Write your rough draft.	Due: ————
REVISING:	Share your rough draft with other members of the class in a rough draft workshop. Discuss what is good about your paper and what needs work.	
REWRITING:	Rewrite your paper based on what you learned from the rough draft workshop.	
PROOFREADING AND REFLECTING:	Have your paper proofread by other members of the class, reflect briefly in writing on what you have learned from it, and turn it in.	Due: ————
SHARING:	Have your paper read by other members of the class to get their reactions to the finished product.	

Worksheet 3: ROUGH DRAFT WORKSHOP

Suggest ideas for improving the paper you have been given by answering the questions below.

1. What are the major goals of the writer of the paper? Write the sentence(s) from the beginning of the paper that state them.

2. How could the beginning of the paper be improved? What could be added to make it more interesting?

3. What is the subject of each paragraph of the paper?

4. What part(s) of the paper could be clearer?

5. What parts of the paper could be improved by adding more detail or description?

6. How could the end of the paper be improved?

7. What is the best thing about the paper?

8. What about the paper needs the most work?

9. Reread the paper and check it for errors in spelling, punctuation, and usage.

Worksheet 4: COMMENT SHEET

NAME: _____ 10

DATE: _____

PROOFREADER 1

I certify that I have carefully read and corrected the final draft of this paper for errors in punctuation and usage.

_____

Proofreader's Signature

PROOFREADER 2

I certify that I have carefully read and corrected the final draft of this paper for errors in spelling.

_____

Proofreader's Signature

WRITER'S COMMENTS

The thing I like most about my paper is:

The thing I like least about my paper is:

The thing I tried most to improve as I wrote this paper is:

Other Comments:

TEACHER'S COMMENTS

Grade _____

Things to work on in your next paper:

©1987 J. Weston Walch, Publisher   *Practical English: A Complete Course*

Chapter Two

USING DIRECT LANGUAGE

It is obvious to most teachers that students have little difficulty communicating with one another orally. High-school classrooms are filled with endless talk about classes, friends, and last Friday's football game. But sometimes, when students sit down to write, they badly abuse the same language they speak so fluently every day of their lives. In an attempt to sound intelligent or literary, their writing becomes wordy and awkward. The common words they are comfortable with disappear and are replaced with others that they can barely manipulate or understand. The result is sentences that are stiff, artificial, and—worst of all—dull.

This unit, which takes about a week and requires no special materials, acquaints students with four common impediments to direct language: passive verbs, false sentence openings, overwriting, and the use of unnecessary words. It includes exercises on each writing problem and a checklist for papers written later in the year. The unit works best if scheduled for a time when students are completing a long reading or writing assignment at home, since it requires little or no homework.

LESSON I

Introduce the unit by passing out Worksheet 1 (Reducing Words). Explain that for the next week the class will learn how to avoid language like the Postal Service example, which is nearly twice as long as necessary to communicate its message effectively. Read the example aloud, and instruct students to reduce its length in any way that seems appropriate without changing or deleting the content. They should make notes and revisions on the example itself, then write a polished version in the space provided at the bottom of the sheet.

When work is completed, have several students write their revised versions on the chalkboard. Here is an example of a successful revision:

> The Postal Service is issuing the Series "D" stamp to avoid shortages of domestic first-class stamps. They will always be worth 22 cents but are not good for international mail. The "D" Series is being used because there was not enough time before increasing rates to produce the billions of new stamps that were needed. (55 words)

Review the changes that were made in the examples on the board, pointing out places for easy cuts in the original. This is a good opportunity to introduce the types of errors listed below that students will learn to avoid later in the unit.

Passive verbs:

1. The "D" Series *has been issued* to avoid any shortages in first-class postage stamps. (Change to an active verb.)

2. Normally six months *are required* to prepare postage stamp designs, produce plates, print and distribute the billions of stamps needed for a change in the first-class letter rate. (Change to an active verb.)

False starts and passive verbs:

1. *It is to be used* domestically just as any other first-class stamp. (Revise opening and change to an active verb.)

2. *It should not be used* for international mail. (Revise opening and change to an active verb.)

Overwriting:

1. The *required lead time* for production and distribution was not available between *determining* the new rate and its *implementation*. (The long words and jargon should be replaced with more direct language.)

Unnecessary words:

1. *It is to be used domestically* just as any other first-class stamp. *It should not be used for international mail.* (These sentences say almost the same thing.)

Tell students that they will become experts at spotting these errors in the next few days.

HOMEWORK:

With the board examples and your explanation in mind, students revise the passage a second time for homework.

LESSON II

Collect the homework and pass out Worksheet 2 (Passive Verbs). Explain that using passive verbs destroys the heart of a sentence, the action described by its verb. Discuss the examples, pointing out the greater liveliness of the active-verb sentences.

To be certain the class understands the differences between active and passive verbs, have them do Exercise A, then correct it with the class.

Next have students suggest several passive-verb sentences, write them on the board, and have the class suggest active-verb alternatives. Assign Exercise B, supervise the students' work, and allow time at the end of the period to correct and collect it.

LESSON III

Today's target is eliminating false sentence starts from student writing. Write the following sentences on the board and have students complete them:

1. I think that this class . . .

2. It is my belief that the varsity football team. . .

3. There is a person in my family who always . . .

Have the students rewrite the sentences without using the words *I*, *my*, and *there*. Volunteers then read their revised versions aloud. They will almost certainly have eliminated the false starts (*I think that*, *It is my belief that*, and *There is*) in all three of these sentences. Point this out.

Pass out Worksheet 3 (False Starts), and go over the false-start examples, explaining that a poor start will cripple a sentence before it has a chance to make its statement. False sentence starts usually result from a lack of confidence about what to say, but a good writer knows where a sentence is going and gets on with it quickly. Assign the exercise on the worksheet. When the class has finished, go over the revisions and collect the work.

LESSON IV

This lesson attacks the problem of overwriting. Pass out copies of Worksheet 4 (Overwriting), and explain that overwriting usually occurs when students are trying too hard to impress others with their writing. Read the example at the top of the sheet, and discuss alternatives for the underlined words. Students revise the paragraph either individually or as a class. Review their changes by writing some on the chalkboard or reading them aloud. A simplified version might be:

> Rain flooded the streets, and the many cars and trucks that clogged the city crawled through the storm. Filthy water flowed in torrents into the sewers.

Students may now complete the exercise at the bottom of the worksheet. You may let the class use dictionaries or you can define difficult words for them to keep the exercise from becoming too tedious. When they have finished, go over their revisions and collect the work.

LESSON V

Today's goal is to make students aware of ideas in their writing that are unnecessarily repeated. Pass out

Worksheet 5 (Unnecessary Words), and go over the introductory paragraph at the top of the sheet. Explain that to avoid repeating themselves, they must be sure of the exact meaning of every word they use. Unless, for example, they remember that all facts are true, they may make the mistake of writing about "true facts."

Students may now complete the exercise at the bottom of the worksheet. When they have finished, go over their revisions and collect the work.

LESSON VI

In this lesson, students apply what they have learned about direct language to their own writing. Schedule it for a time after Lessons I-V have been completed and when the rough draft of a paper is due.

Students arrive with completed rough drafts. Pass out copies of Worksheet 6 (Checklist) and review the terms *passive verbs*, *false beginnings*, *overwriting*, and *unnecessary words*. Go over the worksheet to be sure students understand all the questions. Each student

then uses the checklist to revise his or her own paper and has it checked a second time by a classmate who signs the worksheet as "Evaluator." Students may then begin their final drafts.

FOLLOW-UP ACTIVITIES

1. Repeat Lesson VI several times with different papers until students habitually write with direct language.

2. Encourage students to find and bring to class examples of writing with the problems they are learning to avoid. Schools are filled with them.

3. Worksheet 7 of this chapter (Sentence Length) offers another way of enlivening student language. Writing sentence after sentence of the same length quickly puts a reader to sleep. Good writing uses sentences of varying lengths. Have students use Worksheet 7 to chart the number of words of the first twenty sentences of a paper they are writing. Then have them generalize about the lengths of their sentences and revise if necessary.

Worksheet 1: REDUCING WORDS

Wordy and stiffly written language is everywhere. The passage below comes from the U.S. Postal Service, which used it several years ago on millions of packets of "D" Series stamps that temporarily replaced regular first-class stamps. Reduce the passage from 97 to 60 or 70 words without removing any information.

NOTICE TO CUSTOMERS

The "D" Series stamp has been issued to avoid any shortages in first-class postage stamps. It is to be used domestically just as any other first-class stamp. It should not be used for international mail. The "D" stamp will continue indefinitely to be worth its assigned value. Normally six months are required to prepare postage stamp designs, produce plates, print and distribute the billions of stamps needed for a change in the first-class letter rate. The required lead time for production and distribution was not available between determining the new rate and its implementation. (97 words)

Write your revision of the example below.

_____

_____

_____

_____

_____

_____

_____

_____

_____

_____

_____

Number of words _____

Worksheet 2A: PASSIVE VERBS

A sentence has a passive verb if its subject receives an action rather than performing an action.

PASSIVE: His grave was dug with his bare hands.
ACTIVE: He dug his grave with his bare hands.

PASSIVE: A baby possum was delivered by the stork.
ACTIVE: The stork delivered a baby possum.

Active verbs almost always give sentences more action and make them more interesting, so use passive verbs only when the doer of the action is unknown, unimportant, or obvious.

EXERCISE A

Mark each sentence below **A** if it has an active verb or **P** if it has a passive verb.

———— 1. A jacket with a block "N" on it was lost by his brother.

———— 2. His brother lost a jacket with a block "N" on it.

———— 3. We reached the airport an hour before the plane left.

———— 4. Coffee is grown in Brazil and Columbia.

———— 5. Her homework has been lost for the third time this week.

———— 6. The criminal's escape was feared by the villagers.

———— 7. The small boat sank, but the Coast Guard saved its crew.

Worksheet 2B: PASSIVE VERBS

EXERCISE B

The sentences below have passive verbs. Rewrite them with active verbs on a separate piece of paper.

1. The ball was kicked to the right of the goalpost by Lisner.

2. The pickpocket was noticed by the police before he escaped.

3. Joan and Susan were given free tickets by a friend.

4. The roof of the barn was almost destroyed by hail.

5. After the car was painted at the body shop, it was washed and polished by us.

6. A petition to lengthen lunch has been presented to the principal by the student government.

7. New, painful, high-heeled shoes were worn by her to the prom.

8. Mr. Tweek's class rules were known and understood by everyone.

9. Flags are flown by many Americans on national holidays.

10. Dion's financial problem was solved by getting a weekend job.

11. Their letter was delivered too late by Mr. Arnette to include their ideas in the plan.

12. Fireworks were invented by the Chinese long before gunpowder was known in Europe.

13. By noon Saturday the house had been cleaned and the lawn mowed by us, and a long, pleasant afternoon lay ahead.

14. The door was closed softly by the nurse as she left the room.

15. It was decided by the faculty to postpone the assembly until after final examinations.

Worksheet 3: FALSE STARTS

DATE: _____

Some sentences suffer from weak or false starts that cripple them before they ever get going. False starts usually occur when a writer is not sure of what to write but begins writing anyway. Here are some sentences with underlined examples of false starts.

<u>In my opinion</u>, the situation there is intolerable.
<u>I think that</u> the President did his best to be fair.
<u>It seems that</u> his help just makes matters worse.
<u>It is my belief</u> that they are sure to win the game.

Sometimes revising a sentence with a weak beginning requires more than just removing a phrase; several words must be changed.

BEFORE: *There is* nothing like this anywhere in the state.

AFTER: Nothing like this exists anywhere in the state.

BEFORE: *It was* unfortunate *that* Tina arrived late.

AFTER: Unfortunately Tina arrived late.

EXERCISE: Remove the false starts from each of the sentences below by revising them on a separate piece of paper.

1. There is a boy in my biology class with a mind like a salamander.
2. It is my belief that from now on he will behave differently.
3. There were times when Tina hated him for being right.
4. There will be no practice held tomorrow.
5. I feel almost certain that space travel is a waste of money.
6. This is one thing that I don't know very much about.
7. This is the restaurant where the menu gives you a choice of Chinese, Indian, or kosher food.
8. The thing that enrages me most is teachers who mumble.
9. In my opinion, it seems that his mind is made up.
10. There are some aspects of this problem that will never be understood by me.
11. There is a lot to be said in favor of his point of view.
12. If there is one thing that drives me crazy, it is drivers who follow too closely.
13. There was a crowd of cheering fans outside the locker room.
14. It seems that the boys are more conscious about how they dress than the girls.
15. There are times when it seems that she is not as thoughtful as her brother.

Worksheet 4: OVERWRITING

A common mistake of young writers is trying too hard, and the result is "overwriting." If a writer always chooses the longest and most unusual words, he or she runs the risk of creating a paper that is dull and difficult to understand. Choose the most accurate word, not the one that you think sounds intelligent or literary.

The passage below is badly overwritten. Read it, and think of words to replace the ones that are underlined.

<u>Precipitation</u> flooded the <u>urban thoroughfares</u>, and the <u>multitudes</u> of <u>vehicles</u> that clogged the <u>municipality</u> crawled through the <u>maelstrom</u>. Filthy <u>liquid</u> flowed in <u>Niagaras</u> into the <u>subterranean water disposal network</u>.

Nothing is wrong with the underlined words in the passage above, except that they do not fit what is being said. The writing sounds silly and needs simplification.

EXERCISE: Rewrite the sentences below on a separate piece of paper. Change the parts that are overwritten, using a dictionary, if necessary, to understand what is being said.

1.   Using his talented pedal extremity, Henderson kicked the pigskin through the uprights.

2.   I departed at dawn for a week's sojourn with my avuncular relation.

3.   Easily maintaining his equilibrium, Larry glided down the incline covered with frozen precipitation.

4.   I put aside my school tomes, reclined upon the davenport, and perused the evening gazette.

5.   I passed the afternoon selecting and purchasing disks at a local music emporium.

6.   One's own domicile always gives the greatest solace upon returning from foreign realms.

7.   The multitudes in the tiers around the playing field rejoiced and cried out when Bottoms scored.

8.   To forestall a refusal, I asked Ellen's sibling about her plans for the weekend before requesting her company at the cinema.

9.   My study of species *Homo sapiens* leads me to conclude that the notion of human progress is a myth.

10.   Illumination is required to be extinguished upon vacating the premises.

Practical English: A Complete Course

Worksheet 5:
UNNECESSARY WORDS

Most writers occasionally allow a few unneccessary or repetitive words to slip into their writing. Sometimes these words repeat what is being said, as in "the modern farm practices *of today*" or "*true* facts." Words may also be carelessly repeated by not keeping the entire sentence in mind while writing, as in "This school is a good *school* for electronics."

EXERCISE: Revise the sentences below by crossing out unnecessary words. If a sentence does not need revision, place a **C** next to it in the left margin.

1. Let me refer you back to the first chapter.
2. Ms. Bloom circulated the book around the room for the class to see.
3. The rookie shortstop shows real promise for the future.
4. The meeting will be held Tuesday at 7:00 p.m. in the evening.
5. Her last novel is the best novel she has written.
6. The new gymnasium is extremely large and well-equipped.
7. Both of the two Rasston twins said they will be there.
8. We watched the big, massive clouds building over the level plateau.
9. The pines were outlined in silhouette against the red and scarlet of the dawn.
10. His first film won several awards and is besides an exciting film to watch.
11. Modern automobiles of today, unlike older cars of the past, are efficient as well as comfortable.
12. What the teacher had said was not audible to my ears, so I asked him to repeat it again.
13. My first experience with computers was confusing, but my understanding of computers is now much improved for the better.
14. During her freshman year Suzanne discovered boys.
15. We thought in our minds about how to solve the puzzling problem.
16. The variety of different television programs offered on an ordinary and typical weeknight is marvelous and amazing.
17. He had decided to combine together the two leagues to achieve eventually better competition in the long run.
18. The car lay upside down at the side of the highway, resting on its roof.
19. The final conclusion of the play occurred in the third act when the entire cast sang the song "Oklahoma!"
20. We descended down the cliff and approached the edge of the riverbank.

Worksheet 6: CHECKLIST

Use this sheet to make your writing more concise and direct. Check your paper with what is listed below, then have it double-checked by a classmate who will answer the questions and sign the space above marked "Evaluator."

1. Underline passive verbs and, if it seems appropriate, rewrite the sentences in which they appear in the space below.

2. Circle false or weak beginnings to sentences, and rewrite the entire sentences in the space below.

3. Put rectangles around words or phrases that seem overwritten, and rewrite the sentences in which they appear in the space below.

4. Cross out any unnecessary words with a neat line.

Worksheet 7: SENTENCE LENGTH

DATE: _____

Chart the number of words in the sentences of your paper on the graph below.

SENTENCE NUMBER	WORDS												
	1 5	10	15	20	25	30	35	40	45	50	55	60	
1													
2													
3													
4													
5													
6													
7													
8													
9													
10													
11													
12													
13													
14													
15													
16													
17													
18													
19													
20													

Make a generalization about the lengths of your sentences on another sheet of paper.

Practical English: A Complete Course

Chapter Three

MASTERING SPELLING

We teachers of secondary schools know what a task improving spelling can be. Strategies vary from teacher to teacher. Some of us give random lists of 10 to 25 spelling words a week; some give words with a common spelling focus. Some teachers concentrate on spelling rules and sample students' learnings with rule or unit tests. Some of us select spelling and vocabulary words from books the students are reading or from papers they are writing. Others have simply given up, believing that even after all of our strategies, some students will never learn to spell correctly.

Regardless of our method of attacking or of ignoring the problem, most of us would agree that correct spelling is important for the student. Poor spelling can be linked to poor overall academic success in an otherwise successful student; it can also have a detrimental effect on a student's self-confidence. Poor spelling often leads a student to poor handwriting, because he would rather be reprimanded for bad penmanship than for horrible spelling. As teachers of vocational English, we have a responsibility to prepare our students for success in their vocational training and their jobs after high school. Their ability to spell correctly and to know when to consult a dictionary will in part determine success for many of them. We *can* help the poor speller.

Research has shown us that there are basically three main types of learners: visual, auditory, and kinesthetic. The visual learner looks at something, visually records it in his mind, and recalls it when necessary. The auditory learner is more successful if he hears what is to be learned, says what is to be learned, and then hears it repeated again. The kinesthetic learner, research has recently revealed, needs to be involved by writing, by touching, by manipulating; he must be physically involved in the learning with

more than his eyes and ears. This type of "doing" learning situation becomes more difficult to create the older the student becomes.

1. Write the words to be learned over and over. Change writing styles from print to cursive to capital block letters.

2. Point out to the student the actual part of the word he is missing—the beginning, the middle, the end.

3. Give the student and others words to learn that he uses regularly (*hassle, embarrass, separate*) along with class spelling words.

The spelling lessons can be used throughout the year. They are divided by spelling rules with examples and then appropriate quizzes. "Demon words" will also be presented for study and memory.

LESSON I

Explain to the students that spelling will be an important part of vocational English class. Involve the students in a discussion about the benefits of being a good speller.

Introduce the students to the idea that there are three main types of learners: visual, auditory, and kinesthetic. Using the example of assembling a toy or mechanical device, ask the students to figure out what type of learners they are.

1. Do they like to *read* the directions as they assemble or before they assemble the object? (visual)

2. Do they like to *listen* to the directions as they assemble or before they assemble? (auditory)

3. Do they like to have someone *show* them how to assemble the object? (kinesthetic)

4. Do they like to combine several of the techniques above?

Of course, this is no absolute test, but it can help the student to become aware of *how* he or she learns best.

Ask students to share personal study and learning techniques and experiences. See if the class can identify the type of learning that is involved—visual, auditory, or kinesthetic.

In this unit, spelling rules will be presented with examples. Then spelling quizzes will follow the rules.

Also, "spelling demons" will be presented since they are considered the most troublesome words in American English.

Some teachers select five words a week for intense study and practice and then test at the end of the week.

Another approach is to give one to three of the most commonly misspelled words each day at the beginning of the period.

In either case, the students can evaluate and score the short tests by exchanging papers.

Form the plurals of regular nouns by adding S or ES.

Add ES to nouns that end in CH, S, SH, X, Z and some that end in O. Add S to all other regular nouns.

EXAMPLES: Add S   candle, candles
                        ball, balls

              Add ES   witch, witches
                        brush, brushes

EXERCISE A

Write the following words in their singular and plural forms.

1. ax (or axe) _____

2. book _____

3. punch _____

4. ski _____

5. peach _____

6. pie _____

7. kitten _____

8. wish _____

9. waltz _____

10. bus _____

EXERCISE B

Write five words that end in CH, S, SH, X (and Z) respectively if you can think of some. Then write five regular common nouns. Form their plurals correctly.

SINGULAR	PLURAL
1. _____	_____
2. _____	_____
3. _____	_____
4. _____	_____
5. _____	_____
6. _____	_____
7. _____	_____
8. _____	_____
9. _____	_____
10. _____	_____

Practical English: A Complete Course

WORKSHEET 2

Form the plurals of nouns ending in Y after a consonant by changing the Y to I and adding Es.

Form the plurals of nouns ending in Y after a vowel by adding S.

EXAMPLES:	infirmary	infirmaries
	secretary	secretaries
EXAMPLES:	toy	toys
	key	keys

EXERCISE A

Write the correct plural for each of the following nouns ending in Y.

1. passkey ————————————
2. canopy ————————————
3. identity ————————————
4. buoy ————————————
5. Monday ————————————

6. boy ————————————
7. entity ————————————
8. relay ————————————
9. theology ————————————
10. peculiarity ————————————

EXERCISE B

Think of five more nouns that end in Y, some with a vowel and some with a consonant before the final Y. Then form the correct plurals.

SINGULAR	PLURAL
1. ————————————	————————————
2. ————————————	————————————
3. ————————————	————————————
4. ————————————	————————————
5. ————————————	————————————

Worksheet 3

PART 1

Form the plural of most nouns ending in F by adding S. Form the plural of some nouns ending in F by changing F to V and adding ES.

EXAMPLES: belief   beliefs   thief   thieves
            creampuff   creampuffs   leaf   leaves

EXERCISE A

Write the correct plural for each of the following nouns ending in F. When you are not sure, consult a dictionary. Do not guess!

1. wife _____

2. chief _____

3. chef _____

4. muff _____

5. life _____

PART 2

Form the plural of nouns ending in O following a vowel by adding S. Also form the plural of most musical terms that are nouns ending in O by adding an S.

EXAMPLES: video   videos
            patio   patios
            piano   pianos

Form the plurals of nouns ending in O following a consonant by adding ES.

EXAMPLES: hero   heroes
            torpedo torpedoes

EXERCISE A:

Write the correct plural form of the following nouns ending in O.

1. tomato _____

2. soprano _____

3. potato _____

4. radio _____

5. alto _____

6. tattoo _____

7. shampoo _____

8. cameo _____

EXERCISE B:

Think of other nouns that end in O. Then write them and their plural form.

Practical English: A Complete Course

Irregular nouns do not follow the rules for forming plurals in Lessons II through V.

Some irregular nouns change their spelling and some remain the same in singular and in plural. You have to learn the irregular spellings; there is no rule to cover them all. Consult the dictionary in the singular form and it will give you the plural spelling also.

EXAMPLES: woman   women

             mouse   mice

             trout   trout

EXERCISE A

Write the irregular plurals of the following words. Consult the dictionary when you are unsure.

1. tooth ————————————

2. man ————————————

3. child ————————————

4. foot ————————————

5. goose ————————————

EXERCISE B

Think of other irregular nouns and be sure to spell their plurals correctly. Teach them to the class tomorrow.

Chapter Three

Worksheet 5

NAME: _____ 29

DATE: _____

PART 1

Form the plurals of most foreign words as they are formed in the foreign language. When you are not sure, check the dictionary by looking up the singular form.

EXAMPLES: index   indices or indexes

                    alumnus   alumni

                    alumna   alumnae

EXERCISE

Write the plurals of the following words we have adopted from foreign languages. Check the dictionary when you are not sure.

1. datum _____
2. crisis _____
3. appendix _____
4. matrix _____

PART 2

Form the plurals of most compound words by making the main part of the word plural.

EXAMPLES: brother-in-law   brothers-in-law

                    maid of honor   maids of honor

REVIEW EXERCISE

Write the plural forms of all the following nouns.

1. clock _____
2. contralto _____
3. sheaf _____
4. swatch _____
5. infirmary _____
6. cherry _____
7. wish _____
8. editor in chief _____
9. buoy _____
10. louse _____

Worksheet 6

PART 1

A prefix is a letter or a group of letters added to the beginning of a word to change its meaning. Sometimes it is added to a root to help form a word. The spelling of the word remains the same when the prefixes DIS, IL, IM IN, MIS, OVER, RE, and UN are added to a word.

EXAMPLES: dis + satisfied = dissatisfied

il + luminate = illuminate

im + mobile = immobile

EXERCISE

Correctly spell the following new words.

1. dis + appear _____

2. il + legitimate _____

3. im + mortal _____

4. in + evitable _____

5. mis + shape _____

6. over + ride _____

7. re + entry _____

8. un + noticed _____

PART 2

Form a new word by adding the suffixes NESS and LY to the word's correct spelling.

EXAMPLES: sudden + ly = suddenly

sudden + ness = suddenness

The exceptions to this rule are as follows:

1. Words ending in **Y** usually change the Y to an I before adding a suffix.

EXAMPLES: merry + ly = merrily

stocky + ness = stockiness

2. true + ly = truly

Practical English: A Complete Course

PART 1

Drop the final E before a suffix beginning with a vowel.

EXAMPLES: hate + ing = hating

sincere + ity = sincerity

dominate + ion = domination

The exceptions to this rule are as follows:

1. Keep the final E after C or G when adding A or O to keep the soft G (as in ENRAGE).

    EXAMPLES: outrage + ous = outrageous

    notice + able = noticeable

2. Dye + ing = DYEING so as to separate it from DYING.

PART 2

Keep the final E before a suffix beginning with a consonant.

EXAMPLES: hate + ful = hateful

peace + ful = peaceful

love + ly = lovely

Some of the exceptions to this rule are:

argue + ment = argument

true + ly = truly

EXERCISE

Form the new words indicated.

1. dis + semble _____

2. il + legible _____

3. im + modest _____

4. mis + spell _____

5. true + ly _____

6. sincere + ly _____

7. virtue + ous _____

8. revere + ent _____

9. feisty + ly _____

10. courage + ous _____

Practical English: A Complete Course

Worksheet 8

PART 1

When adding ED, ER, or ING to a one-syllable word ending in a single consonant preceded by a single vowel, double the final consonant.

EXAMPLES: man   manning   manning

span   spanned   spanning

When adding ED, ER, or ING to two-or more syllable words ending in a single consonant preceded by a single vowel, double the final consonant if the accent is on the last syllable.

EXAMPLES: confer   conferred   conferring

propel   propelled   propelling

EXERCISE

Form the new words indicated.

1. propel + er _____   6. chin + ing _____

2. answer + ed _____   7. occur + ing _____

3. plan + ing _____   8. occur + ed _____

4. prefer + ed _____   9. propel + ing _____

5. prefer + ence _____   10. dispel + er _____

PART 2

When you are adding ING to a word that ends in IE, you usually change the IE to Y.

EXAMPLES: die + ing = dying

lie + ing = lying

When you are adding a suffix that begins with a vowel to a word ending in E, you usually omit the final E.

EXAMPLES: care + ing = caring

grate + er = grater

Practical English: A Complete Course

Worksheet 9

When you know that a word has either IE or EI in it, here are the two rules to remember:

1. Write IE when the sound is EE except after C.

    EXAMPLES: niece, piece, conceive, receipt
    EXCEPTIONS: either, neither, leisure, seize, weird

2. Write EI when the sound is not EE and especially when it is A.

    EXAMPLES: neighbor, weigh, height
    EXCEPTIONS: friend, science

EXERCISE:

Following the two rules to help with IE or EI spellings, fill in the blanks below. Note the exceptions beneath each rule!

1. r _ _ gn
2. bel _ _ ve
3. rel _ _ f
4. p _ _ ce
5. fr _ _ ght
6. w _ _ ght
7. conc _ _ ve
8. rec _ _ pt
9. ch _ _ f
10. f _ _ rce

11. pr _ _ st
12. s _ _ ze
13. sc _ _ nce
14. _ _ ther
15. n _ _ ther
16. l _ _ sure
17. ach _ _ ve
18. c _ _ ling
19. rec _ _ ve
20. cash _ _ r

Practical English: A Complete Course

Most Commonly Misspelled Words

After you have studied the basic spelling rules, there is still more you can do to improve your spelling. Learn with your class five of the most commonly misspelled words each week.

1. Study the troublesome parts of the words. In the list those parts are underlined.

2. See each syllable of the word. Then say each syllable. Then write each syllable to form the whole word.

absence
absolutely
acceptance
accepted
accidentally
accommodate
accompany
accuracy
achieve
achievement
acquaintance
acquire
across
actually
administration
admittance
adolescent
advertisement
affectionate
agriculture
aisle
allotment
all right
altar/alter
amateur
analyze
annually
anticipate
apartment

apology
apparatus
apparent
appearance
appreciate
approach
approval
argument
arithmetic
arrangement
athletic
attendance
author
authority
available
awkward

beginning
behavior
believe
benefited
boundary
breath
breathe
brief
business
buying

calendar
campaign

capital
capitol
certificate
character
choose/chose
Christian
clothes
column
commercial
committee
coming
completely
conscious
conscience
controlled
conceivable
controversy
correspondence
criticize
criticism
curious

debtor
deceive
decision
dependent
describe
desperate
develop

disappear
disappoint
discipline
duplicate

easily
effect
eighth
eligible
embarrass
emphasize
environment
equipment
exaggerate
exercise

fascinate
fatal
financial
foreign
forth
fourth

government
gracious
grammar
guarantee

height

imagine
immediately
incidentally
indefinite
innocence
instructor
insurance
intelligent
interest
interfere

laboratory
leisure
license
library
loneliness
loose/lose/loss
luxury

maintenance
maneuver
marriage
medicine
melancholy
minimum
mischief
moral
morale
mortgage
muscle

necessary
neighbor
ninety
noticeable

obstacle
occasion
occurrence
offensive

official
omission
omitted
opportunity
optimist
orchestra
organization
originally

parallel
paralyze
particular
passed/past
peculiar
permanent
perspiration
picknicking
possess
practically
preferred
prejudice
privilege
professor
psychology

receipt
receive
recognize
recommend
referred
repetition
responsibility
restaurant
rhythm
ridiculous
roommate

sacrifice
scarcity
scene

schedule
scholar
scissors
seize
separate
similar
sincerely
skiing
sophomore
specifically
sponsor
studying
succeed
success
sufficient
surprise

temperamental
tendency
thorough
toward
tragedy
truly

unnecessary
using

vacuum
valuable
various
villain

weather
whether
Wednesday
weird
writing
written

yield

An Ongoing Spelling Lesson: Individual Recordkeeping, Practice, and Testing

The English teacher needs to assess a student's spelling ability in his writing assignments. Most teachers do so by circling the incorrect portion of the word, drawing the writer's attention to his error. Some reseachers have indicated that this technique can actually have a negative impact, that it points out and reinforces poor spelling. Perhaps the key to more success lies in the follow-up learning after the spelling errors have been pointed out.

The Spelling Record which follows is an attempt to provide some order to the process of improving an individual student's spelling. The Spelling Record is a place to keep a list of words misspelled on different writing assignments during the year. Besides recording the words on the chart, the student needs to practice writing the words correctly at least ten times each and to practice saying them aloud while visualizing the syllables. Then he needs to be individually tested.

The teacher may designate a part of a class period every two weeks or so for students to test each other in pairs. They can both administer and correct these individualized spelling tests. Because these are actually the words the student has misspelled in his own writing, often he will take this type of spelling assignment more seriously than the spelling rules or the most commonly misspelled words.

The students can keep these papers in a special spelling section of their class notebooks, or they can be stapled into the inside of a class folder which is always kept in the classroom.

SPELLING RECORD

Writing Assignment	Correct Spelling of Words Misspelled (underline problem spots)	Synonym Breakdown of Correct Spelling

Practical English: A Complete Course

Chapter Four

USING LANGUAGE REFERENCE BOOKS

The thesaurus and the dictionary are very useful reference books, not only for school, but for many types of work as well. Familiarizing your students with these books, with all of their offerings, and with how to use them can be a valuable asset to them in high school and beyond.

You will need a class set of dictionaries and thesauruses in order to provide the experiences that follow. If this is impossible, here are a few suggestions:

1. Convince the students of the value of these references and encourage them to purchase a paperback dictionary and a thesaurus on their own. Consult your local bookstore, a discount one if possible, about the current recommended dictionary and thesaurus. Then ask the store to stock up for your students.

2. Get your hands on as many copies of the same thesaurus as you can. If you are able to, acquire some alphabetical and some categorical thesauruses.

Have the class work on the exercises in groups. Be sure each student actually looks up the information several times. Just hearing, reading, or even matching the thesaurus used is not enough. Each lesson in this unit is on a worksheet with directions for the student. Go over the directions with the students; then decide how much of the work you need to do with your class before you turn them loose with their thesauruses.

Worksheet 1A: USING THE THESAURUS

THESAURUS

A thesaurus is a dictionary of synonyms and antonyms. It can be a great help to you as you work on your vocabulary improvement. The best time to use a thesaurus is when you are writing a paper which calls for creativity as well as accuracy. Rather than settle for a common, overused word to describe something, use your thesaurus to find a synonym. A word such as ANGRY, for instance, might call to mind three or four synonyms: MAD, UPSET, SORE, etc. A quick check in the thesaurus under ANGRY would show FUMING, RAGING, FURIOUS, RABID, CROSS, PEEVED, HUFFY, INFLAMED, ENRAGED, INFURIATED, EXASPERATED, FIERY, and so on. Each of these words has a different shade of meaning and will add color to the writing. Just as important, you will add new words to your working vocabulary.

*Use synonyms to avoid redundancy. The THESAURUS can provide the help you need to avoid monotonous repetition. Note the change in the paragraph after the redundant words (in capitals) have been replaced or eliminated:

January in Wisconsin can be bitter cold. The COLDNESS (temperature) often drops to 20 to 30 degrees below zero. THAT'S COLD! (Eliminate.) It is so COLD you can't go outside for fear of HAVING SOME REAL PROBLEMS WITH THE COLD HURTING YOUR HANDS OR FACE (frostbite). On these REALLY COLD (benumbing) days, people are warned against traveling except for an emergency. If the COLD (arctic-like condition) continues for more than a couple of days, almost all traffic stops, since you cannot trust your car to run—even if it does start. Too often a car will stall in the middle of nowhere, leaving a traveler stranded in the EXTREME COLD (frozen air). The only way to beat the incredible COLD (keep as is to draw the paragraph together) of a Wisconsin winter is to huddle around the fireplace and dream of the warm, sunny days of summer.

Thesauruses are arranged in several different ways. If you purchase a paperback thesaurus, you can select one in which the words are simply arranged alphabetically, as in a dictionary. With this dictionary-type of alphabetical arrangement, it is especially important that you go to the dictionary when you aren't sure of the word's exact meaning. Other thesauruses categorize words according to their frame of reference. For example, if you look up the word CHARACTER in the index, you will select from the following frames of reference: NATURE, STATE, CONSTITUTION, NUMBER, ECCENTRIC, and others. Let's say you are writing about someone who is a CHARACTER, an unusual or somewhat weird ECCENTRIC. Turn to the number listed for that type of meaning for CHARACTER. You would find on 504.3, the given number, FREAK, ECCENTRIC, CRACKPOT, etc. Then you could use a different word for A WEIRD CHARACTER if you have used that word before. This sounds a bit confusing, but practice with either or both types of thesauruses will clear up your confusion.

Practical English: A Complete Course

Worksheet 1B:
USING THE THESAURUS

The thesaurus will give you the synonyms for the word you look up. It will also give you synonyms for the different forms of that word. For example, if you look up INTEREST, you will find its synonyms plus the synonyms for INTERESTING and INTERESTINGNESS and TO MAKE INTERESTING. You must chose the right form of the word for your sentence, then the synonym. You may have to consult the dictionary to discover which word is just right.

See the thesaurus entry for ACTION.

EXAMPLE:　ACTION—n.　　action—performance, exercise, pursuit, movement, exertion, execution.

　　　　　　　　　　v.　　act—function, operate, work, take steps, put into practice

　　　　　　　　　adj.　　acting—performing, officiating, operative

　　　　　　　　　adv.　　in the act of—in the midst of, red-handed, actively.

The word ACTION is a noun; its synonyms follow. ACT is a verb, an action word. The adjective for ACTION is ACTING, and the adverb form is the phrase IN THE ACT OF or ACTIVELY. You must be careful to use the right form of the word when you make substitutions in your own writing.

Worksheet 2
THESAURUS EXERCISE

This lesson can be done as a class, with the students looking up words together and orally selecting the best choices.

Read the following paragraph. Use the thesaurus to select better words for the words in capitals. Sometimes you may find it better to eliminate a word altogether. You may have to look up a word you find in the thesaurus, in the dictionary in order to choose the word you really mean. BE CAREFUL TO CHOOSE A WORD IN THE WAY IT IS SUPPOSED TO BE USED, IN THE CORRECT PART OF SPEECH.

The EXCITEMENT (   ) around Northgate High School during Homecoming

Week is unequaled at any other time during the school year. Every activity is designed to

EXCITE (   ) the students and to involve them in the EXCITING

(   ) feeling as they participate with their friends in an EXCITING

(   ) celebration. For four EXCITING (   ) days of Homecoming

Week, the various classes dress in EXCITING (   ) costumes focused on

themes that EXCITE (   ) the imagination. Each day one class performs an

EXCITING (   ) rally to EXCITE (   ) the student body to a level

of ultimate EXCITEMENT (   ). Classes are interrupted by a series of

EXCITED (   ) messengers delivering flowers and EXCITINGLY (   )

romantic notes. The most EXCITING (   ) event of all is, for some, the

Homecoming Game; for others, the Homecoming Dance.

Practical English: A Complete Course

Worksheet 3
THESAURUS EXERCISE

This lesson can be done as a class, with the students looking up words together and orally selecting the best choices.

Read the following paragraph. Use the thesaurus to select better words for the words in capitals. Sometimes you may find it better to eliminate a word altogether. You may have to look up a word you find in the thesaurus, in the dictionary in order to choose the word you really mean. BE CAREFUL TO CHOOSE A WORD IN THE WAY IT IS SUPPOSED TO BE USED, IN THE CORRECT PART OF SPEECH.

I EXPECTED (   ) to earn enough money last summer to completely restore my '57 Chevrolet. How could I ever EXPECT (   ) that the restoration would cost so much? I had EXPECTED (   ) to pay $250 for the rolled and pleated vinyl seatcovers everyone EXPECTS (   ) is closer to $500. The EXPECTANT (   ) painter of my choice EXPECTS (   ) about $200, plus $300 for the preparation body work he EXPECTS (   ) to find the car needs. I guess my EXPECTATIONS (   ) and my realities are a long way apart! I EXPECT (   ) I'll be working several summers to pay for this job.

Practical English: A Complete Course

Worksheet 4
THESAURUS EXERCISE

Read the following paragraph. Use the thesaurus to select better words for the words in capitals. Sometimes you may find it better to eliminate a word altogether. You may have to look up a word you find in the thesaurus, in the dictionary in order to choose the word you really mean. BE CAREFUL TO CHOOSE A WORD IN THE WAY IT IS SUPPOSED TO BE USED, IN THE CORRECT PART OF SPEECH.

My family is quite a MIXTURE (   ) of different nationalities. The MIXTURE (   ) of several cultural backgrounds has produced some interesting effects on my generation. One effect of this MIXTURE (   ) can be easily seen in our physical appearances. Mother and Dad MIXED (   ) her Scottish, blonde hair, green eyes, and fair complexion with Italian curly, black hair, brown eyes, and bronze complexion. The progeny reveal the results of that MIX (   ): three blonde, green-eyed, fair-skinned boys and two curly brunette, brown-eyed, olive-skinned girls. MIX (   ) in Grandma's German reddish hair and freckled face, and you'll find the MIXED (   ) results in three of us having freckles across our noses. Another area in which this cultural MIXTURE (   ) has had its effect is in our diets. A MIXED (   ) meal at our house might consist of Scotch broth, lasagna, schinken mit nudeln, and Scotch shortbread. Although I don't believe it, our family attributes certain character traits to this cultural MIXTURE (   ). My sister's Scottish frugalness and Italian joviality and my brother's German austerity are said to be separate strands of the cultural MIX (   ) that have come through. To me we're all just a nice MIXTURE (   ) of history, culture, cuisine, and national pride!

**Worksheet 5A:
USING THE DICTIONARY**

Most people go to the dictionary to check the spelling of a word or to find a word's meaning. Although you have already consulted a dictionary many times for one of these reasons, you may review some information to help you find words more quickly. What else does a dictionary offer you?

1. A vocabulary of abbreviations.
2. Biographical information on famous people.
3. A pronouncing guide to common English names.
4. A vocabulary of rhyming words.
5. A list of spelling rules.
6. Guides to punctuation, capitalization, and italicization.

While not all dictionaries offer precisely the same information, the dictionary could possibly be your most useful reference book. It's useful not only for school, but for your job as well, if it involves any writing. Lesson V will familiarize you with what your class or personal dictionary offers.

Today's lesson will also review looking up words in alphabetical order, a useful skill to practice at any age.

Open to the Table of Contents of the dictionary you will be using in class or at home. Tell in which *section* of the dictionary you would look for the following information:

1. How to pronounce **morecambe**.

   _____ .

2. What the abbreviation **ct** stands for.

   _____ .

3. What the symbol stands for.

   _____ .

4. Who Lysimachus was.

   _____ .

Practical English: A Complete Course

Worksheet 5B:
USING THE DICTIONARY

5. How to address a letter to a baron's son.

_____ .

6. How to say Yvette and what nationality it originates from.

_____ .

7. How to add the suffix **an/ ian** to geographical and personal names ending in **-a**.

_____ .

8. Whether to capitalize the name of a breed of dog (airedale terrier or Airedale terrier).

_____ .

9. A picture of a mordent or a mortarboard. _____ .

10. The origin of the word **morale**.

_____ .

*This exercise may also be used as practice for going from the Table of Contents to the precise section and page to find the specific information.

Guide words are the words that appear at the top of each dictionary page in heavy, dark print. The word on the left tells the first word that appears on that page, and the word on the right tells the last word that appears on that page. Looking at the guide words, you can see quickly whether the word you are looking for falls somewhere between them.

Check the words that would fall on a page with the guide words **manufacture** and **mare**.

1. marjoram
2. march
3. manuscript
4. maritime
5. mariner

6. maraud
7. maraschino
8. maraca
9. margrave
10. marginal

Practical English: A Complete Course

WORKSHEET 6A: CAPITALIZATION

When you look up a word in the dictionary, you will sometimes see the abbreviation *cap.* in italics before one of the definitions of the word. This means that when the word is used in this way, it must be capitalized.

EXERCISE

Look up the following words and use them in good sentences that show their meanings. If a word can be both capitalized and uncapitalized, use both forms in sentences.

1. god
2. Swiss
3. lord
4. locofoco
5. son
6. democrat
7. republican
8. spinet
9. terrier
10. Finn

EXAMPLE: shawnee

The Shawnee are an Algonquin tribe living in most of the states east of the Mississippi.

1. _____

_____

2. _____

_____

3. _____

_____

4. _____

_____

5. _____

_____

6. _____

_____

7. _____

_____

8. _____

_____

9. _____

_____

10. _____

Worksheet 6B: PRONUNCIATION

Every dictionary gives you the pronunciation of each word. If there is more than one way to say a word, both pronunciations are given. Diacritical marks are the symbols the dictionary uses to show the sounds of the letters. There is a key to these diacritical markings at the bottom of every other page in most dictionaries. There is also a section at the beginning of the dictionary that explains in full the system of sounds the diacritical marks represent.

Look up in your dictionary the following words. Write their pronunciation using diacritical markings. Accent marks appear as an apostrophe at the beginning of the accented syllable. If there are two or more pronunciations, write them all. Then check the key to pronunciation and practice saying each word. Be prepared to say them aloud to the class.

1. finite
2. margarite
3. marguerite
4. shirr
5. jauntiness

6. tutorage
7. mausoleum
8. tauten
9. neuralgia
10. variegate

1. finite _____

2. margarite _____

3. marguerite _____

4. shirr _____

5. jauntiness _____

6. tutorage _____

7. mausoleum _____

8. tauten _____

9. neuralgia _____

10. variegate _____

Worksheet 7: SYLLABICATION AND WORD FORMS

EXERCISE A Syllabication:

When you are writing or typing, it is especially helpful to know where to divide a word if you must at the end of the line. The dictionary divides the words into syllables by using dots (·). Do not confuse these with hyphens (-). Look up the following words and write them in syllables with dots in between.

1. newsworthy _____

2. oxidation _____

3. pathetic _____

4. reconnaissance _____

5. bruise _____

6. contradictoriness _____

7. dragonfly _____

8. penultimate _____

9. syllabication _____

10. journalism _____

EXERCISE B: Different Forms of Words:

The dictionary can be helpful when you aren't sure which form of a word to use. For example, some verbs are not as regular as WALK, WALKED, HAVE WALKED. Take the verb SWIM. If you are writing, "He has s _____ m across this lake many times," but you aren't sure which form to use, consult your dictionary under SWIM. The entry will begin with the word SWIM followed by SWAM and then SWUM. The last entry (either the second or third) is the irregular verb form you need to use with HAS or HAVE, the past participle form of the verb. English has several verbs that are misused often because of their irregular past participles. Another way the dictionary can help you is in determining the comparative and superlative forms of adjectives. Most adjectives work this way: SMALL, SMALLER, (for comparing two), SMALLEST (for comparing three or more). Some adjectives, however, are like GOOD. When you look up GOOD, you will find BETTER and BEST listed immediately after the word GOOD usually. The dictionary also provides irregular comparative and superlative forms for some adverbs like WELL (BETTER and BEST).

**Worksheet 7B: SYLLABICATION
AND WORD FORMS**

EXERCISE B (continued)

Look up the following word forms in your dictionary:

1.   past tense of SHRINK ————————————————

2.   superlative form of CURLY ————————————————

3.   comparative form of BAD ————————————————

4.   superlative form of GOOD ————————————————

5.   past tense of BURST ————————————————

6.   past participle of BURST ————————————————

7.   past participle of BEGIN ————————————————

8.   past participle of RING ————————————————

9.   past participle of DRINK ————————————————

10.   past tense of KNOW ————————————————

Worksheet 8: MEANING

    The most common use for a dictionary besides checking spelling is determining a word's meaning. Some dictionaries give the most commonly used meaning first; then other meanings follow. Some dictionaries give the oldest definition for the word first, then the more recent meanings. Look up the following underlined words and write the correct meaning for that particular sentence.

1. I have never understood my <u>function</u> in this household.

2. Mr. Gische, my calculus teacher, talked for twenty minutes about that particular <u>function</u> in our math homework.

3. That poor child is always the <u>mark</u> among the fourth-grade boys at recess.

4. John Muir's house is the <u>mark</u> that helps me find the Alhambra Avenue exit from the freeway.

5. The boys watched helplessly as their boat <u>sank</u> in the swamp.

6. We watched with agony as my mother's spirit <u>sank</u> during her long illness.

7. With a family of twelve to feed, my grandmother gave rather <u>spare</u> servings of meat but plenty of potatoes and biscuits.

8. Charles will <u>spare</u> you the unpleasant task of unloading the dishwasher tonight.

9. We visited a European discotheque in which the young couples were all dancing the <u>swing</u>.

10. Tom has been watching the <u>swing</u> of the stock market since he made his first big investment.

Chapter Five

UNDERSTANDING AND USING FORMS

In this chapter the student will become familiar with different types of forms he might have to fill out in the working world. Some students will already be familiar with some of the banking forms, the application for employment, and the W-2 form, especially if they are already working.

Use the forms and applications in class, going over each one with the students as you and the class fill one out together. Perhaps you could use an opaque projector or make a Thermofax master for the overhead projector. Then give a blank form or application to each student as classwork or homework.

Worksheet 1: PERSONAL CHECKS

Here is a sample personal check and a check stub. Study them carefully so that you can complete the exercise below. Sometimes the stub information is in a little booklet attached inside the checkbook.

Check No. _6/7_	**THE BANK** No. _6/7_
Date _8/17/82_	_August 17_, 19 _82_
To _Cricket Records_	Pay to the Order of _Cricket Records_ $ _7.42_
For _Louie Boomers_	_Seven and ⁴²/₁₀₀_ _____ Dollars
Old Balance _118.29_	
Deposit _____	_Verna Allwood_
This check _7.42_	
New Balance _104.87_	⑆2100 1020 2⑉ 58⑈080⑈73 2⑊

REMEMBER:
1. Write a check in script; do not print.
2. Do not erase. If you make a mistake, tear up the check and write a new one.
3. Use ink always, preferably not a felt-tip pen.
4. Always complete the stub for your own records.

EXERCISE: You are purchasing a new shirt from The Clothes Horse for $25.71. This is the seventy-first check you have written. Your balance was $127.42. You deposited $100.00 this morning before you shopped.

Check No. _____	**THE BANK** No. _____
Date _____	_____, 19 ___
To _____	Pay to the Order of _____ $ _____
For _____	_____ Dollars
Old Balance _____	
Deposit _____	
This check _____	
New Balance _____	⑆2100 1020 2⑉ 58⑈080⑈73 2⑊

Practical English: A Complete Course

Worksheet 2A: DEPOSIT SLIP

Here is a sample deposit slip for a savings account. Study it carefully so that you will be able to complete the ones on the next page. A checking deposit is made on a form that comes with your checkbook and is only slightly different from this form.

SAVINGS DEPOSIT
United Western Bank

	Dollars	Cents
Currency	7	00
Coins	3	72
Checks *18-23* 1.	15	00
92-004 2.	25	00
33-117 3.	20	00
4.		
5.		
6.		
7.		
$	70	72
	Amount	

Marriot
Branch

Mary Ann Jones
Name

92 Courtland Way
Address

Oraga Ca.   92030
City   State   Zip Code

June 2, 1982
Date

415180
Account No.

REMEMBER: 1. List coins and currency separately in the spaces provided.

2. The check number is the numerator (top number) of the fractions you will find near the upper right corner of every check.

3. Be sure to write your correct savings account number.

EXERCISE: You have received some money for your birthday and you are going to deposit it in your savings account, No. 313452 of the Westmore Branch of the United Western Bank. Here is a list of your gifts: $10.00 cash from Aunt Jo, $2.50 in coins from assorted little cousins, a $5.00 check (13-002) from Uncle Bill, and a $10.00 check (90-456) from Aunt Ruby.

Worksheet 2B: DEPOSIT SLIP

```
┌─────────────────────────────────────────────────────────────────┐
│                       SAVINGS DEPOSIT                             │
│                    United Western Bank        Dollars │ Cents     │
│                                          Currency _____     │
│   _____                         Coins    _____     │
│       Branch                             Checks ___ 1._____     │
│   _____                        ___ 2._____        │
│         Name                                 ___ 3._____        │
│   _____                        ___ 4._____        │
│        Address                               ___ 5._____        │
│   ____  _____  _____                     ___ 6._____        │
│   City   State   Zip Code                    ___ 7._____        │
│   _____                        $ _____          │
│         Date                                                       │
│              _____                                      │
│               Account No.                    Amount                │
└─────────────────────────────────────────────────────────────────┘
```

EXERCISE: Create your own deposit transaction here. Then complete the form
below for your deposit.

_____ in coin   Account No. _____

_____ in currency

Check-bank number _____ for $ _____

Check-bank number _____ for $ _____

Check-bank number _____ for $ _____

```
┌─────────────────────────────────────────────────────────────────┐
│                       SAVINGS DEPOSIT                             │
│                    United Western Bank        Dollars │ Cents     │
│                                          Currency _____     │
│   _____                         Coins    _____     │
│       Branch                             Checks ___ 1._____     │
│   _____                        ___ 2._____        │
│         Name                                 ___ 3._____        │
│   _____                        ___ 4._____        │
│        Address                               ___ 5._____        │
│   ____  _____  _____                     ___ 6._____        │
│   City   State   Zip Code                    ___ 7._____        │
│   _____                        $ _____          │
│         Date                                                       │
│              _____                                      │
│               Account No.                    Amount                │
└─────────────────────────────────────────────────────────────────┘
```

Worksheet 3: WITHDRAWAL SLIP

Here is a sample withdrawal form to remove money from a savings account. Study the form carefully so that you can complete the exercise below.

SAVINGS WITHDRAWAL
Valley Bank

Rockland
Branch

Judy Therriault
Name

24 Madison St.
Address

Rockland, WI   53226
City   State   Zip Code

July 19, 1982
Date

23557-24
Account No.

$72.19
Amount

Seventy-two and $\frac{19}{100}$ Dollars

Judy Therriault
Signature

EXERCISE: You would like to remove $250.00 from the Westmore Branch of the United Western Bank. Your account number is 589643.

SAVINGS WITHDRAWAL
United Western Bank

_____
Branch

_____
Name

_____
Address

_____
City   State   Zip Code

_____
Date

_____
Account No.

$ _____
Amount

_____ Dollars

_____
Signature

Practical English: A Complete Course

Chapter Five

Worksheet 4: APPLICATION FOR CREDIT

Central Bank
Since 1892

Application for Credit

FOR BANK USE ONLY	512074						LOAN OFF NO	MC LIMIT	APPROVING OFFICER	APPROVAL DATE
						C.B.C.	C/C/CTR. OFFICER		

TYPE OF CREDIT REQUESTED

☐ AUTOMOBILE ☐ PERSONAL ☐ MASTERCARD ☐ CENTRAL CASH ☐ OTHER _____

AMOUNT REQUESTED	TERMS REQUESTED	PURPOSE OF CREDIT	OFFICE
$			

I understand I may apply for this credit in my name alone, without my spouse or any other person, regardless of my marital status. I'm applying ☐ IN MY NAME ALONE. ☐ JOINTLY WITH MY SPOUSE. ☐ JOINTLY WITH _____ WHO'S NOT MY SPOUSE (whose separate application is attached). If applicant is married and lives in a community property state such as California, all questions relating to each spouse must be answered even if this is an application for credit in the applicant's name alone.

APPLICANT

	BIRTHDATE MO/DAY/YR	☐ MARRIED ☐ UNMARRIED ☐ SEPARATED	NO. OF DEPENDENTS (INCL APPLICANT)	DRIVER'S LICENSE NO
FULL NAME				
HOME ADDRESS street apt city state	ZIP	HOW LONG? YRS MOS	SOCIAL SECURITY NO	
MAILING ADDRESS if different from above	ZIP	HOME PHONE NO	WORK PHONE NO	
PREVIOUS FULL ADDRESS home (if present under 5 yrs)	ZIP	HOW LONG? YRS MOS	LABOR UNION LOCAL NO	
EMPLOYER NAME and FULL ADDRESS	ZIP	DATE OF HIRE	YOUR OCCUPATION	
PREVIOUS EMPLOYER NAME and FULL ADDRESS (if present under 5 yrs)	ZIP	DATE OF HIRE	YOUR OCCUPATION	
NEAREST RELATIVE NOT LIVING WITH YOU and FULL ADDRESS	ZIP	PHONE NO	RELATIONSHIP	
CLOSE FRIEND and FULL ADDRESS			ZIP	PHONE NO

SPOUSE

	SOCIAL SECURITY NO	DRIVER'S LICENSE NO	BIRTHDATE MO/DAY/YR
FULL NAME			
STREET ADDRESS apt city state	ZIP	HOW LONG? YRS MOS	HOME PHONE NO	WORK PHONE NO
EMPLOYER NAME and FULL ADDRESS	ZIP	DATE OF HIRE	OCCUPATION	
PREVIOUS EMPLOYER NAME and FULL ADDRESS	ZIP	DATE OF HIRE	OCCUPATION	

INCOME   You don't have to reveal income from alimony, child support or separate maintenance unless you want the bank to consider it when evaluating this application.

APPLICANT'S MONTHLY INCOME: GROSS $_____ NET $_____ APPLICANT'S OTHER INCOME (MONTHLY) $_____

SPOUSE'S MONTHLY INCOME: GROSS $_____ NET $_____ SPOUSE'S OTHER INCOME (MONTHLY) $_____

FINANCIAL INFORMATION   If you are married, the bank will assume that all assets and income are community property and all debts are community obligations, unless otherwise indicated.

			ACCOUNT NO
BANK and FULL ADDRESS	ZIP	☐ LOAN ☐ SAVINGS ☐ CHECKING	(SV) (CK)
SAVINGS & LOAN and FULL ADDRESS	ZIP	☐ LOAN ☐ SAVINGS	ACCOUNT NO
CREDIT UNION and FULL ADDRESS	ZIP	☐ LOAN ☐ SAVINGS	ACCOUNT NO

REAL ESTATE

	LANDLORDS OR MORTGAGEES	MO PMT /RENT	BALANCE OWING
☐ BUYING OR OWN ☐ RENTING	NAME _____	(INCL INSURANCE AND PROPERTY TAX) $	$
☐ LIVING WITH PARENTS	FULL ADDRESS		

List all other debts (finance companies, credit unions, credit cards, stores, banks, alimony, child support, separate maintenance).

TO WHOM OWED	ADDRESS OR BRANCH	MO PMT	BALANCE OWING
		$	$
		$	$
		$	$
		$	$
		TOTAL $	$

Is any debt past due? ☐ YES ☐ NO. Are all debts listed? ☐ YES ☐ NO. If you need more space, attach a separate sheet.

Have you or your spouse ever obtained credit under a different name? ☐ YES ☐ NO. If Yes, show name(s): _____

Ever had a judgment against you? ☐ YES ☐ NO   Ever bankrupt? ☐ YES ☐ NO   If yes, what year? _____

Ever had a vehicle or any merchandise repossessed? ☐ YES ☐ NO   IMPORTANT: Mother's Maiden Name _____

ASSET and DEBT IDENTIFICATION   List assets and income which aren't community property and debts which aren't community obligations: show how assets are held and income received (separate property, joint tenancy, tenancy in common) and how debts are owed.

The information I/we have provided with this application is true and correct to the best of my/our knowledge. I/we authorize the bank to gather whatever credit information it considers necessary and appropriate concerning such information. I/we understand that from time to time you may receive information from others and you will answer questions and requests from others seeking credit experience information about my account. I/we understand that this application and any other information used in evaluating this request for credit shall remain the bank's property whether or not credit is granted.

YOUR SIGNATURE _____ DATE _____ YOUR SPOUSE'S SIGNATURE _____ DATE _____
(If you are requesting the financial accommodation jointly with your spouse)

IL 14 (Rev. 2/84)

Practical English: A Complete Course

Worksheet 5A: INDIVIDUAL FINANCIAL STATEMENT

INDIVIDUAL FINANCIAL STATEMENT

INSTRUC-
TIONS: (read
before com-
pleting this
statement)

Regardless of your marital status, you may apply for credit in your name alone.

If you are applying for credit in your name alone or with a person other than your spouse, complete this statement and sign on the reverse.

If you are married and not separated and are a resident of California, information about your spouse must be provided if you intend to use your spouse's income to repay this credit and the Consent To Gather Credit Information must be signed by your spouse. If you apply for credit jointly with your spouse, you and your spouse are to complete this statement and sign on the reverse.

If you are married and not separated, and unless you indicate otherwise, all income and assets will be presumed to be community property and all debts will be presumed to be liabilities of community property.

TO — CENTRAL BANK

NAME IN FULL | SOCIAL SECURITY NO | AGE | MARITAL STATUS ☐ MARRIED ☐ UNMARRIED ☐ SEPARATED | DEPENDENTS NUMBER _____ AGES _____

RESIDENCE ADDRESS (NO., STREET, CITY, STATE, ZIP CODE) | YRS. AT ADDRESS | TELEPHONE & EXT | OCCUPATION

PREVIOUS ADDRESSES IF AT ABOVE LESS THAN 5 YEARS (NO. AND STREET, CITY, STATE, ZIP CODE)
(1)   (2)

EMPLOYER | ADDRESS (NO. AND STREET) | CITY | TELEPHONE & EXT

SPOUSE INFORMATION SECTION

SPOUSE'S NAME | SOCIAL SECURITY NO | AGE

SPOUSE'S EMPLOYER | ADDRESS (NO. & STREET) | CITY | TELEPHONE & EXT

FINANCIAL CONDITION AS OF _____ , 19_____

ASSETS		AMOUNT		LIABILITIES		AMOUNT
CASH	CENTRAL BANK	Office		NOTES PAYABLE TO BANKS	CENTRAL BANK	Office	
	Other Banks				Other (Itemize, Schedule 4)	
STOCKS AND BONDS	Listed (Schedule 1)			OTHER NOTES AND ACCOUNTS PAYABLE	Real Estate Loans (Schedule 2)	
	Unlisted (Schedule 1)				Sales Contracts & Sec. Agreements (Sch. 4)	
REAL ESTATE	Improved (Schedule 2)				Loans on Life Insurance Policies (Sch. 4)	
	Unimproved (Schedule 2)			TAXES PAYABLE	Current Year's Income Taxes Unpaid	
	Trust Deeds and Mortgages (Schedule 3)				Prior Year's Income Taxes Unpaid	
LIFE INSURANCE	Cash Surrender Value				Real Estate Taxes Unpaid	
ACCOUNTS AND NOTES RECEIVABLE	Relatives and Friends (Schedule 4)			OTHER LIABILITES	Unpaid Interest	
	Collectible (Schedule 4)				Others (Itemize, Schedule 4)	
	Doubtful (Schedule 4)					
OTHER PERSONAL PROPERTY	Automobile				TOTAL LIABILITIES	
	Other (Itemize, Schedule 4)				NET WORTH	
	TOTAL				TOTAL	

ANNUAL INCOME	Refer to Federal Income Tax Returns for Previous Year	ANNUAL EXPENDITURES	(Refer to Federal Income Tax Returns for Previous Year)
SALARY OR WAGES		PROPERTY TAXES AND ASSESSMENTS	
DIVIDENDS AND INTEREST		FEDERAL AND STATE INCOME TAXES	
RENTALS (GROSS)		REAL ESTATE LOAN PAYMENTS	
BUSINESS OR PROFESSIONAL INCOME (NET)		PAYMENTS ON CONTRACTS AND OTHER NOTES	
OTHER INCOME DESCRIBE (Alimony, child support & separate		INSURANCE PREMIUMS	
maintenance income need not be revealed if you do not wish to		ESTIMATED LIVING EXPENSES	
have it considered as a basis for repaying this obligation)		OTHER (Alimony, Child Support, Maintenance)	
TOTAL INCOME		TOTAL EXPENDITURES	

LIFE INSURANCE	FACE AMOUNT	BENEFICIARY	COMPANY

CR-17 (Rev. 12/79)

Practical English: A Complete Course

Worksheet 5B: INDIVIDUAL FINANCIAL STATEMENT

Give details of any contingent liability as endorser or guarantor, or on suits or judgments pending. (If necessary, use separate sheet.)

_____

Do you do business with any other bank? _____ If so, give details _____

Have you ever filed any petition under the Bankruptcy Act? _____

Are any of the assets listed on this statement held under a Trust Agreement?   ☐ Yes ☐ No _____

If you are married, are any of the assets described in this statement your spouse's separate property? _____

If so, state which _____

Have your Income Tax Returns ever been questioned by the Internal Revenue Service? _____ If so, most recent year _____

SCHEDULE 1: LISTED AND UNLISTED STOCKS AND BONDS OWNED

NO. OF SHARES OR PAR VALUE	Description	Issued in Name of	Joint Tenancy Ten. in Common Comm. Property	Market Value
LISTED:				
		TOTAL LISTED		
UNLISTED:				
		TOTAL UNLISTED		

Are any of the above listed securities pledged to secure a debt? _____

SCHEDULE 2: REAL ESTATE OWNED (Designate: I - Improved, U - Unimproved.)

Location or Description	Title in Name of	Date Acquired	Cost	Present Value	Trust Deeds, Mortgages or other Liens			
					Unpaid Bal.	Rate %	Monthly Payment	Held By
		TOTAL			X X X	X X X X X	X X X X X X X X X X	

SCHEDULE 3: TRUST DEEDS AND MORTGAGES OWNED

Name of Payer	Legal Desc., Street Address, & Type of Improvements	Unpaid Bal.	Joint Tenancy Ten. in Common Comm. Property	Terms	1st or 2nd Lien	Value of Property
	TOTAL			X X X	X X X X	

SCHEDULE 4: DETAILS RELATIVE TO OTHER IMPORTANT ASSETS AND LIABILITIES

_____

_____

_____

This statement is furnished in connection with an application for credit and is to be regarded as continuous until another shall be substituted for it. If the undersigned, or any endorser or guarantor of the obligations of the undersigned, at any time becomes insolvent, or commits an act of bankruptcy, or dies, or if any writ of attachment, garnishment, execution or other legal process be issued against property of the undersigned, or if any assessment for taxes against the undersigned, other than on real property, is made by the Federal or State government, or any department thereof, or if any of the representations made above prove to be untrue, or if the undersigned fails to notify you of any material change in financial condition as given above, then and in either such case, all of the obligations of the undersigned to or held by you, either as borrower or guarantor, shall immediately become due and payable, without demand or notice. In consideration of the granting or renewing of any credit to the undersigned hereafter, the undersigned hereby waives the pleading of the statute of limitations as a defense to any obligation of the undersigned to you.

I hereby certify that I have carefully read the above statement, including the reverse side, and it is a complete, true and correct statement to the best of my knowledge and belief.

Date Signed _____ , 19_____ .   (Sign Here) _____

(Sign Here) _____

SPOUSE'S CONSENT TO GATHER CREDIT INFORMATION

I authorize the Bank to make whatever inquiries it considers necessary and appropriate for purposes of evaluating this financial statement and reviewing and collecting any credit granted, extended, renewed or continued.

_____   _____

Signature of Spouse   Date

Practical English: A Complete Course

Worksheet 6: SOCIAL SECURITY CARD APPLICATION

SOCIAL SECURITY CARD APPLICATION

DEPARTMENT OF HEALTH AND HUMAN SERVICES
SOCIAL SECURITY ADMINISTRATION

FORM APPROVED
OMB NO. 72-S79002

**FORM SS-5 – APPLICATION FOR A
SOCIAL SECURITY NUMBER CARD**
(Original Replacement or Correction)

MICROFILM REF. NO. (SSA USE ONLY)

Unless the requested information is provided, we may not be able to issue a Social Security Number (20 CFR 422.103(b))

INSTRUCTIONS TO APPLICANT ▶	Before completing this form, please read the instructions on the opposite page. You can type or print, using pen with dark blue or black ink. Do not use pencil.			

		First	Middle	Last
NAA	NAME TO BE SHOWN ON CARD			
NAB **1**	FULL NAME AT BIRTH (IF OTHER THAN ABOVE)	First	Middle	Last
ONA	OTHER NAME(S) USED			

STT **2**	MAILING ADDRESS	(Street/Apt No , P O Box, Rural Route No)

CTY STE ZIP	CITY	STATE	ZIP CODE

CSP **3**	CITIZENSHIP (Check one only)	SEX **4**	SEX	ETB **5**	RACE/ETHNIC DESCRIPTION (Check one only) (Voluntary)
	☐ a. U.S. citizen	☐ Male			☐ a Asian, Asian-American or Pacific Islander (Includes persons of Chinese, Filipino, Japanese, Korean, Samoan, etc., ancestry or descent)
	☐ b. Legal alien allowed to work	☐ Female			☐ b Hispanic (Includes persons of Chicano, Cuban, Mexican or Mexican-American, Puerto Rican, South or Central American, or other Spanish ancestry or descent)
	☐ c. Legal alien not allowed to work				☐ c Negro or Black (not Hispanic)
	☐ d. Other (See instructions on Page 2)				☐ d North American Indian or Alaskan Native
					☐ e White (not Hispanic)

DOB **6**	DATE OF BIRTH ▶	MONTH	DAY	YEAR	AGE **7**	PRESENT AGE	PLB **8**	PLACE OF BIRTH ▶	CITY	STATE OR FOREIGN COUNTRY

MNA **9**	MOTHER'S NAME AT HER BIRTH	First	Middle	Last (her maiden name)
FNA	FATHER'S NAME	First	Middle	Last

PNO **10**	a. Have you or someone on your behalf applied for a social security number before? ☐ No	☐ Don't Know	☐ Yes

If you checked "yes", complete items "b" through "e" below, otherwise go to item 11

SSN PNS PNY	b. Enter social security number	c In what State did you apply?	What year?

NLC	d Enter the name shown on your most recent social security card	e If the birth date you used was different from the date shown in item 6, enter it here	MONTH	DAY	YEAR

DON **11**	TODAY'S DATE ▶	MONTH	DAY	YEAR	**12**	Telephone number where we can reach you during the day	HOME	OTHER

ASD	**WARNING:** Deliberately providing false information on this application is punishable by a fine of $1,000 or one year in jail, or both.

13	YOUR SIGNATURE	**14**	YOUR RELATIONSHIP TO PERSON IN ITEM 1 ☐ Self ☐ Other _____ (Specify)
	WITNESS (Needed only if signed by mark "X")		WITNESS (Needed only if signed by mark "X")

Practical English: A Complete Course

Worksheet 7A: WITHHOLDING CERTIFICATE

You got the job that you applied for. Now your employer wants you to fill out a W-4 Form for income tax purposes. The following terms are necessary for you to know:

- Employee—you; the person who works for a company

- Employer—the company you work for

- Dependents—the people depending on you for support, including yourself

- Exemptions—the number of people depending on you for support, including yourself

- Deductions—the amounts of money withheld from your pay

- - - - - - - - - - - - - - - **Cut here and give the certificate to your employer. Keep the top portion for your records.** - - - - - - - - - - - - - - -

Form **W-4A** Department of the Treasury Internal Revenue Service	**Employee's Withholding Allowance Certificate** ▶ **For Privacy Act and Paperwork Reduction Act Notice, see reverse.**	OMB No. 1545-0010 **1987**

1 Type or print your full name		2 Your social security number
Home address (number and street or rural route)	**3 Marital Status**	☐ Single ☐ Married ☐ Married, but withhold at higher Single rate **Note:** *If married, but legally separated, or spouse is a nonresident alien, check the Single box.*
City or town, state, and ZIP code		

4 Total number of allowances you are claiming (from line G above, or from the Worksheets on back if they apply) . . . **4** _____

5 Additional amount, if any, you want deducted from each pay . . . . **5** $ _____

6 I claim exemption from withholding because (check boxes below that apply):

  a ☐ Last year I did not owe any Federal income tax and had a right to a full refund of **ALL** income tax withheld, **AND**

  b ☐ This year I do not expect to owe any Federal income tax and expect to have a right to a full refund of **ALL** income tax withheld. If both **a** and **b** apply, enter the year effective and "EXEMPT" here . . . ▶ Year 19 _____

  c Are you a full-time student? . . . . ☐ Yes ☐ No

Under penalties of perjury, I certify that I am entitled to the number of withholding allowances claimed on this certificate or, if claiming exemption from withholding, that I am entitled to claim the exempt status.

Employee's signature ▶ _____ **Date** ▶ _____, 1987

7 Employer's name and address **(Employer: Complete 7, 8, and 9 only if sending to IRS)**	8 Office code	9 Employer identification number

Practical English: A Complete Course

Worksheet 7B: WITHHOLDING CERTIFICATE

Form W-4A (1987)

Page **2**

Deductions Worksheet

NOTE: Use this Worksheet only if you plan to itemize or claim other deductions.

1. Enter an estimate of your 1987 itemized deductions. These include: home mortgage interest, 65% of personal interest, charitable contributions, state and local taxes (but not sales taxes), medical expenses in excess of 7.5% of your income, and miscellaneous deductions (most miscellaneous deductions are now deductible only in excess of 2% of your income) . . . . **1** $ _____

2. Enter: { $3,760 if married filing jointly or qualifying widow(er) }
{ $2,540 if single or head of household } . . . . **2** $ _____
{ $1,880 if married filing separately }

3. **Subtract** line 2 from line 1. Enter the result, but not less than zero . . . . . **3** $ _____

4. Enter an estimate of your 1987 adjustments to income. These include alimony paid and deductible IRA contributions . . . . **4** $ _____

5. **Add** lines 3 and 4 and enter the total . . . . **5** $ _____

6. Enter an estimate of your 1987 nonwage income (such as dividends or interest income) . . . . . **6** $ _____

7. **Subtract** line 6 from line 5. Enter the result, but not less than zero . . . . . **7** $ _____

8. **Divide** the amount on line 7 by $2,000 and enter the result here. Drop any fraction . . . . **8** _____

9. Enter the number from Form W-4A Worksheet, line G, on page 1 . . . . **9** _____

10. **Add** lines 8 and 9 and enter the total here. If you plan to use the Two-Earner/Two-Job Worksheet, also enter the total on line 1, below. Otherwise **stop here** and enter this total on Form W-4A, line 4 on page 1 . . . . . **10** _____

Two-Earner/Two-Job Worksheet

NOTE: Use this Worksheet only if the instructions at line G on page 1 direct you here.

1. Enter the number from line G on page 1 (or from line 10 above if you used the Deductions Worksheet) . . . **1** _____

2. Enter "1" if you are married filing a joint return and earnings from the lower paying jobs held by you or your spouse exceed $3,000. Otherwise enter "0" . . . . **2** _____

3. Subtrac⁺ line 2 from line 1 and enter the result here. If you entered "1" on line 2 and combined earnings from all jobs are less than $40,000, enter the result on Form W-4A, line 4, page 1, and **do not** use the rest of this worksheet. Otherwise, continue . . . . **3** _____

4. Find the number in **Table 1** below that applies to the **LOWEST** paying job and enter it here . . . . . **4** _____

5. If line 3 is **GREATER THAN OR EQUAL TO** line 4, **subtract** line 4 from line 3. Enter the result here (if zero, enter "0") and on Form W-4A, line 4, page 1. **Do not** use the rest of this worksheet. . . . . . . **5** _____

6. If line 3 is **LESS THAN** line 4, enter "0" on Form W-4A, line 4, page 1, and enter the number from line 4 of this worksheet . . . . **6** _____

7. Enter the number from line 3 of this worksheet . . . . **7** _____

8. Subtract line 7 from line 6. . . . . **8** _____

9. Find the amount in **Table 2** below that applies to the **HIGHEST** paying job and enter it here . . . . . . **9** $ _____

10. **Multiply** line 9 by line 8 and enter the result here . . . . **10** $ _____

11. **Divide** line 10 by the number of pay periods each year. (For example, divide by 26 if you are paid every other week.) Enter the result here and on Form W-4A, line 5, page 1 . . . . **11** $ _____

Table 1: Two-Earner/Two-Job Worksheet

Married Filing Jointly		All Others	
If wages from **LOWEST** paying job are—	Enter on line 4, above	If wages from **LOWEST** paying job are—	Enter on line 4, above
0 - $6,000	0	0 - $4,000	0
6,001 - 10,000	1	4,001 - 7,000	1
10,001 - 13,000	2	7,001 - 11,000	2
13,001 - 16,000	3	11,001 - 14,000	3
16,001 - 20,000	4	14,001 - 17,000	4
20,001 - 23,000	5	17,001 - 23,000	5
23,001 - 26,000	6	23,001 - 30,000	6
26,001 - 29,000	7	30,001 and over	7
29,001 - 35,000	8		
35,001 - 50,000	9		
50,001 and over	10		

Table 2: Two-Earner/Two-Job Worksheet

Married Filing Jointly		All Others	
If wages from **HIGHEST** paying job are—	Enter on line 9, above	If wages from **HIGHEST** paying job are—	Enter on line 9, above
0 - $30,000	$300	0 - $17,000	$300
30,001 - 47,000	500	17,001 - 28,000	500
47,001 and over	700	28,001 and over	700

Chapter Five

Worksheet 8A: APPLICATION FOR EXAMINATION

An Equal Opportunity Employer
CONTRA COSTA COUNTY PERSONNEL DEPARTMENT
651 Pine Street, Martinez, California 94553

APPLICATION FOR EXAMINATION

POSITION APPLYING FOR

_____
Enter exact Merit System job title

PLEASE TYPE OR PRINT IN INK

DATE RECEIVED		For Personnel Use Only
		Accepted Rejected
		Analyst _____ Date _____
		Reason _____
(21)		(22)

Position Applying for (Show exact title — separate application required for each examination)

PLEASE TYPE OR PRINT IN INK

1. _____ Social Security Number — for Applicant/Employee Record Control (Voluntary)
   (3)

2. Name

   _____ _____ _____
   (4) Last Name   First Name   Middle Name

3. Address

	Test Code Area	OFFICE USE ONLY
	☐ A – Central	
	☐ W – West	
	☐ 3 – East	
	☐ 9 – Special	(12)

   _____ _____ _____ _____ _____
   No   Street (9)   Apt No   City (10)   State/Zip Code (11)

4. Phones

   (___) _____   (___) _____   (___) _____   _____
   (13)   Home (14)   (15) Business (16)   (17)   Emergency (18)

5. If you are **not** a United States Citizen, do you have permission to work in the United States from the U.S. Immigration and Naturalization Service?   Yes ☐   No ☐
   You will be required to submit proof of your permission to work if employed.

6. Have you ever been **convicted** of any offense by any civilian or military court? If yes, please note in Section 15 the date and place of each offense the specific charge, the date and place of conviction and the fine or sentence received. You may omit traffic violations for which the only penalty imposed was a fine of less than $50.00. A criminal record is not necessarily a bar to employment. Each case is given individual consideration, based on job relatedness.   Yes ☐   No ☐

7. Have you ever been discharged, forced to resign, or rejected during a probationary period from any employment within the last ten years?   Yes   No
   If yes, give name and address of employer, reason for each release and dates of employment.
   If answer is yes it is not necessarily a bar to employment. Each case is given individual consideration, based on job relatedness.

8. Are you fluent in any languages other than English? If so, please specify: _____

9. Veterans who qualify to place on "Open" employment lists may be allowed an additional 5% of the total credits earned (providing examination is successfully completed). Acceptable evidence of honorable discharge from active military service (Form DD214) should be submitted with this application, but MUST be submitted or postmarked not later than the final filing date in the examination announcement.

   Do you apply for Veterans Credits?   Yes ☐   No ☐
   (19)

	Verify (V)
	OFFICE USE ONLY

First Name

Middle Name

10. Have you ever worked for Contra Costa County before?   Yes ☐   No ☐

11. Are you currently working in a **permanent** Merit System position for Contra Costa County?   Yes ☐ K   No ☐ A
    Merit System job title.
    (20)

12. List licenses, certificates and/or registrations required for this job (Driver's License, Registered Nurse License, etc.).

TITLE	DATE ISSUED	DATE EXPIRES	NUMBER	Verified By	Lic. No. 1 (23)
_____	_____	_____	_____		Lic. No. 2 (24)
_____	_____	_____	_____		Lic. No. 3 (25)
_____	_____	_____	_____		OFFICE USE ONLY

Last Name

PLEASE TYPE OR PRINT IN INK

AK-1 (4/86)

Worksheet 8B: APPLICATION FOR EXAMINATION (continued)

13. **EDUCATION:** Check appropriate box if you possess one of the following:
☐ High School Diploma   ☐ G.E.D. Certificate   ☐ California High School Proficiency Certificate
Give Highest Grade or Educational Level Achieved _____

Names of colleges/universities attended	Dates Attended	Course of Study/Major	Degree Awarded	Units Completed		Type Degree	Date Degree Requirements Completed
				Semester	Quarter		
A)			Yes ☐ No ☐				
B)			Yes ☐ No ☐				
C)			Yes ☐ No ☐				
D) Other schools/training completed:		Course Studied	Hours Completed		Certificate Awarded		

14. THE FOLLOWING INFORMATION MUST BE FILLED OUT COMPLETELY. Begin with your present or most recent experience and account for all employment for at least the past 10 years or more. Voluntary non-paid experience will be accepted if job-related. Use additional sheets if necessary and you may attach additional information.

A) Dates   Employer's Name and Address   Title   Reason for Leaving
From _____   _____   Duties performed _____
To _____   _____
Total _____   _____
Yrs.   Mos.   Salary per month $ _____
Full time _____   ☐ Volunteer   Hr. Salary
Part time _____   Hrs. per week _____ $ _____

B) Dates   Employer's Name and Address   Title   Reason for Leaving
From _____   _____   Duties performed _____
To _____   _____
Total _____   _____
Yrs.   Mos.   Salary per month $ _____
Full time _____   ☐ Volunteer   Hr. Salary
Part time _____   Hrs. per week _____ $ _____

C) Dates   Employer's Name and Address   Title   Reason for Leaving
From _____   _____   Duties performed _____
To _____   _____
Total _____   _____
Yrs.   Mos.   Salary per month $ _____
Full time _____   ☐ Volunteer   Hr. Salary
Part time _____   Hrs. per week _____ $ _____

D) Dates   Employer's Name and Address   Title   Reason for Leaving
From _____   _____   Duties performed _____
To _____   _____
Total _____   _____
Yrs.   Mos.   Salary per month $ _____
Full time _____   ☐ Volunteer   Hr. Salary
Part time _____   Hrs. per week _____ $ _____

E) Dates   Employer's Name and Address   Title   Reason for Leaving
From _____   _____   Duties performed _____
To _____   _____
Total _____   _____
Yrs.   Mos.   Salary per month $ _____
Full time _____   ☐ Volunteer   Hr. Salary
Part time _____   Hrs. per week _____ $ _____

15. Remarks _____

16. In case of emergency please notify: Name _____
Phone _____ Address _____

17. I authorize the employers and educational institutions identified in this employment application to release any information they have concerning my employment or education, to the County of Contra Costa. Yes ☐ No ☐
May we contact your present employer? Yes ☐ No ☐

18. I CERTIFY that the statements made by me in this application are true, complete, and correct to the best of my knowledge and belief, and are made in good faith. I understand and agree misstatements/omissions of material fact will cause forfeiture of my rights to employment by Contra Costa County.

➡ THANK YOU

_____   _____
DATE   SIGNATURE OF APPLICANT

Practical English: A Complete Course

Worksheet 9: AUTOMOBILE LOSS NOTICE

SET TAB STOPS AT ARROWS

acord. AUTOMOBILE LOSS NOTICE

DATE (MM/DD/YY)

PRODUCER	PRODUCER PHONE (A/C. NO . EXT)	FOR COMPANY USE ONLY		
	COMPANY		POLICY NUMBER	CAT #
	POLICY EFF. DATE (MM/DD/YY)	POLICY EXP DATE (MM/DD/YY)	DATE (MM/DD/YY) & TIME OF LOSS	PREVIOUSLY REPORTED
CODE SUB CODE			A M / P M	YES / NO

INSURED

NAME AND ADDRESS	INSURED'S RESIDENCE PHONE (A/C. NO)	INSURED'S BUSINESS PHONE (A/C. NO . EXT)
	PERSON TO CONTACT	WHERE TO CONTACT
		WHEN
	CONTACT'S RESIDENCE PHONE (A/C. NO)	CONTACT'S BUSINESS PHONE (A/C. NO EXT)

LOSS

LOCATION OF ACCIDENT (INCLUDING CITY & STATE)	AUTHORITY CONTACTED & REPORT NO	VIOLATIONS/CITATIONS
DESCRIPTION OF ACCIDENT (USE REVERSE SIDE. IF NECESSARY)		

POLICY INFORMATION

BODILY INJURY	PROPERTY DAMAGE	SINGLE LIMIT	MED PAY	OTHER THAN COLL DED	OTHER COVERAGES & DEDUCTIBLES (UM. NO-FAULT TOWING ETC)
LOSS PAYEE				COLLISION DED	

INSURED VEHICLE

VEH NO	YEAR. MAKE. MODEL	V I N (VEHICLE IDENTIFICATION)	PLATE NO
OWNER'S NAME & ADDRESS			PHONE (A/C NO EXT)
DRIVER'S NAME & ADDRESS (CHECK IF SAME AS OWNER)		RESIDENCE PHONE (A/C NO)	BUSINESS PHONE (A/C NO . EXT)
RELATION TO INSURED (EMPLOYEE. FAMILY. ETC.)	DATE OF BIRTH	DRIVER'S LICENSE NUMBER	PURPOSE OF USE	USED WITH PERMISSION YES NO
DESCRIBE DAMAGE	ESTIMATE AMOUNT $	WHERE CAN VEHICLE BE SEEN	WHEN	OTHER INSURANCE ON VEHICLE

PROPERTY DAMAGED

DESCRIBE PROPERTY (IF AUTO YEAR. MAKE. MODEL. PLATE NO)	OTHER VEH . OR INSURED PROPERTY YES NO	COMPANY OR AGENCY NAME & POLICY NO	
OWNER'S NAME & ADDRESS		BUSINESS PHONE (A/C NO . EXT)	RESIDENCE PHONE (A/C. NO)
OTHER DRIVER'S NAME & ADDRESS (CHECK IF SAME AS OWNER)		BUSINESS PHONE (A/C NO . EXT)	RESIDENCE PHONE (A/C. NO)
DESCRIBE DAMAGE	ESTIMATE AMOUNT $	WHERE CAN DAMAGE BE SEEN	

INJURED

NAME & ADDRESS	PHONE (A/C. NO)	PED	INS VEH	OTHER VEH	AGE	EXTENT OF INJURY

WITNESSES OR PASSENGERS

NAME & ADDRESS	PHONE (A/C. NO)	INS VEH	OTHER VEH	OTHER (SPECIFY)

REMARKS (INCLUDE ADJUSTER ASSIGNED)		
REPORTED BY	REPORTED TO	SIGNATURE OF PRODUCER OR INSURED

ACORD 2 (8/82-c)   NOTE: IMPORTANT CALIFORNIA, FLORIDA, IDAHO, AND NEW YORK INFORMATION ON REVERSE SIDE   © ACORD CORPORATION 1982

Worksheet 10: SWORN STATEMENT IN PROOF OF LOSS

Form recommended by the
National Board of Fire Underwriters
July, 1950

SWORN STATEMENT IN PROOF OF LOSS

$_____
AMOUNT OF POLICY AT TIME OF LOSS

_____
DATE ISSUED

_____
DATE EXPIRES

_____
POLICY NUMBER

_____
AGENCY AT

_____
AGENT

To the_____

of_____

At time of loss, by the above indicated policy of insurance you insured_____

_____

against loss by_____to the property described under Schedule "A," according to
the terms and conditions of the said policy and all forms, endorsements, transfers and assignments attached thereto.

1. Time and Origin: A _____loss occurred about the hour of_____o'clock _____M.,

STATE KIND

on the _____ day of _____19_____. The cause and origin of the said loss were:_____

_____

2. Occupancy: The building described, or containing the property described, was occupied at the time of the loss as follows,
and for no other purpose whatever:_____

_____

3. Title and Interest: At the time of the loss the interest of your insured in the property described therein was_____

_____No other person or persons had any interest therein or

incumbrance thereon, except:_____

4. Changes: Since the said policy was issued there has been no assignment thereof, or change of interest, use, occupancy,
possession, location or exposure of the property described, except:_____

_____

_____

5. Total Insurance: The total amount of insurance upon the property described by this policy was, at the time of the loss,
$_____, as more particularly specified in the apportionment attached under Schedule "C," besides which
there was no policy or other contract of insurance, written or oral, valid or invalid.

6. The Actual Cash Value of said property at the time of the loss was   .   .   .   .   .   . $_____

7. The Whole Loss and Damage was   .   .   .   . $_____

8. The Amount Claimed under the above numbered policy is   .   .   .   .   . $_____

  The said loss did not originate by any act, design or procurement on the part of your insured, or this affiant; nothing has
been done by or with the privity or consent of your insured or this affiant, to violate the conditions of the policy, or render it void;
no articles are mentioned herein or in annexed schedules but such as were destroyed or damaged at the time of said loss; no
property saved has in any manner been concealed, and no attempt to deceive the said company, as to the extent of said loss, has
in any manner been made. Any other information that may be required will be furnished and considered a part of this proof.

  The furnishing of this blank or the preparation of proofs by a representative of the above insurance company is not a waiver
of any of its rights.

State of_____

County of_____

_____
_____Insured

Subscribed and sworn to before me this_____day of_____19_____

_____Notary Public

TRADE MARK
STANDARD
REG. U.S. PAT. OFF.
JULY 1950

(OVER)

Practical English: A Complete Course

Worksheet 11: REPORT OF TRAFFIC ACCIDENT

SR 1 (REV. 6/86)

STATE OF CALIFORNIA
REPORT OF TRAFFIC ACCIDENT

Every driver of a motor vehicle involved in an accident on a **public street or highway** resulting in injury or death of any person, or property damage to any one person (including the driver) in excess of $500 must within 10 days, report the accident on this form to the Department of Motor Vehicles.
Please use an attachment for any additional vehicles involved, property damage, injuries, deaths, or other information

MAIL THIS REPORT TO
DEPARTMENT OF MOTOR VEHICLES—FINANCIAL RESPONSIBILITY
P.O. BOX 942884, SACRAMENTO, CALIFORNIA 94284-0001

DMV File No. _____
DEPARTMENTAL USE ONLY

PLEASE PRINT

DATE OF ACCIDENT

MONTH	DAY	YEAR 19	HOUR	☐ A.M. ☐ P.M.

PLACE

LOCATION OF ACCIDENT	CITY	COUNTY	PARKING LOT ☐ YES ☐ NO

NUMBER VEHICLES IN ACCIDENT	NUMBER PERSONS INJURED	NUMBER PERSONS KILLED

YOUR VEHICLE	**OTHER VEHICLE**
☐ Stopped in Traffic ☐ Moving ☐ Legally Parked ☐ Pedestrian ☐ Bicycle	☐ Stopped in Traffic ☐ Moving ☐ Legally Parked ☐ Pedestrian ☐ Bicycle
DRIVER'S NAME (FIRST, MIDDLE, LAST)	DRIVER'S NAME (FIRST, MIDDLE, LAST)
DRIVER ADDRESS (NUMBER AND STREET)	DRIVER'S ADDRESS (NUMBER AND STREET)
CITY STATE ZIP CODE	CITY STATE ZIP CODE
DRIVER LICENSE (NUMBER AND STATE) DATE OF BIRTH (MO., DAY, YEAR)	DRIVER LICENSE (NUMBER AND STATE) DATE OF BIRTH (MO., DAY, YEAR)
OWNER OF VEHICLE YOU WERE DRIVING (FIRST, MIDDLE, LAST)	OWNER OF OTHER VEHICLE (FIRST, MIDDLE, LAST)
ADDRESS (NUMBER AND STREET)	ADDRESS (NUMBER AND STREET)
CITY STATE ZIP CODE	CITY STATE ZIP CODE
OWNER'S DRIVER LICENSE (NUMBER AND STATE) DATE OF BIRTH (MO., DAY, YEAR)	OWNER'S DRIVER LICENSE (NUMBER AND STATE) DATE OF BIRTH (MO., DAY, YEAR)
VEHICLE YOU WERE DRIVING (YEAR AND MAKE) BODY TYPE	OTHER VEHICLE (YEAR AND MAKE) BODY TYPE
VEHICLE LICENSE (NUMBER AND STATE) ENGINE OR I.D. NUMBER	VEHICLE LICENSE (NUMBER AND STATE) ENGINE OR I.D. NUMBER
ESTIMATED COST OF REPAIRS $	ESTIMATED COST OF REPAIRS $
Were You Driving a Vehicle Owned by Your Employer and With Permission? ☐ Yes ☐ No	Was he/she Driving a Vehicle Owned by an Employer and With Permission? ☐ Yes ☐ No
EMPLOYER'S NAME AND ADDRESS If Yes	EMPLOYER'S NAME AND ADDRESS If Yes

DAMAGE TO OTHER PROPERTY

NAME OF OBJECT(S)	OWNER'S NAME AND ADDRESS
NATURE OF DAMAGES	ESTIMATED COST TO REPAIR DAMAGE $

INJURIES AND DEATHS CAUSED BY THE ACCIDENT

INJURED

NAME	AGE	☐ Driver ☐ Passenger	☐ In Your Vehicle ☐ In Other Vehicle	☐ Bicyclist ☐ Pedestrian
ADDRESS	TYPE OF INJURY			☐ Fatal
NAME	AGE	☐ Driver ☐ Passenger	☐ In Your Vehicle ☐ In Other Vehicle	☐ Bicyclist ☐ Pedestrian
ADDRESS	TYPE OF INJURY			☐ Fatal

Was a policy of **LIABILITY** insurance or a bond, covering the operation of your vehicle in effect at time of accident? ☐ Yes ☐ No	**DEPARTMENT USE ONLY**
IF YES GIVE NAME OF INSURANCE COMPANY OR SURETY COMPANY (NOT AGENCY) POLICY OR BOND NUMBER	

I CERTIFY UNDER PENALTY OF PERJURY THAT THE ACCIDENT INFORMATION ABOVE AND THE INSURANCE INFORMATION BELOW (IF ANY) IS TRUE TO THE BEST OF MY KNOWLEDGE. (PERJURY IS PUNISHABLE BY IMPRISONMENT, FINE OR BOTH.)

SIGNED AT (CITY)	DATE	► SIGN HERE

Worksheet 12A: APPLICATION FOR EMPLOYMENT

APPLICATION FOR EMPLOYMENT
(PRE-EMPLOYMENT QUESTIONNAIRE)   (AN EQUAL OPPORTUNITY EMPLOYER)

PERSONAL INFORMATION

DATE _____

NAME _____   SOCIAL SECURITY NUMBER _____
LAST   FIRST   MIDDLE

PRESENT ADDRESS _____
STREET   CITY   STATE   ZIP

PERMANENT ADDRESS _____
STREET   CITY   STATE   ZIP

PHONE NO. _____   ARE YOU 18 YEARS OR OLDER   Yes ☐   No ☐

SPECIAL QUESTIONS

DO NOT ANSWER **ANY** OF THE QUESTIONS IN THIS FRAMED AREA UNLESS THE EMPLOYER HAS **CHECKED** A **BOX PRECEDING** A QUESTION, THEREBY INDICATING THAT THE INFORMATION IS REQUIRED FOR A BONA FIDE OCCUPATIONAL QUALIFICATION, OR DICTATED BY NATIONAL SECURITY LAWS, OR IS NEEDED FOR OTHER LEGALLY PERMISSIBLE REASONS.

☐ Height _____ feet _____ inches   ☐ Are you prevented from lawfully becoming employed in the U.S.? ___ Yes ___ No

☐ Weight _____ lbs.   ☐ Date of Birth* _____

☐ What Foreign Languages do you speak fluently? _____ Read _____ Write _____

☐ Have you been convicted of a felony or misdemeanor within the last 5 years?** Yes _____ No _____ Describe:

*The Age Discrimination in Employment Act of 1967 prohibits discrimination on the basis of age with respect to individuals who are at least 40 but less than 70 years of age

**You will not be denied employment solely because of a conviction record, unless the offense is related to the job for which you have applied.

EMPLOYMENT DESIRED

POSITION _____   DATE YOU CAN START _____   SALARY DESIRED _____

ARE YOU EMPLOYED NOW? _____   IF SO MAY WE INQUIRE OF YOUR PRESENT EMPLOYER? _____

EVER APPLIED TO THIS COMPANY BEFORE? _____   WHERE? _____   WHEN? _____

EDUCATION	NAME AND LOCATION OF SCHOOL	*NO. OF YEARS ATTENDED	*DID YOU GRADUATE?	SUBJECTS STUDIED
GRAMMAR SCHOOL				
HIGH SCHOOL				
COLLEGE				
TRADE, BUSINESS OR CORRESPONDENCE SCHOOL				

*The Age Discrimination in Employment Act of 1967 prohibits discrimination on the basis of age with respect to individuals who are at least 40 but less than 70 years of age.

GENERAL

SUBJECTS OF SPECIAL STUDY OR RESEARCH WORK _____

U.S. MILITARY OR NAVAL SERVICE _____   RANK _____   PRESENT MEMBERSHIP IN NATIONAL GUARD OR RESERVES _____

TOPS ⬥ FORM 3285 (84-3)   (CONTINUED ON OTHER SIDE)   LITHO IN U.S.A.

Text running vertically on right margin: LAST   FIRST   MIDDLE

Practical English: A Complete Course

Worksheet 12B: APPLICATION FOR EMPLOYMENT

FORMER EMPLOYERS [LIST BELOW LAST FOUR EMPLOYERS, STARTING WITH LAST ONE FIRST].

DATE MONTH AND YEAR	NAME AND ADDRESS OF EMPLOYER	SALARY	POSITION	REASON FOR LEAVING
FROM				
TO				
FROM				
TO				
FROM				
TO				
FROM				
TO				

REFERENCES: GIVE THE NAMES OF THREE PERSONS NOT RELATED TO YOU, WHOM YOU HAVE KNOWN AT LEAST ONE YEAR.

	NAME	ADDRESS	BUSINESS	YEARS ACQUAINTED
1				
2				
3				

PHYSICAL RECORD:

DO YOU HAVE ANY PHYSICAL LIMITATIONS THAT PRECLUDE YOU FROM PERFORMING ANY WORK FOR WHICH YOU ARE BEING CONSIDERED? ☐ Yes ☐ No

IF YES, WHAT CAN BE DONE TO ACCOMMODATE YOUR LIMITATION?_____

PLEASE DESCRIBE:_____

IN CASE OF EMERGENCY NOTIFY _____
NAME   ADDRESS   PHONE NO.

"I CERTIFY THAT THE FACTS CONTAINED IN THIS APPLICATION ARE TRUE AND COMPLETE TO THE BEST OF MY KNOWLEDGE AND UNDERSTAND THAT, IF EMPLOYED, FALSIFIED STATEMENTS ON THIS APPLICATION SHALL BE GROUNDS FOR DISMISSAL.

I AUTHORIZE INVESTIGATION OF ALL STATEMENTS CONTAINED HEREIN AND THE REFERENCES LISTED ABOVE TO GIVE YOU ANY AND ALL INFORMATION CONCERNING MY PREVIOUS EMPLOYMENT AND ANY PERTINENT INFORMATION THEY MAY HAVE, PERSONAL OR OTHERWISE, AND RELEASE ALL PARTIES FROM ALL LIABILITY FOR ANY DAMAGE THAT MAY RESULT FROM FURNISHING SAME TO YOU.

I UNDERSTAND AND AGREE THAT, IF HIRED, MY EMPLOYMENT IS FOR NO DEFINITE PERIOD AND MAY, REGARDLESS OF THE DATE OF PAYMENT OF MY WAGES AND SALARY, BE TERMINATED AT ANY TIME WITHOUT ANY PRIOR NOTICE."

DATE _____   SIGNATURE _____

DO NOT WRITE BELOW THIS LINE

INTERVIEWED BY _____   DATE _____

HIRED: ☐ Yes ☐ No   POSITION _____   DEPT. _____

SALARY/WAGE _____   DATE REPORTING TO WORK _____

APPROVED: 1. _____   2. _____   3. _____
EMPLOYMENT MANAGER   DEPT. HEAD   GENERAL MANAGER

This form has been designed to strictly comply with State and Federal fair employment practice laws prohibiting employment discrimination. This Application for Employment Form is sold for general use throughout the United States. TOPS assumes no responsibility for the inclusion in said form of any questions which, when asked by the Employer of the Job Applicant, may violate State and/or Federal Law.

Chapter Six

WRITING BUSINESS LETTERS

Writing clear and concise business letters has a practical value that is plain to most students: it can help them get what they want. A good letter makes a good impression and demands attention. Though modern offices rely heavily on telephones and computer networks, the old-fashioned letter is the backbone of business communications, since it provides a record of what was said and when. Moreover, students realize that most of the formal writing they will do following graduation, whether on the job or for personal reasons, will be letter writing.

This unit's goal is for students to learn how to write an effective business letter. Students practice and are tested on business letter form and content, and they compose and mail a real letter inquiring about a "dream" vacation. The unit takes about a week and a half and requires no special materials other than the stamped envelope needed for mailing the vacation letter.

LESSON I

Begin the unit by explaining the importance of business letters. The business letter is the writing form used to communicate with anyone other than friends or relatives. While the exact form may vary from office to office, the basic parts of a business letter and their functions remain the same throughout the business world.

Pass out copies of Worksheet 1 (Letter Form), which is a model of a well-executed business letter. If possible, project the model letter on a screen with an overhead projector, so that you can point out details of the model as you explain them. First discuss the overall neat appearance of the letter: the margins; the vertical alignment of heading, closing, and signature; the skipped lines. Then go over the parts of the letter listed below, emphasizing capitalization, punctuation, and the minimum of abbreviations.

Heading

The address of the person writing the letter and the date it was written. This information assures the writer that the recipient knows his or her address. Skip lines between the heading address and the date and between the date and the inside address.

Inside Address

The full name, title, and address of the person to whom the letter is sent. If the name of the recipient is unknown, a title or department suffices. Skip a line between the inside address and the salutation.

Salutation

This greeting may be made in either of two ways. If the recipient's name is known, use it. If the name is unknown, use *Dear Sir or Madam*. Always follow the salutation with a colon (:) and skip a line between the salutation and the body of the letter.

Body

This is where the letter delivers its message. Most letters students will write consist of two parts: the statement of a problem or situation and a request for action. Point out that the model letter first states that there is a billing problem, then asks that it be corrected. Skip a line between paragraphs and between the body and the closing.

Closing

Any of the following make polite closings to a business letter: *Sincerely yours, Respectfully yours, Cordially yours, Very truly yours.* The closing is followed by a comma, and only the first letter of its first word is capitalized. Skip one or more lines between the closing and the signature.

Signature

The sender's signature concludes the letter. If the letter is typed, the sender's name is typed beneath the signature. When typing, allow four lines for the signature.

When the students understand the parts of the letter, pass out Worksheet 2 (Letter Form Exercise). The three letters on the sheet are spelled, capitalized, and punctuated correctly, but they lack proper business letter form. Students should copy the exercises over onto separate pieces of paper, adding proper form. Supervise students as they work for the remainder of the period.

HOMEWORK:
Students complete the exercises.

LESSON II

Begin by having students check the exercises they did for homework. Using the model on Worksheet 1 and, if possible, the overhead projector, review the details of letter form while the students check their exercise letters. Allow time for corrections and collect the exercises.

Students will now write their first letter from scratch. Write the following assignment on the chalkboard:

> You recently attended a concert and purchased a T-shirt that faded and shrank badly the first time you washed it. Write the promoters of the concert (Music Trends, Incorporated of 1200 Galvaston Boulevard in a nearby city), and explain what you want done. Use your own return address.

Tell students to think about what they want to say in their letters, make some notes, and start writing. When they have completed their rough drafts, pass out Worksheet 3 (Letter Checklist), and go over it with them. This is a sheet they will use to check letter form several times during this unit. Each student should use the checklist and then have his or her letter checked a second time by a classmate who signs the worksheet as "Evaluator." When students are certain content and form are correct, they may begin their final drafts.

HOMEWORK:
Complete final drafts of the letters.

LESSON III

Collect the letters that were completed for homework and tell the class that today they will be writing job application letters.

Begin with a brainstorming session. Have students suggest jobs they have had or would like to have as part-time or summer employment. List their suggestions on the chalkboard. Next, talk to the class about qualifications: the experiences or skills a worker needs to get and hold a job. Have students name four or five qualifications for each job, and list them on the board with the appropriate jobs. Be sure students understand that personal qualities like neatness and reliability can be as important to an employer as work skills like typing and handling money.

When the brainstorming is finished, students will be ready to start writing. Students may choose from the job possibilities on the board. The letters should accomplish three things:

1. Explain who the applicant is.
2. Mention the job being applied for.
3. Discuss the applicant's qualifications.

When students have chosen the job to apply for, they should think about what to write, make some notes, and start their rough drafts. They may invent imaginary names and addresses for employers. Supervise the class as work on the rough drafts continues for the rest of the period.

HOMEWORK:
Complete rough drafts of application letters.

LESSON IV

Today students will check and revise their rough drafts. Begin by passing out copies of Worksheet 3 (Letter Checklist). Students should check their own letters, then have a classmate do the same, just as they did in Lesson II. When this process is completed they may start the second drafts of their letters. At the end of the period, students should turn in their rough drafts, completed checklists, and final drafts.

HOMEWORK:

Students prepare for a test in which they must correctly write a business letter.

LESSON V

Students will be tested today on their knowledge of the business letter. Pass out the following assignment or write it on the chalkboard:

> Imagine that you must write a report on nuclear power for a social studies class. Write a letter to the public relations director of your local power company and ask for any available information. Make the purpose of your request clear.

Remind the class that clarity and completeness are as important as form. They should think about what they want to say and jot down some notes before beginning to write. Give them the period to write and, if time allows, to rewrite.

LESSON VI

Before students proceed to a letter they will actually mail, they will spend a day learning and practicing the proper way to address a letter for mailing. Pass out Worksheet 4 (Letter Envelope) and two copies of Worksheet 5 (Blank Envelopes). Explain the model envelope on Worksheet 4 and assign the exercises at the bottom of the page. Supervise students as they work, and have volunteers put their work on the board, one envelope per student, when they have finished. Review the work on the board, allowing students to check their work, and collect the exercises.

HOMEWORK:

Students should think tonight about where they would like to spend a "dream" vacation. Tell them anything goes: skiing in Switzerland, fishing in Alaska, or sightseeing in Paris. Tomorrow they will start letters inquiring about their vacations.

LESSON VII

Having decided where they would like to go on a dream vacation, students today begin writing letters of inquiry to the tourist bureaus of the cities, states, or countries they hope to visit. Since these letters will actually be mailed, students should be particularly careful deciding what they have to say. Discuss with the class the questions they want to have answered about their trips. Questions might include points of interest, activities available, accommodations, travel costs, and the reasons students have chosen their destinations.

After looking over the ideas on the blackboard and making some notes on what they want to write, students may begin the rough draft of the bodies of their letters. Since they do not yet have the addresses their letters will be mailed to, they should leave room to add them later. Supervise the class as they work for the rest of the period.

HOMEWORK:

Students complete their rough drafts and visit the school or public library to find addresses for their letters. (It might be a good idea to alert your school librarian.) All states and large cities have tourist or visitors' bureaus, and travel information on foreign countries can usually be obtained from consulates or embassies.

LESSON VIII

Students bring their completed rough drafts to class, have classmates check them using Worksheet 3, and complete their final drafts. They then address envelopes and prepare the letters for mailing.

FOLLOW-UP ACTIVITIES

1. Students will enjoy sharing the responses they receive from their vacation letters. Allow time for brief oral reports to the class.

2. From time to time following the unit, set aside a class period to review business letter form and assign one of the following topics. Leave names,

addresses, and other details to the students' imaginations. Continue to use Worksheet 3 to check student work.

a. You have heard of a record club that offers records at discount prices. Write them, asking about details.

b. The first record you ordered from the record club arrived scratched and unplayable. Write them and ask what you should do to receive a refund or a new record.

c. You have heard that a national park in your state is looking for younger people to live and work there for the summer. Write a letter inquiring about the job.

d. Write your local public health department and ask a representative to visit your health science class to discuss services available to teenagers.

e. Write a letter thanking the public health representative who visited your class.

f. Write a letter to the agent of your favorite music or movie performer and ask for an autographed picture.

g. Write a letter to the principal of your school pointing out a problem and suggesting a solution.

h. Write a local television or radio station to complain about a commercial you find annoying.

i. Write a local official, such as the mayor or a county supervisor, to point out a problem.

Worksheet 1: LETTER FORM

Learn the following about the model business letter below:

1. Names of each part of the letter.

2. Places where a line is skipped.

3. Heading, date, and signature are in line vertically.

4. Other details pointed out by your teacher.

274 Elm Avenue
Cragmont, PA 19034   *Heading*

March 12, 1987

Credit Department
Longview Discount Store
1000 Board Street   *Inside*
Larson, PA 19042   *Address*

Dear Sir or Madam:

    Enclosed is a copy of my February bill (account
number 233-01-3478), which includes a charge of
$103.86 for an item purchased in your jewelry
department. While the item purchased is unidenti-
fied on the bill, I am certain that I have made no
jewelry purchases at your store since before
Christmas.   *Body*

    I have enclosed a check for the remainder of my
February purchases ($45.91) and expect that the
remaining balance will be moved from my bill by next
month.

    Please contact me if I can be of further help.
Thank you.

Sincerely yours,   *Closing*

Signature
Dion Larson

Worksheet 2:
LETTER FORM EXERCISES

The exercises below contain a letter which is spelled, capitalized, and punctuated correctly but which is not in proper business letter form. Using Worksheet 1 as a model, rewrite the exercises in proper form on separate pieces of paper.

EXERCISE A

1734 Seventh Avenue Stockton, CA 94364 November 23, 1988 Office of the Principal Ridgemont High School 2350 Crest View Drive Ridgemont, CA 95103 Dear Sir or Madam: While attending a football game at your school last Friday night, I misplaced a blue wool jacket. I was sitting in about the fourth row of the stands on the visitors' side. If the jacket has been turned in to your lost and found, I would appreciate being notified so I can pick it up. Thank you. Sincerely yours, *Annette Winfield* Annette Winfield

EXERCISE B

778 Wailea Drive Hilo, HI 96825 August 23, 1987 Customer Relations Department Quiktix, Incorporated 100 Industrial Circle Suite C Honolulu, HI 96720 Dear Sir or Madam: Two weeks ago I mailed you a check for $54.00 to purchase two tickets for the Fuzzball concert at Sherman Stadium on September 8. I have received no tickets, and I am very concerned since the date of the concert is approaching. Please send me my tickets immediately. Thank you. Sincerely yours, *Jimmy Li* Jimmy Li

EXERCISE C

223 South Avenue Willard, OH 45321 September 2, 1988 Ms. J. R. Rochester Grant High School 2325 Harrington Street Akron, OH 50107 Dear Ms. Rochester: I graduated from Grant High in June of 1987, and I am about to enroll in a community college. Please forward me the information I will need to have my high-school transcripts sent to the school I will be attending. Thank you. Very truly yours, *Lori Schmidt* Lori Schmidt

Worksheet 3:
LETTER CHECKLIST

The items below are important parts of correct business letter form and content. Each time you write a business letter, check what you have written against what is listed below, then have it double-checked by a classmate who should sign the space above marked "Evaluator."

CONTENT

The specific action the letter requests is _____

_____

_____ The requested action is clearly stated.

_____ The letter includes all necessary information and no unnecessary information.

FORM

Overall Appearance

_____ Standard paper size

_____ Wide, even margins

_____ Heading, closing, and signature in line vertically

Heading

_____ Comma between city and state

_____ State abbreviation in capital letters

_____ Month not abbreviated

_____ Line skipped between heading and inside address

Inside Address

_____ Comma between city and state

_____ State abbreviation in capital letters

_____ Line skipped between inside address and salutation

Salutation

_____ Period after *Ms.*, *Mrs.*, or *Mr.*, if used

_____ Colon (:) used after salutation

_____ Line skipped between salutation and body

Body

_____ All paragraphs indented

_____ Lines skipped between paragraphs and between body and closing

Closing and Signature

_____ Only first letter of first word of closing is capitalized

_____ Comma used after closing

_____ Name printed beneath signature, if letter is typewritten

Worksheet 4:
LETTER ENVELOPE

```
Maggie Cline
23 Harper Circle
Oakland, CA 94602


            Mr. Joseph Grant
            Personnel Office
            L. W. Lefort Company
            2503 La Casa Road
            La Mirada, CA 92617
```

Study the model envelope above. Then supply proper punctuation, capitalization, and form to the addresses below as you write them onto the envelopes on Worksheet 5. Use your own return address, or make one up.

1. Kenneth hamanaka   far west publications
   3475 king street   oakley mi 48015

2. general manager   polyform plastics inc
   1556 weston boulevard   reno nv 86715

3. dr elizabeth mitchem   sunset medical group
   344 c street   suite 5   boise id 83701

4. textbook division   arizona department of education
   600 state street   flagstaff az 84528

5. mr michael k munez   accounting department
   heartland box company 2701 third street
   omaha ne 68160

6. lilly mcquiston   mcquiston associates
   5788 commercial parkway   hector ut 82101

Practical English: A Complete Course

Worksheet 5:
BLANK ENVELOPES

Practical English: A Complete Course

Chapter Seven

WRITING A RESUME

The ability to write a concise resume of job skills and experiences is an invaluable tool for students about to enter the job market. A resume is also an excellent way to help students appreciate the marketable skills they have already gained in high school. The importance of composing resumes makes a short unit in resume-writing worthwhile.

These lessons assume knowledge of the business letter (Chapter Six) and work best at the end of the academic year, when students are concerned about finding jobs—either for the summer or following graduation. In this unit, students learn the function of a resume, gather information and write a resume, and prepare a cover letter to accompany it to an employer. The unit lasts about a week, and no special materials are required.

LESSON I

Begin the unit by explaining that a resume (the word means *summary*) is a concise, easy-to-read list of skills and experiences that qualify a job-seeker for employment. In most cases, the goal of writing a resume is obtaining an interview—the next step in the employment process. Students will learn how to write resumes, and, perhaps more importantly, they will learn just how many job skills they already possess. They will also write cover letters to use with their completed resumes.

First students need to gather the information they will use in their resumes. Pass out Worksheets 1-A and 1-B (Resume Questions). Carefully go over each section of the sheets with the class and have them start filling in information as you speak. Your role is helping them remember *all* their work-related experiences. Few students will have entries in all the

categories on the sheet, but most will discover they have more than they expect.

Education and Activities

1. List the last four schools attended. Names, towns, and dates are adequate if the exact street addresses are unknown. Next review with students the job skills they may have gained in school. Obvious skills are learned in business, computer, and industrial arts classes. P.E., music, and art classes help in camp and recreation jobs; psychology and child development classes are useful in child-care work; science classes are good for positions as medical or laboratory aides; and knowledge of a foreign language is always valuable in dealing with the public. Students then list their activities, including experience organizing field trips or fund-raising drives, their special honors or awards, and their work as teacher-aides.

Employment

2. This section is divided into informal jobs that employers might be interested in (like yard work, housework, painting, and housesitting) and formal work with fixed hours and regular wages. If students cannot remember all the names and addresses needed to complete this section, they may finish it tonight after finding the information they need at home.

Personal

3. Here students include additional information about themselves such as the ability to type, handle cash, or drive. Be sure students understand that the ability to deal courteously with the public is an extremely important job skill.

References

4. Students must think of people outside their immediate families whom an employer could contact to verify that they are honest, dependable, and hard-working. Remind students always to ask permission before giving the name of a reference to a prospective employer.

Career Goal

This entry asks students about their post-graduation goals, a factor which may be of considerable interest to an employer.

Students spend the rest of the period completing their worksheets.

HOMEWORK:

Students gather needed information and complete their worksheets. It might also be useful for students to show their worksheets to close friends or relatives and ask if there is anything they may have forgotten to include.

LESSON II

Check the resume question worksheets for completion and tell students that they are about to begin work on the rough drafts of their resumes. Pass out Worksheet 2 (Resume Form). Explain that while resumes exist in many forms, all serve the same purpose: to make information about an applicant's qualifications easily available to employers who must pick the best prospects from many applicants. Remind students that a resume is a summary of their skills and should not include details that would be better covered in a job interview. All information is condensed into a single page and presented in sentence fragments for brevity. Experiences are listed in reverse chronological order, the most recent first. Point out the following details about the resume's form:

1. The resume is headed with name, address, and telephone number with ZIP and area codes.

2. All information is divided into three sections: Education and activities, work experience, and personal information.

3. List schools with the current one first. Primary schools and street addresses need not be included. Include school and community activities here.

4. List past jobs with the most recent first. Begin with the title of the highest position you held, then give the name, city, and state of the firm. Briefly describe the most important responsibilities held and any promotions. Informal jobs and long-term volunteer work may be included if they involve skills or responsibilities similar to those needed for paid work.

5. Personal information includes any additional job-related skills not already mentioned. The birthdate need only be stated if you are not legally an adult. Include all skills and special interests in which an employer might be interested and finish this section with a long-term career goal.

6. Mention the availability of references, but do not include them. When an employer contacts an applicant about references, it is an indication of serious interest.

The students are now ready to begin work on their rough drafts. They should carefully go over their resume question sheets, mark the information they want to include on their resumes, and start writing, using Worksheet 2 as a guide. Let them work under your supervision for the rest of the period.

HOMEWORK:

Complete rough drafts of resumes.

LESSON III

Students arrive with their completed rough drafts. Write the guidelines below on the board and review them. Have students check their resumes and exchange papers so that classmates can double-check them.

1. Proofread the resume to correct every error in content, form, spelling, punctuation, and grammar. Such errors give employers the impression the applicant is sloppy and illiterate.

2. To keep the resume brief, sentence fragments may be used. Worksheet 2 is a guide.

3. The finished resume should be on standard 8½ by 11 inch paper. (It should be typewritten if actually submitted to an employer.)

When the rough drafts have been carefully corrected, students may write their final drafts. Collect both drafts at the end of the period.

HOMEWORK:

Students should bring the help-wanted sections of current, local newspapers to class tomorrow.

LESSON IV

Today students are to imagine that they are actually seeking a job and will compose cover letters similar to those that would accompany their resumes to employers. Pass out Worksheet 3 (Cover Letter) and go over the assignment, explaining the need for a cover letter to make a resume more effective. This is also a good time to review the proper form for a business letter. (See Chapter Six.)

The students are now ready to start work. They first choose jobs to apply for, using either the help-wanted ads they have brought to class or the ones on the lower half of Worksheet 3. Then, using the guidelines on Worksheet 3, they carefully write the rough drafts of their letters. They may work on their rough drafts for the rest of the period.

HOMEWORK:

Complete rough drafts.

LESSON V

Today students will revise and rewrite their cover letters. Each student should check his or her own paper and have it double-checked by a classmate. Pass out Worksheet 3 (Letter Checklist) from Chapter Six, write the following guidelines on the board, and go over them.

1. Does the cover letter mention each of the following?

   a. the exact position being applied for

   b. how you found out about it

   c. the hours you can work and the date you will be able to start

   d. any skills or experiences not mentioned in your resume, but useful for the job.

   e. a request for an interview

   f. your phone number

2. Check the form of your letter with the Letter Checklist. When the rough drafts have been revised, students may write their final drafts. Rough and final drafts are due at the end of the period.

FOLLOW-UP ACTIVITIES

1. Following this unit students are usually very interested in the local job market. It would be a good time to invite a speaker who knows something about the kinds of employment available locally to students. Likely candidates include a school guidance counselor and a representative from a county or state youth employment agency.

2. The class will probably be interested in a discussion of where working members of the class are employed and how they were hired. How did students first find out about their jobs? How did they apply? What were their interviews like? What things do they think were crucial in landing their jobs? How are their jobs different from what they thought they were going to be like when they applied?

3. Students who actually use their resumes and cover letters may want to share their responses with the rest of the class.

Chapter Seven

Worksheet 1A: RESUME QUESTIONS

NAME: _____

DATE: _____

Answer the questions below to gather information you will need as you begin writing your resume.

EDUCATION AND ACTIVITIES

List the names and addresses of the last four schools you have attended, most recent school first. Include dates.

1. _____   3. _____
   _____   _____
   Dates _____   Dates _____

2. _____   4. _____
   _____   _____
   Dates _____   Dates _____

List any skills you have learned in school that could be used on a job. Keep business, computer, and industrial arts classes especially in mind.

_____

_____

_____

List any school or community activities (teams, clubs, service groups, church groups, etc.), including positions of responsibility held.

_____

_____

List any honors or awards you have received.

_____

_____

EMPLOYMENT

Informal jobs: List any jobs you have done, whether for pay or not, for friends or relatives. Include dates.

1. _____ Dates _____

2. _____ Dates _____

3. _____ Dates _____

Practical English: A Complete Course

Worksheet 1B: RESUME QUESTIONS

Formal jobs: List any jobs you have had with regular hours and pay, whether part- or full-time. Include addresses of employers and dates.

1. _____
_____ Dates _____

2. _____
_____ Dates _____

3. _____
_____ Dates _____

PERSONAL

List any special interests or activities you have not already mentioned.

_____

_____

List any skills you have not already mentioned that might be of use on a job.

_____

_____

REFERENCES

(For use when requested by a potential employer)

List the names and addresses of three people who know you well and would be willing to act as a reference for you. If possible, include an employer, a teacher, and a friend of the family.

1. Name _____ Phone _____
Address _____

2. Name _____ Phone _____
Address _____

3. Name _____ Phone _____
Address _____

CAREER GOAL

Write the job you would like to have when you are finished with your education. List any special training or certificates you will need for the job.

_____

Worksheet 2: RESUME FORM

RESUME

Lori Stanfield
260 Mill Road, Apt. 205
Herman, IL 60814
(312) 555-1257

EDUCATION and ACTIVITIES

1986 to Present:	Taft High School, Herman, IL 60807
1979 to 1986:	Oak Grove School, Dodd, IL 60912
School Activities:	Future Business Leaders' Club Marching Band Track Team
Community Activities:	Teen Club, St. John's Church, Herman, IL

WORK EXPERIENCE

November 1986 to present:	Assistant Manager, La Fleure Women's Wear, Herman, IL Supervised store and two other employees in owner's absence. Promoted to position from salesperson.
June 1986 to September 1986:	Part-time Salesperson, women's wear department of Clausen's Department Store, Herman, IL
June 1985 to September 1985:	File clerk, Dynacorp Enterprises, Boxwood, IL Filed and did general office work.

PERSONAL

Born:	Omaha, NE; August 3, 1969
Special Skills:	Types 30 words per minute Operates cash register Red Cross First Aid Certificate Speaks some Spanish
Special Interests:	Clothing design Art and drawing
Career Goal:	To own and operate a retail women's wear store

REFERENCES FURNISHED UPON REQUEST

Practical English: A Complete Course

Worksheet 3: COVER LETTER

Because your resume is a general description of your skills, it should be accompanied by a carefully written cover letter that stresses why you are particularly qualified for the job you want.

Check the help-wanted ads of your local newspaper or use the ads below to choose a job; then write a cover letter to accompany your resume to a prospective employer. Assume all addresses are in your town, and be sure to include each of the following:

1. proper business letter form
2. the exact position being applied for
3. how you found out about the job
4. the hours you can work and the date you will be able to start
5. any skills or experiences not mentioned in your resume but useful for the job
6. a request for an interview
7. your phone number

HELP-WANTED ADVERTISEMENTS

PART-TIME sporting goods salesperson. Afternoons and weekends. Must be well-groomed and able to deal with the public. No experience necessary. Apply Harry Rose, Champion Sporting Goods, 3421 Hayes Avenue.

GAS STATION attendant. Saturdays only. Wait on customers and help with simple auto maintenance. Resume to Wilbur Wong, 5701 Route 95.

MOTHER'S HELPER to work in my home weekdays, 3 to 6 p.m. Care for 2- and 4-year-olds and help with housework. Contact Thelma Banducci, 25 A Street.

PHONE INTERVIEWER for market research company. Must have patience and good speaking voice. Apply Box 12, this newspaper.

RECREATION AIDES. Summer openings for athletic young people able to work with kids. Apply Janet Owens, Recreation Dept., City Hall.

COUNTER PERSON for fast-food restaurant. Part-time evenings and possible summer work. Contact Emilio Martinez, El Taco Pizzeria, 133 Kennedy Drive.

SUPERMARKET BAGGER. Strong, fast teen to work after school, weekends. Harry Ojakian, Harry's Market, 6500 Mission.

COUNTY YOUTH Employment Services is now taking resumes from young people seeking work. Hundreds of jobs. Write Youth Employment Service, Rm. 300, County Office Building, 1000 Stanwell Drive.

Chapter Eight

INTERVIEW PAPER: WRITING ON THE JOB

It is a sad fact that many students practically never write unless an assignment forces them into it. They see writing as a school activity, largely devoid of value outside of school, and have no notion of how many occupations rely on writing skills.

Changing this view of things is the first goal of this unit, in which students interview employed adults about work and the role of writing in it. Additionally students learn how to prepare, conduct, and edit a successful interview paper, and develop a sense of the difference between spoken and written language.

The unit starts with a discussion of jobs in general and writing on the job in particular. Students read and study models of the kind of paper they will write. Then each student finds an appropriate subject for an interview; learns some basic interviewing techniques; conducts an interview; writes, revises, and rewrites the interview; and shares it with the rest of the class. The usual writing process is followed, but the emphasis is different, since the content of the paper comes from the interviewee, and the writer spends more time planning, organizing, and editing than generating words.

The project is quite a change from most schoolwork and can be a welcome reprieve from other assignments. As described here, the unit takes about two weeks to complete. Two model interviews are included for duplication as a class set.

No introduction to this unit should neglect to mention the book that inspired it, Studs Terkel's *Working* (Avon Books, 1975). This thick collection of interviews with people in all walks of life, from news carrier to strip miner to film critic, is a marvelous springboard for discussion about work and career choices. Its language is readily accessible to students of all levels and abilities. A week or two reading selected interviews from it will provide lively discussions and excellent models of interview writing.

LESSON I

Introduce the unit by telling the class that for the next couple of weeks they will be thinking, discussing, and writing about the importance of writing on the job. The paper they write will result from an interview with someone who writes regularly as part of his or her work.

Today the class will discuss work, writing, and the relationship between them. The goal of the discussion is to have the class see that school writing is usually quite different from nonschool writing. School assignments are most often exercises completed for a teacher and a grade, rather than attempts to communicate useful information to someone who needs it.

Use the open-ended questions below as a guide for the discussion.

Discussion Questions

1. What is work? Is it the same for all people? How is work different at home, at school, or on the job? Is it possible to work while playing (games, sports, etc.)?

2. What did you like or dislike about a particular job you had to do? What is a "good" job? What circumstances would make you quit a job?

3. What satisfactions, separate from wages, can be gained from work?

4. When is writing work? When is it pleasurable? When does it give the satisfaction of a well-done job?

5. How much writing do you do at school? For yourself at home? On jobs you have had? Keep in mind all instances of writing, including things quickly jotted down.

6. When you write at school, what are you usually trying to communicate? To whom? For what purpose? How about what you write at home? At work? What differences are there between school and nonschool writing?

7. What teachers or assignments have you had that helped you to become a better writer? Why were these experiences successful?

Conclude with a summary of what has been said about work and the distinctions between school and nonschool writing.

HOMEWORK:

Tonight students have two tasks to complete. The first is to read the two job-writing interviews with the nurse and the cabinetmaker (See the end of this chapter). Pass out duplicated copies, and tell the class that this is the kind of paper they will write next. As they read, they should ask themselves how the subjects of the interviews feel about their work and why writing is important to them. Secondly, students should start thinking about whom to choose as a subjects for the interviews they will write. The subjects should be adults with full-time jobs that require some formal or informal writing. Relatives and friends are good candidates, and high schools are full of people who must regularly write. The subjects must also be available to be interviewed between Lessons V and VI, so let the class know when this will be. Allow several days of alternate work or a weekend between the lessons, if possible.

LESSON II

Today students discuss the model interviews they read last night to determine how the interviewees feel about their jobs and how they use writing. Use the questions below to talk about first one interview and then the other.

Discussion Questions

1. How does the subject of the interview feel about the job? What are the best parts of the job? What are the worst? What satisfactions do they receive? What about each job reminds you of work you have done at school, at home, or for wages?

2. What kind of writing does the interviewee do? Who reads what is written? Why is accuracy important?

3. What process does the interviewee follow when writing? Under what conditions is the writing done? (Note that the cabinetmaker rewrites at home and that the nurse sometimes remembers things she wishes she had written.)

4. How is the writing of the interviewee similar to and different from school writing in purpose? In audience?

5. What is the purpose of the descriptive introductions to the interviews? What do they include, and how do they add to the papers?

6. How is the language of the interviews different from what you would find in a newspaper or textbook? What makes the interviews sound like people talking? Is the usage of the interviewees always perfect?

Conclude with a summary of what has been said. At this point the class should understand that writing on the job usually requires the same basic process they use in class, but that it also requires a sense of audience and a responsibility for accuracy missing from most school assignments. They should also see the difference between the spoken language of the interviews and the more formal writing they usually see in print.

Allow students to keep their copies of the model interviews to refer to later as they work on their papers.

LESSON III

Pass out Worksheet 1 (Assignment and Guidelines), and go over it to explain the entire interview assignment. Remind the class again of the time period between Lessons V and VI when the interview must be held. Point out that this paper uses the same stages in the writing process that they are accustomed to, but that this time their task consists more in eliciting a good response from the subject and in organizing what is said, than in producing the words of the paper. The assignment encourages students to rely on a tape recorder during the interview. This works well because it allows the interview to become a discussion between the student and his subject. An interview with an inexperienced notetaker tends to become a stop-and-go affair with long pauses while the student tediously inscribes what is said. Noticing when the student is and is not taking something down can also be a distraction to the subject.

When the assignment is understood, it is time to start thinking about how to conduct the interviews. Ask each student to compose a list of five questions about work and writing that would result in good answers. Tell the class to keep the model interviews and the class discussion in mind and to think of questions that would be revealing if they were asked of them in an interview. They should avoid questions that invite one-word anwers.

When they have worked for about ten minutes, have each student read his best question aloud. This is a time for students to gather additional ideas from their classmates to improve their own question lists. Point out virtues and problems in the questions read aloud, and help students rephrase questions that could be answered in one word.

HOMEWORK:
Each student comes to class tomorrow with five questions that will be the basis of the interview.

LESSON IV

The class as a group will have an opportunity to try out interview questions on one or two practice interviewees today. Students with jobs make good subjects, but student body officers, teachers, administrators, and other adults on campus may also be invited to class to be interviewed.

Begin by checking that all students have completed their list of interview questions. Point out that

the practice interview is an opportunity to see how the questions have written will work, so each student should pick one or two questions to try. Remind the class that their goal is to have the subject reveal interesting things about his or her work and use of writing. Students should begin with general questions and use follow-up questions like the ones suggested on the assignment sheet to elicit detailed, anecdotal responses.

Let the interviewee take center stage. Retire to the rear of the room and interrupt the proceedings only when the interview is straying from the topic or when an obvious follow-up is being missed. When the interviews are completed, briefly discuss with the class what sorts of questions were most successful. Ask what parts of the interviews they found most interesting and why.

LESSON V

Today students will continue to practice their questioning techniques, but each one will work one-on-one with another student. Divide the class into pairs, and tell them each to think of some work that they have done over a period of at least a few weeks and that they can answer questions about in a simulated interview. A paying job is the ideal chioice, but work done for school, neighbors, or parents will also fit the bill. The questions about writing can be answered with reference to writing the students do in school. The point here is not so much to duplicate exactly the situation of the interview they will do later with an adult as it is to practice asking general questions and pursuing detailed answers.

One student interviews the other for about fifteen minutes, using the questions he or she has developed and practicing following-up questions. Then the students switch roles, with the interviewer becoming the interviewee and vice versa. End the period by reassembling the class and discussing their experience. Ask which questions worked best and which led to dead ends. What worked well as follow-up questions?

The students are now ready to undertake the formal interviews for the papers they will write. Refer to the information on conducting and transcribing the interview on Worksheet 1, and point out the following:

1. Students should remember to note details they may want to use in their introductions.

2. Transcribing the interview sounds more difficult than it is. Some parts of the interview may not be worth putting into writing at all. If the interviewee has talked about matters that are dull or far removed from the topic being pursued, students should feel free to delete what was said.

3. Removing the interviewer's questions to create a monologue is not difficult if the responses are seen as paragraphs or sections of a paper, rather than specific answers to questions. Point out how easily the model interviews move from a topic suggested by one question to a topic suggested by another.

4. Students will also find that oral language is full of fragments and interrupted sentences that they will want to change. Tell them that when they actually start putting their tape-recorded interviews on paper they should feel free to alter words or phrases here and there to make the language flow smoothly.

In any case, the transcript they bring to class next time is only a rough draft, and they will make major changes in it before it is turned in.

HOMEWORK:

Conduct the interview, transcribe it as a monologue, add an introduction, and bring a legible copy to class. Allow several days for this assignment.

LESSON VI

Begin by checking to be sure all students have finished their rough drafts. They are now ready to start shaping their interviews into final form.

Ask the class to divide into pairs, and pass out a copy of Worksheet 2 (Rough Draft Workshop) to each student. Go over the worksheet, and explain that the goal today is to get suggestions from their partners for improving their interviews. Papers are exchanged; each student signs the "Evaluator" line of the other's paper and reads the paper, making suggestions. When

both papers have been read and commented on, students explain the written comments and marks on the papers to one another.

Students now ask themselves the same questions about their papers that their partners did on the worksheet. When they have done this, they are ready to start their final drafts. Ask them to try to maintain the conversational style of the interviews as they rewrite, regardless of how great the changes in organization. Students keep their rough drafts and workshop sheets to turn in with the final draft.

LESSON VII

As students rewrite their papers, you may want to give them a day in class to work. Remind them when the final draft is due, and make yourself available to help, especially with organizational problems.

LESSON VIII

Final drafts are now due, but first students take time for a final proofreading and to think over what they have done. Pass out Worksheet 3 (Comment Sheet), and have the class break into groups of three. Each writer should have his final draft proofread by the two other members of his group. The first reader checks for errors in punctuation and usage. The second reader concentrates solely on spelling, reading the paper backwards from the last word to the first, so that each word is checked individually. Each reader signs the Comment Sheet in the appropriate place. When proofreading is finished, the writer answers the questions under Writer's Comments.

Students turn in their work at the end of the period. They should include:

1. the final draft

2. the Comment Sheet

3. the rough draft

4. the Rough Draft Workshop Sheet

5. a blank sheet of paper to be used for reader comments

LESSON IX

As a final activity for this unit, students share their finished papers. As students arrive, desks should, if possible, be arranged in a single large circle. Pass out the interview papers at random; write the following directions on the board, and go over them:

1. Quietly and carefully read the paper you have been given.

2. Write a note to the paper's writer on the blank page. Here are some things you might include:

    a. What did you like best about the paper?

    b. What did you learn from reading the paper?

    c. What kind of person does the subject of the interview sound like?

    d. What does the point of the paper seem to be?

    e. What about the paper is better than your own paper?

3. Sign the note, and pass it to the person on your right. Wait to receive a paper from the left.

The teacher's job during the period is to keep papers moving so that each is read several times. Allow time at the end of the period for students to read the comments on their papers, then collect the papers for grading.

FOLLOW UP ACTIVITIES

1. The interviewing skills in this unit may be further developed in the interview that is part of the job research paper in Chapter Nine.

2. After students have taken on the role of interviewer, an interesting discussion on employment interviews is possible. While the goal of such an interview is obviously very different from the interview they have conducted, students may now have insights into what makes someone look good in an interview and how best to deal with interview questions.

94

INTERVIEW MODEL
Tim Ingham
Cabinetmaker

Tim wears a faded red T-shirt as he sits at his wooden kitchen table. He sports a head of shaggy brown hair and a bushy moustache. The kitchen contains a refrigerator, a bookshelf, a desk, and a router table.

I'm a journeyman cabinetmaker for a fixture company in Oakland that makes bank, office, and commercial cabinetry. The company does nice quality work. The last couple of days I've been working on some planter boxes for a bank office. We've made these in the past, and this is the new model which is far better constructed than the older ones. Usually my foreman makes shop drawings based on something an architect has done, and I work from those drawings and a materials list. Sometimes when things are busy we'll work directly from the original architect's blueprints.

What I like about my work is primarily the work itself. I enjoy building things. I enjoy starting with raw materials and going from an idea (whether it's my own or somebody else's) and seeing something sort of grow out of these raw materials, knowing all the time I can do it as sloppily or as perfectly as I want. It's basically competing with myself that I like best. Your skills sort of grow, and it's a really good feeling to be confronted with a problem and draw on previous experience and say, "Hey, this would be a good place to use that technique again." The challenge is always there, as long as I remind myself that it's there.

There are some things about the job I could easily do without. The owners of the shop are annoying because they're unpredictable. You get the feeling they're saying, "Is everybody working as hard as they need to work, as fast as they can?" They try to keep us on our best behavior at all times—not talking unless it has to do with the job. The environment also bothers me because it's really unhealthy. There's always dust, and there's always fumes from glue, and you just can't get away from it. When things get very busy I tend to forget to put on my dust mask or my goggles.

One of the sidelines of the job is that sometimes I will be sent out of the shop to install things that we have made. I like to install because I get to work away from the shop and away from the things I don't like there. The writing part of my job happens when I'm working outside of the shop. Nine times out of ten, if I'm sent out of the shop to some bank or stock brokerage or department store, in addition to installing what we've already built in the shop, there's some remodeling that goes on. That means that I'll consult with whoever's in charge and discuss with him what needs to be done in addition to what I've been sent to do. All of this has to be written down and transmitted back to my company. I remember one instance at Capwell's Department Store. I resurfaced their customer service counter with a new sheet of Formica, and they needed a new drawer put under it to match an old drawer that was already there. Everything about that old drawer had to get relayed back to my company if they were going to make a bid on a new one. You can't have someone driving from Hayward to Oakland to make sure the drawer they're making

© 1987 J. Weston Walch, Publisher

Practical English: A Complete Course

Tim Ingham (continued)

is the same as the one in place. What I did in that case was ask the manager exactly what he wanted, and then I asked all the pertinent questions. Do you want the same kind of lock on the drawer? Do you want the same key or a different key? Do you want a cash till inside it? Do you want a cheaper drawer than the old style, or the same thing with the dovetails and hardwood sides? I write all this information down, and then I get out my tape measure and measure the old drawer. Usually I also make a quick little sketch.

A lot of stuff can't be shown in a drawing, because even the best cabinet drawings don't show realistic details at all. They show no joinery, edging, things like that. A client may think he's getting one thing, and he'll get something else unless it's all spelled out. The written descriptions have to be very specific, because in my trade drawings are often misunderstood. The person who drew them doesn't communicate with the people who build from them. The better I do describing a job, the more chance my company will get the work, and the more chance I'll be able to work away from the shop again, which is what I like to do most.

Often I will return home at the end of the day with my scratchy notes on the back of napkins or boxes or whatever I have around, and I neaten it up and rewrite it. If you're talking about a piece of paper generating work or generating money, it's something important. Once I had to describe 270 boxes—all different dimensions—so we could build them, and somebody else could install them in counters. If the instructions weren't understandable, there could have been four days labor for four people that would have been wasted. The money in a case like that really starts mounting up.

What I write doesn't just get read by one person. It gets filed away in the job file, and it's needed in order for the company to tally up labor and materials later on. It also might be used to verify what we did for the customer. It might get sent to the company that orders the work to get the purchase order so my company gets paid.

Most of what I know about writing I learned in a journalism class I took once, not in any English class. This class required a *lot* of writing. The teacher was a no-nonsense teacher. He said if you're going to write about something, get your facts straight. He said he wasn't going to waste his time reading dull stuff that you wrote five minutes before class. His class helped a lot.

Some people I work with didn't get past maybe the eighth grade, maybe sophomore in high school. Maybe they're from out of the country and didn't go the school much at all. They tend to relay things verbally to the company when they come back from the job. My company's had me outside a lot. I think it's because I can communicate on paper. If you're being walked through ten different rooms of an office where there are twenty different jobs that have to be relayed back to the company, you have to be able to write it all down clearly. It's impossible to do that all in your head. I think that being able to look at something and then transmit it in writing has a lot to do with me being able to continue to work outside the shop. So being able to write lets me do the kind of work I want where I want to do it—away from the shop.

INTERVIEW MODEL
Mary Chatsworth
Nurse

She has been a nurse for about two years, and she looks harried after a day on the job. Her living room is filled with antique oak furniture. A huge wardrobe sits against one wall, and a hall tree stands near the door. She nestles in an overstuffed chair covered by an afghan, curling and uncurling herself as she talks.

There's a lot of writing in nursing, and it's a pain in the neck. I float, and in nursing that means I go to psychiatric units, surgical units, medical, maternity—you name it. Generally I have maybe four patients. One or two of them will be total-care patients, so I have to do everything for them, including making sure the food gets into their mouths. Today I was on a medical psychiatric unit. I spent a lot of the day talking to one woman. She was paralyzed, but she could look at you, focus, and see what you were doing. To get her to cooperate, it's important to establish a good relationship. You have to talk therapeutically, and with every patient it's different.

When something important happens with a patient, you hear it from another nurse; you correspond. Somewhere in the day you have a moment to talk, to keep track of what's going on with a patient.

I enjoy nursing because it has a lot of little tiny ego-builders. That's what I like about it. The human contact, the exchange, the patient saying "thanks," the patient improving, the patient building a trusting relationship with you, the patient moving a finger and knowing you have helped that happen. Those are the things you do it for. If they don't have confidence, you give them confidence. You're the one who goes in and takes care of that patient for eight hours, and you're the one who's responsible. You make some important decisions yourself.

Sometimes it's very depressing, but you develop defenses. And if you're in a good nursing unit you develop camaraderie. Everybody depends on everybody else. If somebody dies that you were very close to, your co-workers have a way of consoling you. You know that you aren't responsible for the death. You continually say to one another: "You did a good job today." It helps you survive. The stress of the job gets handled with mutual support.

The writing you do is information that other people need to know: other nurses, doctors, pharmacists, even lawyers. If you have something really intense going on, something life-threatening, you have to write it up while things are happening. You keep track of what's going on in crash-cart notes. You're writing all the time—this or that is happening to the patient. Then later you transfer it all to the patient's chart. In an emergency, you have two or three doctors in the room and three nurses. One nurse does the medication; one nurse arranges the crash cart, the room, and does the running; and

Practical English: A Complete Course

Mary Chatsworth (continued)

the other nurse is constantly taking notes on what is happening. Things are going on so fast that you really need someone to keep track of all that's happening. Typically you might have someone in heart failure. So you've got fluid coming in, and they're trying to keep the lungs clear. They're trying to stimulate the heart with various medications or doing C.P.R. It's all very dramatic, but you've got to take clear notes. Life is at stake.

The normal everyday writing tells what is happening to a patient on your shift. Hospitals recognize that nurses should have time enough during a shift to write what is called **SOAP** notes. It's an acronym. The letters in **SOAP** stand for what's in the notes. **S** is for subjective observations. That's what the patient says is going on—how he feels. **O** is for objective. That's what you observe is happening, data like the vital signs, the bowel sounds, whatever is going on medically with the patient and his problem. **A** is for assessment. That's what you think all the objective data mean. Where does this patient stand in his recovery? Is he doing well? What needs to be watched? **P** is for plan. It's your opinion of what the nurses who follow your shift ought to do—what needs to be watched and so on.

There's also a thing called a treatment rand. This contains all the pertinent information on a patient: the diet, the activity level, what you can do with a patient—get him up, walk him down the hall—the medications the doctor has ordered, specimens you have to collect, tests to be taken. All the details of what's supposed to happen and when it's supposed to happen. During the day you constantly get orders from physicians and put them on the rand. There's a section for the doctor's notes; there's a section for nurses' notes—the SOAP notes—and there's a section for vital signs, lab tests, x-rays. The important writing I do is in the nurses notes, the SOAP notes.

Hospitals recognize that nurses need time during their shifts to write down these notes, but you only have about half an hour to do notes for all four patients. You just sit right there in the nurses' station with doctors and nurses running in and out. Usually everybody knows at that time in your shift you need to write, and they let you just sit there and write, but it can be hard to concentrate. You're pretty tired, so sometimes I come home and rest for two hours, and then I know what I really should have written. When that happens it bothers me. The chart is a legal document, so in addition to the welfare of my patients, I'm also thinking of the legal aspect of what I've written in case there's a lawsuit.

Other nurses depend heavily on what I've written—especially the "plan" part. The doctors use the nurses' notes sometimes, too. That way they can find out what has been really going on with the patient, because the nurses' notes are usually more specific than what other doctors write.

I think my notes are a lot better than when I started nursing. They're more specific; they're to the point; I don't throw in a lot of unneeded words. One of my teachers when I was in nursing school really worked hard at getting us to write good notes. She criticized

98

Mary Chatsworth (continued)

me if what I wrote wasn't clear, concise, and easily understandable. And short. That's important, too. You have a page about the size of a piece of binder paper, and you only have about a third of that to write all your SOAP notes on. You have to include all the important things that happened to that patient during the day. That teacher of mine was really a help at getting me to say a great deal in just a few words. She would read over my student-nursing notes and then catch me on my own and tell me that I'd made a big story out of a small thing and that I could have said it in just a few words. Just short and simple sentences, clear, and to the point. Things like: "The patient said he doesn't feel well today," or "Temperature 38.2 degrees Centigrade," or "The patient had a disturbing visit from relatives today," or "Try to sit down and talk with the patient."

There isn't enough time for all the writing and all the work, so sometimes you just stay late and do it. It's that important.

Worksheet 1: ASSIGNMENT AND GUIDELINES

Your assignment is to hold an interview with someone who has a job which requires some kind of writing. Make a written record of what he or she says about the job and why writing is important to it.

THINKING AND PLANINNG

Before you interview, have a clear idea of the questions you will use and the areas you will cover. The class activities in the next few days will help you prepare a good set of interview questions and sharpen your interviewing skills.

DOING THE INTERVIEW

When you arrive for your interview, jot down some notes about your subject's personal appearance (features, age, clothing, gestures, etc.) and the room you are using for the interview. You will use these details in an introduction similar to ones that start the model interviews.

Take as few notes as possible during the interview. Your writing will slow things down and distract the subject. Instead, if your subject agrees, use a tape recorder so you won't worry that you are missing something.

Limit yourself to four or five major questions, spending five or ten minutes on each, and use follow-up questions to draw out details from your subject. Here are some example questions to use when you want your subject to say more about something:

1. Why do you feel that way?
2. What is an example of that?
3. What happened that shows that?
4. What more do you have to say about that?

WRITING AND REVISING

Next, transcribe your interview, that is, set it down on paper, using the interview models as a guide. Notice that the questions of the interviewer have been removed, and the interview has become a monologue—a long, uninterrupted talk by the subject. This is done by removing the questions and replacing them with transitional phrases and new paragraphing. More about this later.

Add an introduction, and bring your transcript to class on the day it is due. Use the suggestions you receive during the rough draft workshop to cut unneeded or dull sections and to decide how you will organize, begin, and end your paper. More on this later, too.

REWRITING, PROOFREADING, REFLECTING, AND SHARING

Write your final draft, have it carefully proofread, reflect on what you have done on a comment sheet, and turn your paper in when it is due. The finished interview will be read by several other members of the class.

Worksheet 2: ROUGH DRAFT WORKSHOP

Suggest ideas for improving the paper you have been given by answering the questions below.

1. Does the paper start interestingly? Suggest another part of the paper that could be used as a beginning by marking it in the margin with a **B** for beginning.

2. What parts of the paper are dull, wordy, or unnecessary? Mark them with a **C** to suggest that they be cut out.

3. What are the minor topics of the major parts of the paper? List them, and suggest an alternate order for them.

4. Is the ending of the paper good? Does it sum up the subject's attitude toward the job or writing? Suggest another part of the paper that could be used as an ending by marking it **E** for ending.

5. State what seems to be the point of the paper in a single sentence.

6. What is the best thing about the paper?

7. What about the paper needs the most work?

8. Reread the paper, and check it for errors in spelling, punctuation, and usage. Mark any words that are overused or inappropriate with a **D/T**, indicating that the writer should consult a dictionary or thesaurus.

Worksheet 3: COMMENT SHEET

_____

PROOFREADER 1

I certify that I have carefully read and corrected the final draft of this paper for errors in punctuation and usage.

Proofreader's Signature

PROOFREADER 2

I certify that I have carefully read and corrected the final draft of this paper for errors in spelling.

Proofreader's Signature

WRITER'S COMMENTS

The thing I like most about my paper is:

The thing I like least about my paper is:

The thing I tried most to improve as I wrote this paper is:

The most important thing I learned from writing this paper is:

Other Comments:

TEACHER'S COMMENTS

Grade _____

Things to work on in your next paper:

Chapter Nine

PERSONAL JOB RESEARCH PAPER

This writing project takes students further than their Personal and Career Goals paper. Furthermore, it should use skills acquired or refreshed in the chapters on the writing process, spelling, using reference books, letter writing, and job-writing interviews. This is actually a culminating project for the term and can be a four-to-six-week project, depending on the class' capabilities and on the amount of class time given to the students to work.

The following materials and resources are needed:

- people to interview
- people to job-shadow
- permission to leave campus for an interview during school hours if necessary
- permission to be excused from one-half or one whole day to job-shadow a person
- cooperative and resourceful librarian
- plain paper or stationery and envelopes
- cassette tape recorders and tapes
- *An Oral History Primer* by Gary L. Shumway and William G. Hartley, Box 11894, Salt Lake City, UT 84147
- several copies of telephone yellow pages
- information about jobs/careers of parents of students in class or in school

LESSON I

Ask the students to think way back to Chapter One: The Writing Process and the Personal and Career

Goals Paper that they wrote. Have the students take out their papers and all their prewriting to help them get started on this project. (Either arrange to have them bring it to class today, or, if it is filed in the classroom, distribute the Personal and Career Goals Paper and prewriting.)

Explain that the students are going to write a Personal Job Research Project. This will not necessarily be the type or style of research paper they may have worked on in a social studies class. Most of the information that will go into this paper will not come from books but from interviews and observations of working people and from correspondence with working people. Assuming that you have given them some advance notice about beginning the thinking phase of the project today, ask them each to write on the top of a page the career they are now most interested in pursuing. Walk around the room to see if the career choice needs to be narrowed down a bit. For example, a student who writes "stenography" might really be interested in "courtroom stenography." A "designer" might be actually interested in "men's fashion design."

To continue the thinking process and to draw from a previous source, ask them to look over their Worksheet 1 from the Personal and Career Goals Paper. Their thinking task, which is part of the prewriting, is to think of any questions they have about this job and any questions they would like to ask someone who have this job now. Tell them not to worry about which questions they will use in the paper, just to write whatever comes into their minds. This list of questions is to be continued for homework.

LESSON II

Begin class by asking students to share with a partner their choice of job and the questions they would like to know about the job and about a person who has that job now. Partners should listen and suggest other questions to be added to the list.

Next pass out Worksheet 1, the Explanation of Personal Job Research Project worksheet. Go over the entire project with the class. You can assign some or all of the due dates. You can also ask for volunteers to bring in the equipment the class will need. After you go over the entire sheet with the class, you can ask each student to tell the class his job-topic for the research paper. The class, listening carefully, can tell which of their friends, parents, or community members actually hold that position. This may be of great help to students in arranging for interviews and job-shadowing.

Allow time for questions if possible, or assign students to review the project explanation for homework and to bring questions to class tomorrow.

After class:
If you have a cooperative and resourceful librarian in your school or community who has time to help with classroom projects, give him or her a list of the students' topics. Ask the librarian for a list of useful and available publications and any suggestions about places to write to or people to contact. The third way your resource person can help is to provide you with titles of filmstrips, videos, or films that are available on any of the job topics; perhaps providing you with a catalogue of district or county media available would be possible.

If you have a career center, let the person in charge know of the topics also. Then on library day students can visit whichever center has the more useful information for them.

LESSON III

Today's work will focus on planning using the questions the students wrote about their topic. Also useful for the second phase of today's topic will be any suggested names or businesses that students gave each other in their exchange of resources.

Using the phone directories for your community plus other resources that students have discovered, students are to write to the individuals or organizations for information. They should write the question(s) from their question sheet that might be answered and additional questions or information of a specific nature. Wherever possible the full address is to be written also. Students may work in pairs using phone di-- rectories.

The second phase of today's lesson is to indicate which questions on their question sheet might be answered in a publication of some kind. They are to write what kind of a publication they will look for, being as specific as possible.

QUESTIONS: Where can you go to school in this area to learn to be a chef?

UNNACCEPTABLE ANSWER: pamphlets

ACCEPTABLE ANSWER: pamphlets from career section in library
community college course catalogue
yellow pages in telephone directory

Circulate around the room, checking on progress, giving ideas, and encouraging resourceful thinking.

LESSON IV

Take the class to the library. Their primary task is to find out where to write for information. The librarian may have rounded up some leads, and the *Reader's Guide to Periodical Literature* might give the students some ideas. Another place for some students might be the career center in your high school, especially if the career resource person has had time to do some preliminary legwork for your students. Take two days for this if necessary.

LESSON V

During class: Explain to the students that the business letters requesting specific information need to be written and mailed very soon so that responses will be received in time to help with the project. Students are to write at least two business letters to request information. They have already studied the business letter format earlier in the course, so use Worksheets 2 and 3 only if you feel the students need the review. Have students write one business letter in class, following the directions on Worksheet 1. They will need to refer to their work from yesterday for names and addresses. Telephone directories will be needed today by some of the students.

HOMEWORK:

Students are to complete the first business letter. They are to have a parent or another adult proofread the letter, looking for the organization and content required by Worksheets 2 and 3, good sentences, correct spelling, and good punctuation. They are to bring the original, rough draft of the letter with corrections on it to class tomorrow. They are also to bring plain paper or stationery and two envelopes if they would like to write their letters by hand. If they would like to type it at school, make arrangements if possible. If they would like to type it at home, tell them you must see the corrected, revised rough draft before the typing is done.

LESSON VI

Have students write their second business letter in class, following the directions on Worksheets 2 and 3. As they write, confer with individual students at your desk, going over the first business letter and its corrections, making any necessary changes.

HOMEWORK:

Students who have had a conference about the first letter should write in ink or type a perfect copy on plain, unlined paper. They may make a carbon copy unless they plan to photocopy it for inclusion in their paper. Students who have not had the conference should finish the second letter and follow Lesson IV's directions for proofreading and revising.

LESSON VII and VIII

Continue conferences with individuals about business letters, noting progress of each student. Students will be at different stages in their two business letters as you confer with them. The conferees after the first day will probably have only one conference.

If possible, have carbon paper available for duplicates of letters. Remind students that a carbon, Xerox, or handwritten copy of each business letter must be included in the project.

LESSON IX

Using Worksheet 2, have students address the two envelopes for their two letters. Credit each student with his finished envelopes before they are mailed.

Tell students to make interview appointments during the next three days for next week (after Lesson XIV). Preparation for the interviews will take place in class on the days of Lessons XI through XIV. Change it to an earlier day if you need to. Have students submit to you the names and positions of their interviewees, places of interviews, and times of interviews. Make necessary arrangements for those students who need to be excused from classes for an appointment. Encourage interviews before or after school hours. Provided on page 107 is a student sign-up sheet for you to duplicate.

Also explain the concept and process of job-shadowing. Shadowing a person at work means being with him or her during regular working hours or part of them, observing, taking notes, writing down questions you would like to ask later about your observations. The shadow (the student) is to be as inconspicuous as possible, allowing the worker to fulfill his regular responsibilities as normally as possible. Later, after the shadowing, the two need to find a time for questions and explanations. (In the high school in which we teach, we have participated in a shadowing program to allow teachers to become more aware of the students' total day. We each followed a randomly selected student through a complete school day of six class periods; then we met with other "shadows" after school to share our observations.)

Ask the students to set up a job-shadowing time. See what you can do to arrange for partial or whole day school absences to accommodate the shadowing schedules. Have students complete the shadowing schedule chart and the school's required paperwork.

LESSON X

Today's lesson focuses on notetaking in the school or public library. Using the board and Worksheet 5, show students the differences between: A. a summary, B. a paraphrase, and C. a direct quote.

Explain that you will teach them three different kinds of notetaking and that they must decide which will be the most useful for each source in the library. Be sure that students know that when taking notes, they should jot down page numbers; titles of articles, pamphlets, and books; authors; publishing companies and places; dates of publication. Order isn't important; you'll give them a bibliography lesson soon.

HOMEWORK OR CLASSWORK:
Have students complete Worksheet 6.

LESSON XI

Explain that a research paper requires a complete bibliography, or alphabetical listing of all the sources used on the paper, at the end. Tell the students to use Worksheet 7 to write the necessary information for all books, magazines, pamphlets, films, and other sources that they will use on the project. A lesson on writing bibliography in its correct format will come later.

Tell the students that it will be helpful in preparing the bibliography if they have kept an accurate record of the sources they have used.

Today will be a preparation day for the interview. Have the students take out their preliminary questions about the job they are researching in Lessons I and II. The booklet *An Oral History Primer* by Gary Shumway and William Hartley gives some very helpful hints about interviewing.

Review the difference between an open-ended question and a closed question. The former allows the interviewee some choice in his answer and gives him more freedom to respond individually. The latter requires a specific and limited response.

CLOSED QUESTION:

How many years did you study or train to be a cabinet maker?

OPEN-ENDED QUESTION:

What led you to a career as a cabinetmaker?

Have students look over their preliminary questions to see which are open-ended and which are closed. Then ask them to prepare a second, revised list of at least ten open-ended questions to be used for their job interview. Tell them that there may be times when they need to ask a closed question, but a whole interview of closed questions would be very stiff and confining for the interviewee. Remind them that there are certain questions that will encourage your interview subject to say more about a topic. See Worksheet 1, Assignment and Guidelines, from Chapter Eight.

LESSON XII

Look over the students' lists of questions for their job interviews. Have them share in groups of three the questions they have formed for their job interviews. Tell them to circle the five most important questions they have to ask their interviewee about his or her job. Hand out Worksheet 1 from Chapter Eight as a review, and spend class time going over it. The two interviews differ in that the first one focused on the writing involved in a person's job and this interview seeks to reveal the interviewee's job experience in all of its phases. This interview does not concentrate only on the writing exclusively but also asks about writing as one part of the job.

If time permits, set up another interview with a teacher, administrator, or another adult on campus whose present position or former position is of interest to the students. See Chapter Eight, Lesson IV. Inform the students of the subject to be interviewed so they can prepare questions.

LESSON XIII

Interview the adult on campus, using especially prepared questions. (Chapter Eight, Lesson IV)

LESSON XIV

See Chapter Eight, Lesson V.

Students are now ready to complete their job interviews outside of class.

LESSON XV

Use Worksheet 7 today, reminding the students to use some of their time to do research on their job, take notes, and keep a record of their sources. This is a bibliography guide to show them how to organize and order their collected sources of information.

LESSON XVI and XVII

After students have conducted their interviews, transcribed them as monologues, and added introductions that capture the setting (sounds, smells, sights, feelings) and the appearance of the interviewees, follow Lessons VI through VIII of Chapter Eight. Students will use Worksheets 2 and 3 in order to evaluate their own and others' interview papers.

LESSON XVIII

Distribute the Job-Shadowing Guidelines, Worksheet 8. Go over the students' role in observation and notetaking. Allow several days for the shadowing to take place while the students in class can work on research, rough draft writing about research findings, and improving the quality of the rough draft with a partner.

LESSON XIX through XXI

As students return from their job-shadowing experiences, have them begin working on their rough drafts using Worksheet 9. This process should take several class periods with your help and several nights of homework. Use Worksheet 9 as the culminating activity for the shadowing phase of the project.

Remind students after the Comment Sheet has been filled out to bring in all notes from publications to class tomorrow.

LESSONS XXII and XXIII

Students are to have all their notes from published sources in class today. With this mass of paperwork, the primary task is to decide on an order for the presentation of the information.

Tell the students to look through their original questions first and then their notes. Then they should list the order of the divisions (topics) in their paper. They can then number the list and number the sections in their pages of notes to correspond to the job topic they fall into. This task of organizing is the biggest job of all and should be given at least one day and one night to complete—more if a group requires more time and supervision.

Before students start to compose the explanatory paper from their notes, they need to be sure to have direct quotes in quotes so they can accurately footnote. They need to be aware of the sections that are paraphrased or summarized and can be credited in the bibliography only.

Next begins the actual composing process, the synthesizing of the notes that explain those aspects of the job that the student researched into one coherent paper. When the body of information has been organized and written, the introduction and the conclusion can be written. The introduction should have one main statement about the job and several other supporting statements that will be explained and exemplified later in the paper. The conclusion may be a brief summary in reverse order of the introduction or the student's response to this wealth of information he or she has assimilated.

HOMEWORK:
Finish writing the rough draft of the research paper.

LESSON XXIV

Follow directions for Lessons VI through VIII of Chapter Eight, perhaps condensing into two sessions. Use Worksheet 9 for the rough draft evaluation.

LESSON XXV

Footnoting should not be neglected, as plagiarism is a crime we do not wish to foster. The simple form is to place the number after the last word quoted, above and to the right, like this: "... linen."[1] The bottom of the page will reveal the source:

[1] John Mallonee, *Eyesight is Essential*, p. 91.

For several footnotes from the same sources or for more complicated situations, refer the students to the footnote worksheet, Worksheet 10.

The final lesson concerns the bibliograpy and the Table of Contents. Again use Worksheet 7 as a collection of models of different kinds of publications. Point out to the students that these models are not in alphabetical order on the worksheet (because they are arranged categorically) but that their job project bibliographies must be in alphabetical order.

The Personal Job Research Paper should contain the following information:

Title
The Story of a Search
Questions About the Job
Business Letter
Response
Preliminary Interview Questions
Interview Paper
Job-Shadowing Paper
Research Response
Bibliography

AT END OR IN ANOTHER FOLDER OR NOT SUBMITTED
Comment Sheets
Worksheets
Notes
Rough Drafts

HOMEWORK:
Complete the bibliography tonight.

LESSON XXVI

Have the students exchange their bibliographies, checking their partner's entries for alphabetical order as well as completeness and order for each entry.

Today students will begin in class their Story of a Search. In this page (or two) they should take the reader on their journey of job discovery. They use their own words, their own voice, their own "I." They can mention any discoveries that surprised them and what influence, if any, their job reserach project has exerted on them.

HOMEWORK:
Complete the Story of a Search. Finish preparing all papers for inclusion in your folder. Be ready to turn project in on due date—as announced by teacher.

LESSON XXVII

Use Worksheet 11 before collecting the projects. Give one more night for final spelling corrections if possible.

NAME: _____

DATE: _____

-POST- **INTERVIEW INFORMATION**

Student	Interviewee	Job Title, Company	Date	Place	Time

Practical English: A Complete Course

-POST-

INTERVIEW INFORMATION

Student	Interviewee	Job Title, Company	Date		Place	Time

Practical English: A Complete Course

Worksheet 1: PERMISSION FORM

PERMISSION FORM

_____ grants _____
(Interviewee)   (Interviewer)

permission to use the contents of his or her job-shadowing notes in his or her research project

for _____ at _____
     (Name of Class)

_____ .
(Name of School)

_____
(Date)

_____
(Signature of Interviewee)

PERMISSION FORM

_____ grants _____
(Interviewee)   (Interviewer)

permission to use the contents of his or her job shadowing notes in his or her research project

for _____ at _____
     (Name of Class)

_____ .
(Name of School)

_____
(Date)

_____
(Signature of Interviewee)

Worksheet 1A: EXPLANATION OF PERSONAL JOB RESEARCH PROJECT

During this unit of study you will be working on a major research project. Since it will be about a job you are interested in, make all the research meaningful. Where you go to get your information, how you find your information, and your ideas while you are working will all be a part of this paper so SAVE ALL YOUR NOTES.

The following resources will be needed for the class to complete this project:

1. plain paper or stationery and envelopes
2. cassette tape recorders with microphones
3. blank cassette tapes
4. telephone books with yellow pages
5. working people to interview
6. working people to job-shadow
7. typewriters or word processors

The following requirements will be the beginning steps of the project. We will work on these steps together:

1. The questions you have about the job; what you wish to discover during your research.

2. The names or titles of people and their businesses to whom you will write business letters requesting information.

3. The names of titles of people and their businesses whom you will telephone or write requesting:

    A. interview appointments
    B. job-shadowing times

4. The questions you will ask in your interview (at least ten). See Step 1.

5. The items from Step 1 (questions) for which you can find answers in a publication such as a book, magazine, or pamphlet.

Due dates will be announced for each part of the project. Progress checks will be made along the way; all notes will receive credit, as will participation in each phase of the project. Use this sheet to record due dates.

NAME: _____ 113

Worksheet 1B: EXPLANATION OF   DATE: _____
PERSONAL JOB RESEARCH PROJECT

The project will consist of the following:

1. Title page
2. Table of contents
3. Your questions about your topic
4. Your business letters (carbons or copies)
5. Responses to your letters
6. Preliminary interview questions
7. Your interview paper
8. Your job-shadowing observation paper
9. Your research findings from written sources
10. Your personal response, a summary of and reaction to your findings
11. Bibliography

The papers are to be written in ink (or typed or word-processed) and are to be *secured* in a folder. All notes, rough drafts, and worksheets are to be included behind the final copies of the writings if your teacher requests them.

Worksheet 2: BUSINESS LETTER MODEL

1945 Davis Drive
Miami, Florida 33168
April 10, 1988

Darnella School of Modeling
202 Castle Court
Danville, California 94526

Dear Sir or Madam:

   I am a high-school senior preparing a research project on the career of modeling. Since I plan to become a model, I am especially interested in your school.

   If you have a course catalog or any kind of a brochure describing your program, I would appreciate receiving it. Also, if you have any information especially for young men, I have some friends who would be interested.

   It would be very helpful if you could send me the information by April 24, as that is the deadline for our research. Thank you very much.

                              Sincerely yours,

                              Lynne La Bue
                              Lynne La Bue

Notice these facts about the business letter:

1. The HEADING is written a few spaces from the top on the right third of letter. Follow the punctuation.

2. The INSIDE ADDRESS is written a few spaces below and to the far left or the heading. The first line should be the name or title of the person to whom you are writing.

3. The GREETING is to a general person if you do not have a name or a title in the inside address. Notice the COLON.

4. The BODY of the letter will usually be two or three clear, concise paragraphs. In the business letter you may or may not indent.

5. The CLOSING is a few spaces below the last line of the letter and directly under the heading. Capitalize the first word only ("Sincerely," "Yours truly"). Use a comma.

6. Write your SIGNATURE above your printed or typed name.

Practical English: A Complete Course

Worksheet 3: BUSINESS LETTER

On this paper write a business letter requesting information that will specifically help you with your research paper.

A. Use your name, address, and the actual date in the heading.

B. Be sure to write the name or title, or both, of the person you wish to receive your letter, not just the organization.

C. The body should consist of the following, in three paragraphs:

   1. An explanation of your project.
   2. A specific request for information—exactly what you want them to send you or what you want to know.
   3. A thank-you for their "prompt reply," since time is a crucial factor.

Worksheet 4: BUSINESS LETTER ENVELOPE

```
Lynne La Bue
1945 Davis Drive
Miami, Florida 33168


              Principal or Director
              Darnella School of Modeling
              202 Castle Court
              Danville, California 94526
```

NOTE: A.   Your RETURN ADDRESS includes your name and address. Follow the punctuation.

        B.   Put the person's name or title above the organization in the ADDRESS.

        C.   Keep margins straight in both addresses.

        D.   Do NOT put a comma between the state and ZIP code.

ASSIGNMENT: Address the envelope below as you actually will address the envelope for your business letter to request information for your project. After the teacher checks this practice envelope, address your actual envelope.

Worksheet 5: NOTE-TAKING

Always carefully write down for each source of information: the title of the article, pamphlet, or book; the author; the publishing company and place; the date of publication; the page numbers used, especially for any direct quotes you may use in the paper.

QUESTION: What are the routine duties of a California Highway Patrol officer?

1.   The SUMMARY is what you write when you want to condense what you have read into only a few sentences. Because you will write the book title and page number, you can always go back to it if you need more details.

A CHP officer's main duties on the road include patroling, giving tickets, and taking charge of a highway emergency. Off the road he helps teach traffic safety.

(Career for Women, California Highway Patrol pamphlet, p.1)

2.   The PARAPHRASE is what you write when you change each sentence of a certain section into your own words and take notes, sentence by sentence.

An officer's main duty is ensuring good use of roads and helping drivers. Officers often cruise roads, warn bad drivers, and give tickets or make arrests. The officer is in charge in any road emergency. He also helps in education, investigation, and officer assistance.

(Career for Women, California Highway Patrol pamphlet, p. 1)

3.   The DIRECT QUOTE is exactly what the author wrote. You write the author's words using quotation marks before and after (" ") and using three dots (. . .) when you leave out some words or sentences.

"An officer's primary concern is with the safe, proper use of the highways and to provide assistance to the motoring public. Officers routinely patrol freeways and rural roads, warn drivers against improper practices, and when necessary, make arrests or issue citations to appear in court. The officer takes charge in roadway emergencies . . . and does all that is necessary to restore order and care for the injured. Highway Patrol officers also assist in traffic safety education programs, conduct special investigations, and render assistance to other police officers."

(Career for Women, California Highway Patrol, pamphlet, p.1)

Worksheet 6: NOTE-TAKING EXERCISE

QUESTION: What can you expect during your first one to two years after completing training to become a California Highway Patrol officer?

Using the source information that follows, take notes in the following three ways.

Upon graduation, new officers are assigned to various locations within the state where they must complete a 12-month probation. This includes a "break-in" period during which their Academy training is applied in the field under the direct supervision of a training officer. Most new officers spend their first two or three years on patrol before being considered for special duty assignment.

California Highway Patrol: A Challenging Profession, CHP pamphlet, p.15.

1. SUMMARY

2. PARAPHRASE

3. DIRECT QUOTE

Worksheet 7: MODEL BIBLIOGRAPHY

The bibliography shows which sources you have used in writing your research paper. It must be arranged in alphabetical order using the first letter of the first word in the entry, whether it is a person's last name or a title.

Here is how to write the entries for different kinds of sources:

1. BOOK WITH ONE AUTHOR
   Karolevitz, Robert F. *Doctors of the Old West.* New York: Superior Publishing Company, 1967.

2. BOOK WITH TWO AUTHORS (or more)
   Bennett, Hal, and Mike Samuels, M.D. *The Well Body Book.* New York: Random House, Inc., 1973.

3. BOOK WITH AN EDITOR
   Teyler, Timothy, J., ed. *Altered States of Awareness.* San Francisco: W. H. Freeman and Company, 1954.

4. BOOK WITH ONE SECTION READ BY YOU
   Wickes, Frances G. *The Inner World of Choice.* Englewood Cliffs, N.J.: Prentice-Hall, Inc., 1963, pp. 76-96.

5. MAGAZINE ARTICLE WITH AN AUTHOR
   Dole, Jeremy H. "Behind the Great Muppet Capers." *Families,* Vol. 1, No. 2 (May 1981), pp. 98-108.

6. MAGAZINE ARTICLE WITH NO AUTHOR GIVEN
   "Teen-Agers and Sex: The Price of Freedom." *Families,* Vol. 1, No. 2 (May 1981), pp. 4347.

7. PAMPHLET WITH NO AUTHOR GIVEN
   "Revised U.S. Edition of Royal Canadian Air Force's *Exercise Plans for Physical Fitness.* Canada: Simon and Schuster, 1962.

8. ENCYCLOPEDIA ARTICLE WITH AUTHOR
   Cowan, Ian McT. "Mammals," *The New Book of Popular Science.* Danbury, Conn.: Grolier Educational Corp. 1979, Vol. 5, pp. 2-12.

9. ENCYCLOPEDIA ARTICLE WITH NO AUTHOR GIVEN
   "O'Keefe, Georgia," *The World Book Encyclopedia,* 1981 ed. Chicago: World Book-Childcraft International, Inc., Vol. 14, pp. 539-540.

10. NEWSPAPER ARTICLE
    Sniffen, Michael J. "CIA Spy Chief Resigns; Casey Has Problems." *Contra Costa Times,* July 15, 1981, p. 1.

11. OTHER MEDIA
    Record
       Lightfoot, Gordon. *Gord's Gold.* Burbank: Warner Brothers, 1975.
    Film Loop
       Super Eight. "Surfing in Hawaii." Fanciful Films, 1969.

Practical English: A Complete Course

Worksheet 8: JOB-SHADOWING GUIDELINES

THINKING AND PLANNING

This phase was accomplished when you selected the person you would like to job-shadow back in Lesson X. You want to observe a person working at a job you might consider in the future.

JOB-SHADOWING

When you arrive for your job-shadowing, carefully look around. Notice the surroundings, your subject's work environment. Write down your perceptions of sights, sounds, and sensations (physical feelings, tastes, smells). Also, during the day jot down notes about your subject's appearance (features, age, clothing, gestures, activities, attitude, any changes you notice).

YOU ARE TO BE A SHADOW, NOT AN ACTIVE PARTICIPANT, NOT AN INTERVIEWER. Explain this concept to your subject before you begin the workday. Also, ask him to sign the permission form to enable you to use the observations from your shadowing in your Job Research Paper.

As you shadow your subject, take notes on his behavior, being as specific as possible. Precise, descriptive phrases will really help you put together an interesting paper. Jot down any questions that you have about what you are observing. Ask them during a convenient break or at the end of the session.

WRITING AND REVISING

Now you are ready to write a rough draft of the shadowing experience, using your notes as your source (instead of a reference book!). First, create an interesting introduction by setting the scene with your notes about time and place. (See JOB-SHADOWING, paragraph one, above.) Then continue the day chronologically with your observations, inserting the information you discovered during your post-shadowing question session wherever necessary. Break for paragraphs when there is a change in activity, locale, or phase of operation. You have to decide where these breaks should come, but keep the paper chronological. End the paper with a paragraph of your impression of the job as a result of the shadowing.

Bring your rough draft transcript to class on the day it is due. Use the suggestions you receive during the rough draft workshop to enliven dull sections, to cut where necessary, and to decide whether your opening and ending are successful. You will also receive help with transition, spelling, sentence structure, usage, and word choice.

REWRITING, PROOFREADING, REFLECTING AND SHARING

Write your final draft, have it carefully proofread, reflect on what you have done on a comment sheet, and turn in your paper when it is due. The completed job-shadowing paper will be read by several other members of the class.

Worksheet 9: COMMENT SHEET

PROOFREADER 1

I certify that I have carefully read and corrected the final draft of this paper for errors in punctuation and usage.

_____
Proofreader's Signature

PROOFREADER 2

I certify that I have carefully read and corrected the final draft of this paper for errors in spelling.

_____
Proofreader's Signature

WRITER'S COMMENTS

The thing I like most about my paper is:

The thing I like least about my paper is:

The thing I tried most to improve as I wrote this paper is:

Other comments:

TEACHER'S COMMENTS

Grade _____

Things to work on in your next paper:

NAME: _____

Worksheet 10: JOB-SHADOWING ROUGH DRAFT WORKSHOP

DATE: _____

Suggest ideas for improving the paper you have been given by answering the questions below.

1. Does the paper begin interestingly? What more could be included to "show" the reader the setting? Sights? Sounds? Feeling sensations? Tastes? Smells? What more could be included to "show" the reader the subject? Features? Age? Clothing? Gestures? Mannerisms or personality?

2. What parts of the paper are dull, wordy, or unnecessary? Mark them with a **C** to suggest that they be cut out. Make comments here.

3. What are the major topics or major parts of this paper? List them, and suggest any changes in the paragraph division or arrangement here.

4. Is the ending of the paper good? Does it sum up the shadow's impressions of a day on the job well? Suggest any other parts of the paper that you feel the writer should consider for use in the ending by marking them **E** for ending. Comment here.

5. State what seems to be the main impression of the shadow in a single sentence.

6. What is the best thing about the paper?

7. What about the paper needs the most work?

8. Reread the paper, and check it carefully for errors in spelling, punctuation, and usage. Mark any words that are overused or inappropriate with a **D/T**, indicating that the writer should consult a dictionary or a thesaurus.

Worksheet 11: FOOTNOTES

The first time a work is mentioned, the footnote should give: author's name, title of the work, and page number.

[1] Andrew Cortez, *The Hills of Martinez*, p. 11.

If the source is a magazine article or a short writing in a book, follow this example:

[1] Andrew Cortez, "Shell Ridge," *The Hills of Martinez*,
     p. 22. **

**If you need to take two lines to write a footnote, you indent the second line five spaces.

It is acceptable in this form of a research paper to put only the information given above in the footnote; the rest of the publication information will be given in the bibliography. In some more formal papers, however, all of the bibliographical information is given in the footnote also.

SOME MORE FOOTNOTE POINTERS:

■ Refer to one page as "p. 60."

■ Refer to more than one page as "pp. 60-61." (not "60-1" or "160-2")

■ When references (footnotes) to the same work follow each other without any intervening footnote, even though the footnotes are separated by several pages, the abbreviation "ibid." (for the Latin IBIDEM, "in the same place") is used to repeat as much as is appropriate.

[1] Brandon Michaelis, *Karate Instruction*, p. 83

[2] *Ibid.*, p. 88

■ When references (footnotes) to a work previously cited follow other intervening footnotes, the abbreviation "op. cit." (for the Latin OPERE CITATO, "in the work cited") is used.

[1] Andrew Carson, *Professional Skateboarding*, p. 121.

[2] Peter Schlag, *Olympic Gymnastics*, pp. 82-83.

[3] Carson, *op. cit.*, pp. 133-134.

■ Do not use "op. cit." if you are citing two different publications by the same author. This is too confusing for the reader.

■ Depending upon the type of paper and the instructor's preference, the footnotes may be numbered consecutively from the beginning to the end of the paper, or they may begin with number one on each new page.

PART II

Ongoing Skill Development

Chapter Ten

DEVELOPING VOCABULARY

Most approaches to teaching vocabulary begin with a teacher handing students a list of words they have never seen before. This poses two potential problems: the students may see learning such a list as a meaningless exercise and they may never develop the habit of noticing and learning the many new words they encounter every week.

This program attempts to remedy both of these problems. It provides a regular routine for vocabulary development and encourages students' responsibility for learning by having the class develop weekly lists of vocabulary words. Using this method, each student suggests a word for vocabulary study each week, and students develop the habit of noticing and looking up the unfamiliar words they meet.

The program takes only one day per week but should be continued for a substantial portion of the year. One day a week for ten weeks is a minimum for students to establish "new-word awareness." More than a semester, however, and the routine will probably become tedious.

LESSON I

About a week before you plan to start your vocabulary program, take part of a period to introduce it to the class. Explain that the purpose of the program is to develop vocabulary in three ways: (1) by making students aware of the new words around them, (2) by having the class develop its own lists of vocabulary words, and (3) by establishing a regular schedule of quizzes.

Pass out Worksheet 1 (Explanation and Word). Go over the sheet, explaining that each student must complete the information on a new, interesting, and

useful word before an assigned day the following week. Point out that they must not only suggest a word; they must also name its part of speech, briefly define it, give the place and sentence in which they found the word, and write an original sentence using the word correctly.

Emphasize that the goal is to make them more aware of words they don't know. If they keep their eyes open, they will probably run into several appropriate words each week. Books, magazines, newspapers, television, and the conversation of family and friends are full of useful new words. Some words, however, are better than others, and students should avoid obscure words and jargon. Terms picked up in specialized classes will probably not be useful to the rest of an English class.

HOMEWORK:

Students locate vocabulary words, fill out worksheets, and bring them to the class on the assigned day.

LESSON II

Today will be the first regular vocabulary day. Collect the sheets on which students have suggested words. Out of the thirty or so words handed in, quickly select the twenty that are most appropriate in usefulness and level of difficulty for the students to learn.

Introduce the twenty words you have selected. Write each word and its definition on the chalkboard or overhead projector. Most students find the words are easier to remember if they are placed in context. An example of what to write on the board for the word *lexicon* would be:

a *lexicon* of slang: dictionary or glossary

Read the source sentences and student-written sentences aloud and use them for context ideas, while students copy down the words and definitions. A convenient way to do this is to fold a piece of binder paper vertically and write the words on one side of the fold and the definitions on the other. This way the words can be covered for study later.

At the end of the period, remind the class that a week from today they will be quizzed on ten randomly selected vocabulary words from the list they have suggested. The quiz will provide definitions, and students will supply the correctly spelled vocabulary words that fit them. Pass out a copy of Worksheet 2 (Word and Quiz). Students will use a copy of this worksheet each week for the remainder of the vocabulary program. Next week is Week Two, and the worksheet should be numbered accordingly. Before the next quiz day, students should fill in the information on a new vocabulary word. They will then write the answers for their first quiz on this sheet. Completed quizzes that do not include a new word suggestion will not be counted.

HOMEWORK:

Students prepare for the following week's quiz and find new words to suggest for study the following week.

LESSON III

Begin class with the vocabulary quiz by writing the definitions of ten of last week's words on the board or overhead projector. Students write their quiz answers at the bottom of their copies of Worksheet 2 and turn them in. These sheets should already have new vocabulary suggestions on the top half.

As you did in Lesson II, select twenty words from those suggested by the class, and spend the period introducing them. Students will prepare for another quiz and provide another word for next week. This routine continues for the remainder of the vocabulary program.

HINTS AND SUGGESTIONS

1. Since the vocabulary lists will be written on the chalkboard and will vary for each class you teach, be sure you have an accurate list of the vocabulary words and definitions before the board is erased.

2. Notice how easily the quizzes are corrected. You or a student aide need only check for the correct word and spelling. A class set should take no more than five or ten minutes.

3. Students who are absent the day a new vocabulary list is introduced can get their words from classmates. Make-up quizzes, including all the words covered since a previous make-up, may be offered occasionally, perhaps once or twice a marking period.

VARIATIONS AND FOLLOW-UP ACTIVITIES

1. Substitute posters or collages for the word-suggestion worksheet. Students make and present illustrations of their words and definitions.

2. Some teachers like to reinforce the weekly vocabulary list with a mid-week activity. Having students write sentences using the assigned words is a common activity.

3. As a means of reviewing words from past lists, occasionally have a quiz on all the words previously covered.

4. Worksheets 3 and 4 of this chapter (Menu Words and Menu Word Quiz) offer a variation on the weekly routine. They consist of a list of French words that students might encounter on restaurant menus. The lesson works especially well around prom time. A matching quiz on the words is also included.

Worksheet 1: EXPLANATION AND WORD

Week One

In the weeks to come you will be responsible for improving your vocabulary by doing two things:

1. Bringing to class a word that you think other students would benefit from learning.

2. Learning a list of words suggested by other students.

The first words to learn will be assigned next week, when members of the class will make their first suggestions. In the next few days, keep your eyes open for words you do not know. When you encounter one, jot it down, look it up, and fill in the information below so you can suggest the word for the class to learn.

_____

Suggested Word: _____ Part of Speech: _____

Definition: _____

Place I found the word: _____

Sentence where I found the word: _____

_____

_____

_____

My sentence using the word: _____

_____

_____

_____

Practical English: A Complete Course

Worksheet 2: WORD AND QUIZ

Week Number: _____

Suggested Word: _____ Part of Speech: _____

Definition: _____

Place I found the word: _____

Sentence where I found the word: _____

_____

_____

_____

My sentence using the word: _____

_____

_____

_____

_____

QUIZ

In the spaces below, write the words whose definitions you are given.

1. _____

2. _____

3. _____

4. _____

5. _____

6. _____

7. _____

8. _____

9. _____

10. _____

Practical English: A Complete Course

Worksheet 3: MENU WORDS

Learn the English meanings of these common French words that you might encounter on a restaurant menu.

1.	à la carte	with a separate price of each menu item
2.	agneau	lamb
3.	apéritif	appetizer
4.	beurre	butter
5.	bifteck	steak
6.	boeuf	beef
7.	cafe	coffee
8.	champignon	mushroom
9.	chocolat	chocolate
10.	crême	cream
11.	dessert	dessert
12.	entrée	main dish of a meal
13.	escargot	snail
14.	filet	slice of meat with bone removed
15.	fromage	cheese
16.	gâteau	cake
17.	glacé	ice cream
18.	haricot	bean
19.	jambon	ham
20.	legume	vegetable
21.	oeuf	egg
22.	oignon	onion
23.	poisson	fish
24.	potage	soup
25.	poulet	chicken
26.	sauté	fry in sauce
27.	veau	veal
28.	viande	meat
29.	vin blanc	white wine
30.	vin rouge	red wine

Worksheet 4: MENU WORD QUIZ

Write the letter of the correct English word next to the French word that means the same thing. Not all of the English words will be used.

1. _____ beurre

2. _____ cafe

3. _____ chocolat

4. _____ escargot

5. _____ a la carte

6. _____ jambon

7. _____ fromage

8. _____ creme

9. _____ saute

10. _____ vin rouge

11. _____ oeuf

12. _____ poisson

13. _____ poulet

14. _____ dessert

15. _____ filet

16. _____ glace

17. _____ agneau

18. _____ champignon

19. _____ oignon

20. _____ legume

21. _____ entree

22. _____ boeuf

23. _____ bifteck

24. _____ aperitif

25. _____ vin blanc

26. _____ potage

27. _____ gateau

28. _____ veau

29. _____ viande

30. _____ haricot

ENGLISH WORDS

a. separate price for each menu item
b. lamb
c. appetizer
d. butter
e. steak
f. beef
g. coffee
h. mushroom
i. chocolate
j. cream
k. dessert
l. main dish of a meal
m. snail
n. turkey
o. slice of meat with bone removed
p. cheese
q. cake
r. ice cream
s. bean
t. ham
u. potato
v. vegetable
w. egg
x. onion
y. fish
z. soup
aa. chicken
bb. fry in sauce
cc. veal
dd. meat
ee. white wine
ff. red wine

Practical English: A Complete Course

Chapter Eleven

CORRECTING SENTENCE ERRORS

Chapters Eleven, Twelve, and Thirteen provide exercises for a systematic program to combat common language errors. Only as a part of a regular composition program, however, will they really help students master the language rules necessary for good writing. It is an unfortunate fact that assigning language exercises usually results in little more than improving students' ability to do language exercises. Unless the work mimics situations students encounter in proofreading their own work, the exercises serve little purpose.

For this reason, many of the exercises in these three chapters resemble samples of student writing. Some take the form of paragraphs rather than sentence lists, and some contain several different kinds of errors on a single page. The goal is to train students not only to find and correct errors but also to improve their proofreading skills. The sheets assume that students are familiar with only the most basic grammar terms: subject, verb, noun, and pronoun. More advanced concepts are defined as they occur and are used only when absolutely necessary.

While the sheets may be used consecutively to form units of several weeks' duration, it is usually more effective to set aside a day or two a week for language study and use the sheets throughout the year. In this way, students will see mastering these skills as a year-long commitment and avoid learning them for a quiz on one day only to forget them the next.

The sheets in all three final chapters are organized to introduce a series of rules and reinforce them with exercises and quizzes. Included are six types of worksheets, described below in the order they usually occur:

1. *Explanation Worksheets* explain a set of related language rules and provide examples. These are followed by exercise, editing, and quiz worksheets that provide work on the material the explanation worksheet outlines.

2. *Exercise Worksheets* provide practice of the rule explained on the previous explanation worksheet. An explanation sheet and exercise sheet together constitute a day's lesson. The teacher explains the material on the explanation worksheet; the students complete the exercise; and the teacher and class check the work for errors.

3. *Editing Exercise Worksheets* provide additional practice in mastering the set of rules on the most recent explanation sheet, but students now search for errors in a writing passage. These sheets make good homework assignments on the day an explanation worksheet is introduced.

4. *Unit Quizzes and Tests* cover the rules on the most recent explanation worksheet. They include both sentence lists and writing passages and may be used as additional exercises rather than as quizzes.

5. *Cumulative Tests* cover rules introduced on the most recent explanation worksheet as well as those covered on previous worksheets in the chapter. The emphasis, however, is on more recent work.

6. *Unit Tests* occur at the ends of Chapters Eleven and Thirteen. They cover all the work in the chapters they conclude.

Chapter Eleven tackles problems of sentence fragments, run-ons, subject-verb agreement, pronoun-antecedent agreement, and pronoun case. Cumulative tests conclude each of the main sections of the chapter and a Unit Test concludes the chapter.

Worksheet 1A: SENTENCE FRAGMENTS—EXPLANATION

A SENTENCE FRAGMENT

A sentence fragment is a part of a sentence or an incomplete sentence. It is a piece or a fragment of a whole sentence.

INCOMPLETE THOUGHT

A sentence fragment is missing the subject or the predicate of the sentence. Something is missing: either the main person or thing or what he or it is doing.

The movie at the Century V. (Is What? or Who saw it? or What about it?)

Only put me in for two innings. (Who did?)

The movie at the Century V is a classic, *Citizen Kane*.

I saw *the movie at the Century V* three times last month.

The coach *only put me in for two innings.*

—ING VERB ALONE

A verb ending in —ING can never be used as the **MAIN** verb in a sentence.

The boy heading the soccer ball.

A new employee being in charge of the computer program today.

My dad putting in the new water pump.

My girlfriend designing and constructing our new dining table.

Sentence fragments like these can be corrected in several ways. One way to improve them is to replace the —ING verb with another form of the verb with the same or similar meaning.

My dad *put* in the new water pump.

Another way to correct the situation is to insert a helping verb before the **—ING** verb. (am, is, are, was, were)

My girlfriend *is* designing and constructing our new dining table.

Other **—ING** verb fragments are improved by using the fragment as part of an expanded sentence.

The boy heading the soccer ball was on my select team last year.

A new employee being in charge of the computer program today, I think I will run it through myself later.

I watched *my dad putting in* the new water pump.

Commas are sometimes needed for these phrases, especially if they are extra (unnecessary to the meaning of the sentence phrases).

The captain, heading the soccer ball, scored the final goal.

Practical English: A Complete Course

Worksheet 1B: SENTENCE FRAGMENTS—EXPLANATION

BECAUSE, IF, WHEN, ETC.

A sentence that begins with BECAUSE, IF, WHEN, (and the words listed below) must have *two parts* or it will be a fragment.

Because Tom really needed that job.

If I had only been on time.

When sports equipment needs replacing.

These sentences need two parts: BECAUSE, IF, WHEN (or dependent clause) part and the part to which it is joined (the independent clause).

Because Tom really needed that job, the manager chose him instead of Mike.

If I had only been on time, I might have encouraged my sister to run that race.

When sports equipment needs replacing, the team's manager has to prove his case to the division manager.

I might have encouraged my sister to run that race if I had only been on time.

NOTICE that the comma is needed when the BECAUSE, IF, WHEN begins the sentence but not when it begins the second part of the sentence.

Besides BECAUSE, IF, WHEN, there are several other words to beware of using as sentence starters. Use of these words at the beginning may result in fragments *unless* the sentence has two parts.

After	Since
Although	So
As	Till
As Long As	Though
Every Time	Unless
In Case	Until
While	

Say each of these words in front of this good sentence, and see how it becomes a fragment.

I receive a Christmas bonus.

Now create two-part sentences with the clauses you said aloud. The clauses can be either the first or second parts of two-part sentences.

Example: After I receive a Christmas bonus, I will let you know how good my job is. OR I will let you know how good my job is after I receive my Christmas bonus.

Worksheet 2A: SENTENCE FRAGMENTS—EXERCISE

Construct complete sentences from the fragments below.

1. The *Elfquest* series of four books.

   _____

   _____

2. My former Cub Scout den mother.

   _____

   _____

3. Used to direct the Martinez High School marching band.

   _____

   _____

4. Her sister training the summer engineering student workers.

   _____

   _____

5. His hair glowing wildly with phosphorescent paint.

   _____

   _____

6. Because the pole vault is his best event.

   _____

   _____

7. When our family attended the Winter Olympics.

   _____

   _____

8. If I had taken bookkeeping and accounting in high school.

   _____

   _____

Worksheet 2B: SENTENCE FRAGMENTS—EXERCISE

9. Since Phil was my father's boss at the plant.

   _____

   _____

10. Although I had never written a resume before.

   _____

   _____

Indicate whether the following are sentences (**S**) or fragments (**F**).

——— 11. I might attend a community college.

——— 12. While I am working full-time.

——— 13. My friend doing both at the same time.

——— 14. If I decide to go on to a four-year college.

——— 15. All my community college credits will be credited.

Worksheet 3: SENTENCE FRAGMENTS—EDITING EXERCISE

The passage below contains both complete sentences and sentence fragments. Correct any sentence fragments that you find by making them into complete sentences. You may attach fragments to complete sentences (if the new sentence makes sense), add words to fragments, omit words in fragments, or change verb forms in fragments.

The new County Community Services Department is hiring this month. Weatherization engineers, crew foremen, designers, installers. When I heard about the new positions, I went down to the department for some information.

Sending me out to watch a weatherization crew at work. Seemed to be a good way to "tell" me about the job. One worker was having a time. The front door, which was rotting at the bottom. Another one added aluminum siding to cover cracks in the wall. Because the team also caulked the edges of doors and windows. I could tell that this would cut down on heating costs. I could see the value of learning this kind of work.

My junior-high camp buddy, Joe, replacing a broken window on one side of the house. When he told me he was learning a lot by working with his crew everyday.

As I looked in the window, I saw a worker covering the water heater with a blanket. A fairly simple way to conserve heat and therefore, money.

As I heard the crew foreman talking to the owner of the house. I realized that this was being done as a county service. Being done free for someone who couldn't afford to weatherize his home.

I made my decision that afternoon. Definitely the job for me right now. Earning money, learning useful skills, and helping people who can't help themselves.

Worksheet 4A: SENTENCE FRAGMENTS—UNIT QUIZ

Indicate **S** for sentence or **F** for fragment.

———— 1. The students enjoyed the speaker.

———— 2. Since the apples are not ripe.

———— 3. Her horse loping around the ring.

———— 4. Because they made me feel welcome.

———— 5. When I had to go, they didn't try to stop me.

———— 6. She was strapping her skis to the van.

———— 7. Then Dan shouting angrily at her.

———— 8. A $75.00 pair of running shoes.

———— 9. Spaghetti and ravioli with meatballs.

———— 10. Running on foggy or rainy days is great.

Convert each fragment below into a complete sentence. Use each method at least once: add a part needed, omit a word or words, or change a verb form.

1. The dog barking wildly at the fire engine.

   _____

   _____

2. The eerie midnight call of the foghorn.

   _____

   _____

3. When the pine tree crashed through our garage roof.

   _____

   _____

4. The red wagon wheels lending themselves to the new go-cart.

   _____

   _____

Worksheet 4B: SENTENCE FRAGMENTS—UNIT QUIZ

5. Only half a minute sooner.

_____

_____

6. As soon as I saw the map of the ancient explorers' routes.

_____

_____

7. Conversion of a chemical plant into a polymer plant.

_____

_____

8. Because he learned to walk before he ever crawled.

_____

_____

9. The cat leaping gracefully onto the roof of the treehouse.

_____

_____

10. If that had been my new Mercedes.

_____

_____

**Worksheet 5A: RUN-ONS
EXPLANATION**

A RUN-ON sentence is two or more sentences written as one sentence. It usually is composed of two sentences separated by a comma or two sentences not separated at all.

Here are some RUN-ONs. Can you hear and see two sentences with each one?

Darren paid twenty dollars for the ten-speed now he had to get it into operating condition.

Jennifer tried to find a summer job, babysitting was becoming rather tiresome for her after three summers with the Millers.

There are four ways of correcting RUN-ON sentences:

METHOD ONE

Divide the separate thoughts in the RUN-ON into two separate sentences. Use a period and a capital letter.

RO The Trojan War lasted ten years *the Iliad* **S** tells the story of that war.

S   The Trojan War lasted ten years. *The Iliad* tells the story of that war.

METHOD TWO

Join the two sentences within the RUN-ON into a compound sentence by using a comma and a coordinating conjunction (and, but, or).

RO I didn't pass my driver's test, I can't drive to the party tonight.

S   I didn't pass my driver's test, and I can't drive to the party tonight.

METHOD THREE

Use a semicolon between the two sentences.

RO My brothers and I grew up in the country, we really miss it now.

S   My brothers and I grew up in the country; we really miss it now.

Practical English: A Complete Course

**Worksheet 5B: RUN-ONS
EXPLANATION**

METHOD FOUR

Using a subordinate conjunction (from the following list), make one part of the RUN-ON into a dependent clause. You will need a comma if the dependent part is *first*.

After	Since
Although	So
As	Till
As long as	Though
Because	Unless
Before	Until
Every time	When
In case	While

Do these sound familiar? We learned these when we talked about sentence fragments. They are useful to remember!

RO I lost my brother's baseball glove he is really going to be furious.

S Since I lost my brother's baseball glove, he is really going to be furious.

RO Tory arrived at Northgate after the football team had been selected, he became the starting quarterback.

S Although Tory arrived at Northgate after the football team had been selected, he became the starting quarterback.

Worksheet 6: RUN-ONS
EXERCISE

Correct the following RUN-ONS by changing them into well-structured sentences by one of the four methods explained on Worksheet 5. Use each method at least once.

1. I was the main witness, I saw the car drive through the store window.

   _____

   _____

2. I've got a new job after school it's helping me to organize my time.

   _____

   _____

3. We planted a vegetable garden the first five years we lived here, we haven't had one in two years because of the baby.

   _____

   _____

4. Mark is a very intelligent young man he hides his intelligence from his co-workers.

   _____

   _____

5. My grandfather swears like a sailor my dad never says a swear word.

   _____

   _____

Indicate **S** for sentence and **RO** for run-on.

_____ 6. The Rodgers' old Jeep doesn't run the way it used to.

_____ 7. Reed's handwriting is illegible, I advised him to buy a typewriter or a printer for his computer.

_____ 8. That job has a lot of appeal for me the wages, the working conditions, and the vacations are fine.

_____ 9. Because he used to be my boyfriend, we are still good friends.

_____ 10. Although he used to be my boyfriend, we are still good friends.

**Worksheet 7: RUN-ONS
EDITING EXERCISE**

      The passage below contains many run-ons. Convert them into well-constructed sentences using the four methods from Worksheet 5.

Terry laughed at herself all the way home from her first afternoon at work, the ad had said, "Advancement depends on individual skill, and speed. Many opportunities. Call now." There certainly had been many opportunities, but her speed and skill hadn't exactly made her a prime candidate for advancement.

What a chuckle her family would have over her first job she had found the ad, answered it, interviewed, been hired, and worked an afternoon. She'd done all that in two days, forty-eight hours. What exactly was she doing to earn her tuition for beauty school she knew her family would ask her.

Would you believe tying flies for a fish-and-tackle shop? Gray Gnat and Royal Coachman and Yellow Humpy were her specialties today, who knows what tomorrow will bring?

Maybe this job would be useful after all, she was still chuckling as she envisioned the hairdo of the future, complete with Gray Gnat and Royal Coachman and Yellow Humpy on top.

Worksheet 8A: RUN-ONS
UNIT QUIZ

Convert the following RUN-ONS into well-constructed sentences. Use each of the four methods at least once.

1. There have been many movies lately about outer space the earliest space travel film was George Melies' *A Trip to the Moon.*

    _____

    _____

2. The most thrilling space-type film for me was *Close Encounters of the Third Kind*, the possibility of alien beings contacting earthlings really is exciting.

    _____

    _____

3. Early science-fiction films often portrayed space creatures as harmful *E.T.* presented a different view, one of a gentle and friendly outer-space visitor.

    _____

    _____

4. Film viewing has always interested me now I am thinking about film making.

    _____

    _____

5. George Lucas practically started creating movies in his own backyard maybe I could get started locally too.

    _____

    _____

**Worksheet 8B: RUN-ONS
UNIT QUIZ**

Correct any RUN-ONS in the passage below. Use several different methods of converting them into good sentences.

The use of computer technology is rapidly changing the movie industry, the coming of sound to the movies was an earlier and equally significant technological advancement. In 1926 Warner Brothers produced *Don Juan*, a silent film with accompanying musical score on records the picture used a device called a Vitaphone. But talking pictures really started in 1927 when Warner Brothers used the Vitaphone to produce *The Jazz Singer*, starring Al Jolson. This picture revolutionized the movie industry, just think, someday we'll read about how films like *Star Wars* and *Tron* were early examples of an equally significant movie revolution. Since I missed the "talking revolution," this is a revolution I want to be a part of.

Practical English: A Complete Course

Worksheet 9: RUN-ONS
CUMULATIVE TEST

Correct the sentence fragments and run-ons in the passage below. Then rewrite the passage, making sure that your version is composed of well-constructed sentences.

Teenagers have an interesting diet. It seems to fall into four main food categories: french fries, Whoppers or Big Macs, nachos, and large Cokes. Large Cokes being the basic liquid in the teenager's diet. Injected intravenously when they are hospitalized or their growth will be stunted.

In addition to large Cokes, which are ingested at any time during the day or night with or without solid food. The french fries are the main solid staple in the teenager's diet without this one element of especially greasy potato strips the meal or snack is incomplete in nourishment.

The Big Mac or Whopper is a dessert, added whenever the spending money allows. The Big Mac or Whopper is most often a snack, eaten between "meals" which Mom prepares these super burgers supply the real vitamins and minerals to counteract the ones Mom thinks are in the eggplant parmagiana. And the fresh spinach and mushroom salad.

Nachos supplying the finishing touch to any meal or snack with their tantalizing prepared-weeks-in-advance cheese sauce. A substitute may be made when warm nachos and cheese are not a possibility nacho chips or Doritos sometimes sour cream and onion potato chips. To add vegetables and dairy foods and make the folks happy.

There's no doubt about it. When you question a teenager about his diet, you can be sure that it will cover fully the four basic food groups. Large Cokes, Big Macs or Whoppers, french fries, and nachos.

Worksheet 10A: SUBJECT-VERB AGREEMENT—STANDARD AGREEMENT & COMPOUND SUBJECTS EXPLANATION

SINGULAR AND PLURAL

"Number" in grammar means either singular or plural. A word is singular if it refers to one person or thing. A word is plural if it refers to more than one person or thing.

AGREEMENT

In English a verb must agree with its subject in number. Both must be singular or both must be plural. This shouldn't be too difficult, because in English verbs are different in the singular and plural forms ONLY in the third person and ONLY in the present tense. The third-person present singular form ends in S.

I)		He)	
You)		She) works
We) work		It)	
They)			

YOU is always used with the plural form of the verb, even if it is only referring to one person.

You write, interview, talk, work. (all plural forms)

There is one verb (TO BE) that causes people a lot of trouble sometimes. It has different forms for singular and plural as well as for present and past.

PRESENT		PAST	
I am	We are	I was	We were
You are	You are	You were	You were
He, She, It is	They are	He, She, It was	They were

Underlined are the most common trouble spots. If they sound perfectly normal to you, don't worry about them at all. If they sound strange, try to practice saying them so you can say them automatically.

Practical English: A Complete Course

Worksheet 10B: SUBJECT-VERB
DATE: _____
AGREEMENT—STANDARD AGREEMENT
& COMPOUND SUBJECTS EXPLANATION

Important: The subject of a sentence is never found in a prepositional phrase. Be careful not to choose a noun or pronoun following one of these words or phrases as the subject:

about	together with	on	as well as
along with	under	through	of
among	in	to	during
at	into	with	for
by	like	within	from
over	between		

There are other prepositions besides these. Just be careful of the words separating the main subject from the verb it must agree with.

Her mother and nurse will accompany her.

Peanut butter and jelly is my favorite sandwich.

Bacon and eggs looks good to me.

COMPOUND SUBJECTS

Compound subjects joined by AND are plural.

John and Elizabeth are visiting us.

Exception—Some compound subjects are thought of as a single person or thing. When this is true, you must use a singular verb.

Singular words joined by OR, NOR, EITHER-OR, NEITHER-NOR are singular.

Neither Carson nor Adams is working.

Either Brandon or Devin is hiding.

Is the salary or the vacation bothering you?

When a singular word and a plural word are joined by OR or NOR, the verb agrees with the subject word nearer to it.

Either my puppy or my kittens *disturb* my parents at night.

Neither his sisters nor his brother *knows* where Jeff is today.

Practical English: A Complete Course

NAME: _____

Worksheet 11A: SUBJECT-VERB AGREEMENT—STANDARD AGREEMENT & COMPOUND SUBJECTS EXERCISE

DATE: _____

Underline the verb that agrees with the subject.

1. The leaves on the birch tree (is, are) falling.

2. My allowance, together with my birthday money, (is, are) enough for these new Nikes.

3. Either Barbara or Elaine (is, are) going to be elected president of the club.

4. Our scout den and our leader (is, are) going to attend Scout Jamboree.

5. Almost all the sailboats in the race (has, have) capsized at least once before.

6. Neither the bing cherry tree nor the peach trees (bears, bear) fruit anymore.

7. The teacher, as well as the principal, (attends, attend) every student-parent conference.

8. Sardines or cheese (is, are) an excellent source of calcium.

9. Running or Jazzercising (is, are) going to be my daily exercise during the school year.

10. Whoppers or Big Macs (fills, fill) me up at lunchtime.

Complete the following sentences using only *present* tense verbs. Remember to make the verb agree with the subject. Make the sentence at least *ten* words long. Use no past tense verbs.

1. Jackie and Barr _____

    _____

2. Baseball or football _____

    _____

3. My dad, as well as my uncles, _____

    _____

4. Either Shannon or Gina _____

    _____

Practical English: A Complete Course

Worksheet 11B: SUBJECT-VERB   DATE: _____
AGREEMENT—STANDARD AGREEMENT
& COMPOUND SUBJECTS EXERCISE

5.   The majority of the voters _____

_____

6.   That photo of my fourth-grade classmates _____

_____

7.   Neither my record nor my tapes _____

_____

8.   The coaches or the managers _____

_____

9.   Neither the losers nor the winner of the race _____

_____

10. Ralph, together with Carmen and Kathy, _____

_____

Underline the verb that agrees with the subject.

1.   I wish that you (was, were) my partner.

2.   We (was, were) swimming when he arrived.

3.   He said that you (is, are) going with him.

4.   They (was, were) witnesses to the crime.

5.   John answered the doorbell that they (was, were) ringing.

Worksheet 12: SUBJECT-VERB AGREEMENT—INDEFINITE PRONOUNS EXPLANATION

SINGULAR INDEFINITE PRONOUNS

The following indefinite pronouns are singular and need singular verbs.

each	one	no one	anybody
every	everyone	nobody	someone
either	everybody	anyone	somebody
neither			

Each boy swims at his own pace.

Each of the boys swims at his own pace.

Everyone in that crowd was singing with me.

Neither of my reasons sounds very convincing.

PLURAL INDEFINITE PRONOUNS

The pronouns BOTH, MANY, FEW, and SEVERAL are plural indefinite pronouns.

Several of the instructors are learning to fly from my uncle.

Both of the cars are in running condition.

SINGULAR OR PLURAL INDEFINITES

The words some, NONE, ALL, ANY and MOST are singular when they refer to a quantity, or a part of something. They are plural when they refer to several things.

Some of the job applications *are* interesting.

Some of the salad *is* mine.

All of the swimmers *were* on my team last year.

All of the birthday cake *was* served.

Practical English: A Complete Course

NAME: _____ 153

Worksheet 13A: SUBJECT-VERB AGREEMENT—INDEFINITE PRONOUNS EXERCISE

DATE: _____

Underline the verb that agrees with its subject in number. Remember that singular verbs end in **S** (unlike singular nouns).

1. Each of the players (receives, receive) his own uniform before the season begins.
2. All of the Pirates (is, are) in Mrs. Garfield's second-grade class.
3. Both of my cousins (serves, serve) the ball like a pro.
4. Many of the applicants (has, have) years of working experience.
5. It occurred to the manager that one of his employees (was, were) failing to lock up his station at night.
6. Some of the luggage (seems, seem) to be missing from the ship.
7. How could it be that nobody (wants, want) to chair the committee for the dance?
8. None of the apples (was, were) damaged in packing.
9. Few of the magicians (performs, perform) as dramatically as Adam does.
10. One of the worst situations (was, were) created by both girlfriends appearing at the dance.
11. Every bike and skateboard (is, are) to be locked up in the storage room during the meeting.
12. Everyone in the family album (looks, look) like my grandfather.
13. Somebody in that supermarket (was, were) yelling for assistance.
14. I found that neither of the boys (laughs, laugh) loudly enough for that part in the play.
15. I'll bet that anyone in this crowd (cheers, cheer) with more enthusiasm than he does.

Worksheet 13B: SUBJECT-VERB AGREEMENT—INDEFINITE PRONOUNS EXERCISE

DATE: _____

Compose five sentences of at least *eight* words each, using five of the following indefinite pronouns. Be sure to make the verb agree with its singular or plural subject.

each	one	no one	anybody
every	everyone	nobody	someone
either	everybody	anyone	somebody
neither			

1. _____

   _____

2. _____

   _____

3. _____

   _____

4. _____

   _____

5. _____

   _____

**Worksheet 14: SUBJECT-VERB
AGREEMENT—SUBJECT
FOLLOWING VERB EXPLANATION**

HERE AND THERE

When a sentence begins with HERE or THERE, you must look ahead to find the subject. Then be sure to make the verb agree with its singular or plural subject.

Incorrect	Here is my warm-ups.
Correct	Here are my warm-ups.
Incorrect	There's the racquets I was looking for.
Correct	There are the racquets I was looking for.

WHO, WHAT, WHEN, WHERE, WHY, HOW

In questions beginning with WHO, WHAT, WHEN, WHERE, WHY, or HOW, you must look ahead to find the subject. Then make the verb agree with its singular or plural subject. Sometimes it helps to convert the question into a statement, omitting the question word, or interrogative.

Incorrect	Who's the guys on that team?
Correct	Who are the guys on that team?
Incorrect	What's the worst problems you've had?
Correct	What are the worst problems you've had?

DON'T and DOESN'T, DO and DOES

The words DOES and DOESN'T are used with singular nouns and with the pronouns HE, SHE, and IT. The words DON'T and DO are used with plural nouns and with the pronouns I, WE, YOU, and THEY.

The counselor does/doesn't

He does/doesn't

She does/doesn't

It does/ doesn't

The counselors do/don't

I do/don't

You do/don't

We do/don't

They do/don't

Practical English: A Complete Course

Worksheet 15A: SUBJECT-VERB AGREEMENT—SUBJECT FOLLOWING VERB EXERCISE

Underline the verb that agrees with its subject in number. Remember to look ahead to find the singular or plural subject (when it is not at the beginning), and make the verb agree with it.

1. The boys on the soccer team (does, do) need a physical examination before the season begins.

2. It (doesn't, don't) look like rain.

3. Here (is, are) the problems I created for the math quiz.

4. (Who's, Who are) your favorite runners of the marathon?

5. All of us (does, do) the selecting of the team name.

6. Why (is, are) Casey and Chad on the same team?

7. Onto the field (runs, run) my little brother whenever he can.

8. There (seems, seem) to be several under-14's without a team this season.

9. Not one of the players (kicks, kick) with her left foot on this team.

10. How (does, do) those coaches make it to a 5:00 practice?

11. When (is, are) the trophies going to be awarded?

12. In the bleachers (sits, sit) my former junior-high coach.

13. (Here's, Here are) my fiancee and her parents.

14. Why (does, do) he insist on protesting every call in his team's baseball games?

15. There (happens, happen) to be one very qualified referee for this soccer game.

Practical English: A Complete Course

Worksheet 15B: SUBJECT-VERB AGREEMENT—SUBJECT FOLLOWING VERB EXERCISE

Read the following sentences carefully. If the subject and verb are in agreement, write **C** for correct in the space provided. If the subject and verb are not in agreement, write **I** for incorrect. Then change the verb to agree with its singular or plural subject.

_____ 1. Below the old bridge waits a hungry troll.

_____ 2. There's the golden eggs the goose laid.

_____ 3. Here are my favorite book of fairy tales.

_____ 4. Why does the fairy tale always have magic in it?

_____ 5. There is neither a handsome prince nor an ugly frog in this tale.

_____ 6. What are the story "Snow White and the Seven Dwarves" about?

_____ 7. There's many reasons why I still read fairy tales and folk tales.

_____ 8. Why do those children watch cartoons instead of reading a book?

_____ 9. On my bookshelf wait my favorite collection of Grimm's fairy tales.

_____ 10. Here's the story and the song of "Puff, the Magic Dragon."

Worksheet 15A: SUBJECT-VERB AGREEMENT—SPECIAL SUBJECTS EXPLANATION

COLLECTIVE NOUNS

Collective nouns are nouns that name groups of individual people or things. A collective noun can be considered singular or plural depending upon the meaning of the sentence.

army	mob	class
audience	club	flock
team	committee	group
herd	assembly	crowd
jury	cast	family

These are a few collective nouns. Can you think of any more?

In deciding whether a collective noun is being used in a singular or plural sense, read the sentence carefully. When the collective noun refers to a group that acts as one unit, the noun is singular. When the collective noun refers to the individual parts or members of the group, the noun is plural.

As a unit, this soccer *team* outplays all others in its age group.

Today the *team* practice whichever skill they are weakest in.

The whole *faculty* is supporting the Miles for Meals Walk-a-thon.

The *faculty* are still deciding who will walk and who will be rest station supervisors.

NOUNS ENDING IN -S

There are several nouns that end in -S and take a singular verb.

checkers	dominoes	economics
mathematics	mumps	physics

Mumps *is* the only childhood disease I didn't have.

Today physics *was* my most challenging class.

Practical English: A Complete Course

Worksheet 16B: SUBJECT-VERB AGREEMENT—SPECIAL SUBJECTS EXPLANATION

Some nouns name single objects but take a plural verb.

eyeglasses	glasses	pants
scissors	shorts	pliers
tweezers	vise grips	

Who knows where the scissors *are*?

I'm sure my glasses *were* right on this table; I can't see without them.

TITLES

Titles are considered singular even though they may be plural in form.

Streets of Fire is a very violent film.

The Purple Decades by Tom Wolfe *chronicles* the Sixties well.

"Rotten Peaches" by Elton John *tells* of a life gone sour.

Worksheet 17A: SUBJECT-VERB AGREEMENT—SPECIAL SUBJECTS EXERCISE

Each sentence below contains a collective noun. Write the collective noun in the space provided. Then write whether it is singular or plural in that sentence—**S** or **P**.

1. _____ , _____ The assembly seems to be really enjoying the magician's performance.

2. _____ , _____ The mob behave as totally different people than they are in a different situation.

3. _____ , _____ The jury is giving its unanimous verdict at this time.

4. _____ , _____ I want to know when the committee reaches its final step in the process.

5. _____ , _____ Do you think the cast are practicing their parts when they are not at rehearsal?

6. _____ , _____ The flock is heading south, flying directly over my valley.

7. _____ , _____ Mrs. MacLellan said this class was the liveliest junior class she had ever taught.

8. _____ , _____ Why are the herd scattering wildly in so many different directions?

9. _____ , _____ The crowd is moving toward the front of the school.

10. _____ , _____ The team is practicing with a visiting Canadian team today.

Worksheet 17B: SUBJECT-VERB AGREEMENT—SPECIAL SUBJECTS EXERCISE

Underline the correct form of the verb. Remember these are special subjects!

1. Physics (uses, use) all the knowledge and concentration that I have.

2. My scissors (cuts, cut) very badly since you trimmed your dog's hair.

3. *The Three Musketeers* (was, were) the book I reported on to the class.

4. Do you think economics (helps, help) you make financial decisions that will affect your career?

5. She can't believe that mathematics (stretches, stretch) her ability to figure things out.

6. The new pants nearly (falls, fall) off me when I take a breath.

7. Dad's pliers (is, are) supposed to be in his toolbox.

8. My father even said that *The Adventures of Buckaroo Bonzai* (was, were) a hilarious and entertaining film.

9. These tweezers (needs, need) to be replaced.

10. "Those shorts (looks, look) like something the cat dragged in," said my mother.

Practical English: A Complete Course

Worksheet 18A: SUBJECT-VERB AGREEMENT—NUMBERS AND AMOUNTS EXPLANATION AND EXERCISE

AMOUNTS

Subjects referring to amounts take singular verbs when the amount is considered a single unit. Usually periods of time, fractions, weights, measures, and amounts of money are singular.

Twenty dollars is what the Northgate High Madrigals charged to come sing at Grandma's eightieth birthday party.

Three-fourths of that huge cake is already gone.

Four years seems like a long time to be in high school.

A NUMBER OF SEPARATE ITEMS

When the amount is considered a number of separate items, the subject and verb are plural. This usually just sounds right to your ear.

Forty students tried to sign up for that photography class.

All twelve doughnuts are in the bakery box.

AMOUNTS SEPARATED FROM VERB BY PREPOSITIONAL PHRASE

When a subject is separated from the verb by a prepositional phrase, the verb is singular if the subject is considered a single unit or thing. The verb is plural if the subject is considered several things or plural.

Three cups of sugar *is* what the recipe calls for. (single unit)

Two-fifths of the campers *are* from Michigan. (several people)

Four boys from Mrs. Okawachi's class *are* always getting into trouble. (single unit)

Two-thirds of the honey *is* mine. (single unit)

Construct a sentence in which the verb agrees with the given subject in number. Be sure to use the present tense of the verb and to have at least eight words in each sentence.

1. Five tons of grain _____

    _____

2. Two-thirds of the junior class _____

_____

3. Eighty-five pounds of sugar _____

_____

4. Twenty boys _____

_____

5. Seven miles _____

_____

6. Eighteen years _____

_____

7. Ninety-nine cents _____

_____

8. Fifty dollars _____

_____

9. Fifteen inches _____

_____

10. Thirty-seven children _____

_____

11. Four-fifths of the class _____

_____

12. Two tons of wheat _____

_____

13. Eight girls on the team _____

_____

14. Nine pounds of peanuts _____

_____

15. One-third of the team _____

_____

Practical English: A Complete Course

Worksheet 19A: SUBJECT-VERB AGREEMENT—EDITING EXERCISE

The passage below contains many errors in subject and verb agreement. In the space above the words correct any errors in agreement that you find. Only correct the verb forms. Only use the present tense of the verb.

Greta would never forget ther first experience with summer camp. She arrived a day late. The camp for advanced Girl Scouts were a mistake in the first place. She had only joined the scout troup a month ago, and the troop was not serious scouts. Peaches and Mary Lou was her best buddies in the den, but neither Peaches nor Mary Lou were able to come to Camp Chickaronda.

"You girls is really going to like it here," promised the Camp Director, "and here is fun plus learning for all!"

Inwardly Greta groaned. "Why don't my mother ever involve me in these decisions?" she asked herself. "Oh, well!" she picked herself up. "Some of this experience have to be fun!"

"This morning each of you girls select a buddy," announced Mrs. Chirpini. "Greta, one Treetopper or two Pathfinders is still available for your buddy. How do one of these girls look to you?"

Greta grimaced as she selected Treetopper Tina. Trying to make conversation later, she asked Tina, "What's your favorite songs?"

Worksheet 19B: SUBJECT VERB AGREEMENT— EDITING EXERCISE

Tina quickly replied, "Anchors Aweigh" are my all-time favorite! Every girl in my troop back home know all the words. In fact, anyone who don't can't join the troop."

Greta grunted that she couldn't believe everyone in the troop love that song. Then she added to be friendly, "Both the scouts and your counselors is very good at singing."

That evening after the Treetoppers sang their rendition of "Anchors Aweigh," Greta delighted them all with "The One-Eyed-One-Horned-Flying-Purple-People-Eater." Thirty Girl Scouts are all very impressed with Greta's historical knowledge of the Fifties.

NAME: _____ 166

Worksheet 20A: SUBJECT-VERB AGREEMENT—UNIT QUIZ

DATE: _____

Read the following sentences carefully. Write **C** for correct if the subject and verb are in agreement. Write **I** for incorrect if the verb does not agree with its singular or plural subject. Then write the correct form of the verb in the *present* tense above the existing verb.

_____ 1. Sports interest Adam much more than mathematics does.

_____ 2. The senior class has decided on their various costumes for Homecoming Week.

_____ 3. *Star Wars* was my favorite film for a long time.

_____ 4. *Raiders of the Lost Ark* are at the top of my list too.

_____ 5. Either he or his sisters are supposed to cook the dinner.

_____ 6. Where's the bicycles?

_____ 7. Neither the students nor the teacher knows the answer to that one.

_____ 8. *Aesop's Fables* are on my bookshelf.

_____ 9. Through the pine trees blow a lovely breeze.

_____ 10. Every fork and spoon is washed.

_____ 11. The family are going to take turns having Grandma come to visit.

_____ 12. The counselor, as well as the psychologist, is evaluating the boy's problem.

_____ 13. Is there first-class seats on this plane?

_____ 14. The flock were attacking each other.

_____ 15. A bike with hand brakes are what I want for my birthday.

_____ 16. No one in my club wants to be the president.

_____ 17. Brandon and Stephen fight all the time.

_____ 18. Some of the vegetables is rotten.

_____ 19. Few of the dockworkers support the drive to strike.

_____ 20. The dresses on the top rack is beautiful.

Practical English: A Complete Course

Worksheet 20B: SUBJECT-VERB AGREEMENT—UNIT QUIZ

Read the following passage. Correct any errors in subject and verb agreement that you find.

Greta grinned as she read the entries in her journal from Camp Chickaronda.

"A shower to these campers are a tin can with holes in it and a pitcher of water."

"There's buddy burners to cook on and sit-upons to sit on."

" 'Smiles' or 'Hiking Along' are the tune for each day."

"Each girl in the different troops have to carry a compass at all times."

"Neither the mosquitoes nor the cabin's yellowjacket have any resting time."

"The book I brought to read, *Favorite Ghost Stories*, are really scary."

"Mumps are going around Cabin 3 like wildfire."

"The Kirby family takes turns writing letters to Kelly so she won't be homesick."

"My mother don't have any idea what she has gotten me into here. I wish you was here, Mom, so I could show you."

"Neither my Treetopper buddy nor my Trailblazer swimming buddy have ever been away to camp before."

"All of the girls in Tina's troop do know the words to a weird song."

"I can't wait till my mother asks me, 'Who's your new friends from Camp Chickaronda?'"

"Under my bed is so many spiders and ants I check my shoes each morning."

"Here's a couple of drawings I made after the nature hike."

"My tweezers are my most valuable possession here. They've removed most of the cabin floor from my feet."

"Two weeks seem like a long time to be at camp but it's passing quickly. I think I might come back next year."

Worksheet 21: SUBJECT-VERB AGREEMENT—CUMULATIVE TEST

Directions: Read the following passage. Correct any errors in subject and verb agreement that you find.

I have to drive too, and the posters along the freeway is making it a bit difficult for me to concentrate these days. Who's all these beautiful girls telling me to drink milk and listen to the radio and come to Tahoe? Even mumps have a billboard pushing for the MMR vaccination. All of these ideas are great if you don't mind being blasted all the time with visual images.

I think television advertising must be getting too expensive. *Hill Street Blues* are attracting a lot of viewers, and the stations are charging a lot for commercial spots. Companies are getting smart. An ad in the church bulletin or a mini-poster on a parking meter is reaching many people for less money. Advertisers may be trying new forms of advertising, but two-thirds of the advertising is still done on prime-time television.

Worksheet 22: PRONOUN-ANTECEDENT AGREEMENT—EXPLANATION

PRONOUN-ANTECEDENT

A pronoun is a word such as I, YOU, HE, SHE, or IT that takes the place of a noun. The antecedent of a pronoun is the word to which the pronoun refers.

Catherine is a prima ballerina.

She is the best dancer I have seen.

She is a pronoun referring to *Catherine*, the noun in the previous sentence.

ANTE means before, and the antecedent usually comes before the pronoun. Sometimes, however, the order is reversed and you have to figure out just where the antecedent is.

Because *he* is my eldest son, I place great responsibility on Carson.

PRONOUN-ANTECEDENT AGREEMENT

A pronoun should always agree with its antecedent in gender and number. Gender refers to use of a masculine or feminine pronoun. Number refers to singular or plural.

John prepared *his* favorite meal for the family.

Elizabeth decided to challenge *her* supervisor's order.

Brian and Sarah really like *their* new school.

In the first example, HIS is the pronoun used to refer to John, a male. In the second example, HER is the feminine pronoun used to refer to Elizabeth. Brian and Sarah are two people, so a plural pronoun must be used. In English, we have no masculine or feminine plural pronouns, so THEY is used for feminine plural, masculine plural, and both feminine and masculine plural.

As soon as a young person applies for a position at this store, the supervisor calls *him* for an appointment.

When the gender of the antecedent is unknown, as it is in "a person," English traditionally uses the masculine pronouns to refer to the antecedent. "She" or "her" may be used as an alternative to male pronouns when the antecedent is unknown. You could say "him or her," "he or she," "his or her," but it is a bit long, especially if you have to write it several times.

SINGULAR INDEFINITE PRONOUNS

Indefinite pronouns are always singular. Other pronouns in the sentences must agree with these *singular* indefinite pronouns. It is worth your time to memorize them:

each	one	nobody	somebody
every	everyone	anyone	either
everybody	anybody	neither	no one
someone			

Practical English: A Complete Course

Worksheet 23A: PRONOUN-ANTECEDENT AGREEMENT—EXERCISE

Read the following sentences aloud. They are all correct in agreement but they may sound strange to you. All of the pronouns that refer to the singular indefinite pronouns are singular. Notice the gender (masculine or feminine) that is used in each sentence.

1. Each person in my class entered something of *his* own making or raising into the county fair.

2. Every teacher in the school told *his or her* class about us.

3. Either of the girls who entered the jam and jelly contest could have won with *her* creation.

4. Neither of the boys who raised cattle planned to sell or slaughter *his* steer.

5. One of the kids named *his* pig Wilbur after his favorite character in *Charlotte's Web*.

6. Everyone in the eleventh-grade class was especially proud of *his or her* own participation.

7. Why did everybody decide to support *his* teacher's impossible idea?

8. There was no one in the whole class who could think of a time when *his* own idea had been laughed at or ignored by the teacher.

9. Besides, nobody wanted *her* failure to participate to break the perfect plan.

10. We all agreed that anyone who tackled the raising of an animal had *his* hands full for months.

11. My father said that anybody who entered would receive *his* own prize of personal accomplishment.

12. Someone at the newspaper wrote about us. In *her* words we were "a most unusual group of young people."

13. Our teacher said at the fair, "Somebody had better take a picture of us, and *he'd* better do it before I cry!"

Practical English: A Complete Course

Worksheet 23B: PRONOUN-ANTECEDENT AGREEMENT—EXERCISE

Indicate proper agreement of pronoun and antecedent by underlining the correct choice in each of the following sentences.

1. Any man who climbs that mountain is risking (his, their) life foolishly.

2. Several women at my dad's trucking company handle (her, their) rigs better than many of the men.

3. A superior student, such as you have described, would not jeopardize (his, their) future by cheating on a final exam.

4. Someone in Sharon's P.E. class left (her, their) shoes on the court.

5. Either of the boys might have held (his, their) breath for another minute.

6. Everyone at baseball camp agreed to send (his, their) buddy a school picture in the fall.

7. I find no one who has tattooed (himself, themselves) in here.

8, 9, 10. Each bulb in my garden surprises me as (it, they) (produce, produces) (its, their) own special surprises.

Construct from the following phrases sentences with at least ten words. Be sure that the sentence contains at least one pronoun that refers to the antecedent given. (Remember that verbs in the present tense must also agree with their subject.)

EXAMPLE: A few of the boys

A few of the boys forgot *their* towels

11. Either Mary or Sylvia

12. Both of my best friends

13. No one in this dormitory

14. Every person that I talk to

15. Anyone who wants to

Worksheet 24A:
PRONOUN-ANTECEDENT AGREEMENT
EDITING EXERCISE

The passage below contains many errors in pronoun-antecedent agreement. Some sentences are completely correct. Make any corrections that you believe are necessary to make the pronoun agree with its antecedent.

Koko, a 230-pound female gorilla, is learning to communicate with people and other animals. Both of Koko's parents came from Cameroon in West Africa, and their daughter is now a Californian. No one in their right mind would believe Koko can actually talk but maybe one could allow themself to believe that Koko can communicate.

Dr. Francis Patterson is a psychologist who has been working with Koko for thirteen years. A psychologist is a person who concentrates their study on why people behave as they do. Dr. Patterson, however, works with Koko and several other animals instead of with people. For the past thirteen years, Dr. Patterson has been teaching Koko American Sign Language, a system of hand and body movements to help someone who is deaf communicate their feelings. Everybody who "talks" this way is expressing their ideas by "signing."

One day Koko signed that she wanted a cat. Dr. Patterson gave Koko a cat picture and a toy cat, but neither did their job of making Koko happy. Koko had someone else in mind, and she knew them when she saw them. Dr. Patterson gave Koko a little tailless kitten, whom Koko named All Ball. Every day held their special times when Koko would hold All Ball, petting him and signing "Soft good cat." When All Ball was killed by a car, Dr. Patterson told Koko. Both of them shared their silent sorrow, and then Koko made a crying sound.

Practical English: A Complete Course

Worksheet 24B: PRONOUN-ANTECEDENT AGREEMENT EDITING EXERCISE

Soon after, Koko received a new kitten she named Lips. Anyone can see for themselves how Koko loves Lips, as she cradles him and signs "Love, love, love."

Each of Koko's visitors comes away with their own personal amazement. Some say Koko is smart because she lived at Stanford University for awhile and learned from their doctors. Some sign their own messages to Koko, and she signs back. But everyone agrees that in their mind, Koko is a most unusual gorilla.

Practical English: A Complete Course

NAME: _____

Worksheet 25A: SENTENCE FRAGMENT, RUN-ON, SUBJECT-VERB AGREEMENT, AND PRONOUN-ANTECEDENT CUMULATIVE TEST

DATE: _____

Correct the sentence fragments and run-ons; add words where necessary. Correct the subject and verb agreement, being sure to keep the verb in the *present* tense. Correct the pronoun and antecedent agreement.

Have you played any Trivial Pursuit games lately? If you have, you know the topics that makes people test their knowledge of sports records. The most pinch hits by a lefthander. The most errors by a short stop in a nine-inning game. The fewest assists by a catcher in a full season.

Some records are really important. Like Roger Maris' sixty-one home runs in 1961 and Hank Aaron's 755 career homers. Joe DiMaggio's fifty-six game hitting streak in 1941 are the toughest record to break. In major league baseball's 109-year history, no one of the batters have hit safely in more than forty-four games.

Either Joe DiMaggio of the New York Yankees's sports clips or Joe DiMaggio of the coffeemaker commercial are the strong batter and centerfielder. He was thirteen years in the majors, Joe rarely struck out. Joe, as well as his fans, are still amazed at his 361 home runs and only 369 strikeouts. We was all Joe's fans in the forties.

Every one of your parents remember Joe's fifty-six game hitting streak, it began on May 15, 1941, with a single. There was lots of good hitters with a twenty-game hitting streak. Who's the hitters whose streaks went higher?

Practical English: A Complete Course

Worksheet 25B: SENTENCE FRAGMENT, RUN-ON, SUBJECT-VERB AGREEMENT, AND PRONOUN-ANTECEDENT CUMULATIVE TEST

Wee Willie Keeler of the Baltimore Orioles held the record at forty-four games in 1897. Joe's team in 1941 also remember their individual reactions when Joe broke the record.

Mathematics are really important when it comes to recordkeeping. Fifty-six games is the record, no one has matched it yet. When DiMaggio singled and doubled against the Cleveland Indians. The end came the next night against Cleveland. The third-baseman throwing him out twice. Nobody in their right mind wanted to see Joe stop hitting safely. Someone I know said that he saw Joe go zero for three, with a walk that night.

Each number in the record books are impressive for Joe DiMaggio. During the streak Joe batted .408 and hit fifteen home runs, he batted in fifty-five. For the full season he hit .357 with thirty homers and 125 RBI. The Yankees winning the pennant easily.

Maybe someday a player will break Joe's record, but don't hold your breath for them to appear.

NAME: —————————————————————

Worksheet 26A: PRONOUN CASES NOMINATIVE EXPLANATION

DATE: —————————————————————

Pronouns take the place of nouns in a sentence. Pronouns have different forms or cases, depending on how they are used in a sentence.

SUBJECT PRONOUNS

When a pronoun is used as the subject of a sentence, the pronoun is in the nominative case and is called a SUBJECT PRONOUN.

My sister is in your office.
She is in your office.

That boy took the last Coke.
He took the last Coke.

Those kittens are adorable.
They are adorable.

When a pronoun by itself is the subject of a sentence, you do not usually have a problem choosing the proper form. These are the nominative pronouns to use for subject pronouns:

I, YOU, HE, SHE, IT, WE, YOU, THEY

COMPOUND SUBJECTS WITH PRONOUNS

When a subject is compound and consists of a noun and a pronoun or several pronouns, you must still use the nominative form for the subject pronoun. One way to be sure is to say the sentence with only the pronoun as the subject.

Matt and *I* play on the same polo team.
(*I* play on the same polo team.)

Darin invited Shana and *him* to his party.
(Darin invited *him* to his party.)

Juan Carlos chose Jonathan, Adam, and *me* to play with him.
(Juan Carlos chose *me* to play with him.)

SUBJECT PRONOUNS IN PREDICATE

The predicate is the part of the sentence containing the verb; it says something about the subject. When a pronoun in the predicate renames the subject and follows a linking verb, use a subject pronoun.

Practical English: A Complete Course

Worksheet 26B: PRONOUN CASES: NOMINATIVE EXPLANATION

LINKING VERBS

Linking verbs do not show action. They just "link" the subject to the predicate. Think of them as an "equals" sign.

AM, IS, ARE, WAS, WERE, BE, BEING, BEEN, SEEMS, BECOMES

The police officer is *she.*
(*She* is the police officer.)

The police officer = she
    (Subject)   (Subject Pronoun)

His co-workers are Paul and *I.*
Paul and *I* are his co-workers.

His co-workers = Paul and I
    (Subject)   (Subject Pronoun)

It sometimes helps to change the order of words in a question or inverted sentence.

Was it (he, him) on the phone?
(*He,* him) was on the phone.

John said it was (I, me) who would get the job.
(John said (*I,* me) was it who would get the job.)

NAME: _____

Worksheet 27A: PRONOUN CASES: NOMINATIVE EXERCISE

DATE: _____

Underline the correct pronoun in each sentence.

1. My brother and (I, me) rode our dirt bikes to the creek.

2. (They, Them) and my grandparents drove a camper out to San Francisco.

3. Frank and (he, him) play golf every Saturday morning.

4. It was either Gina or (she, her) who interviewed the applicants.

5. The new secretary in our office must be (he, him).

6. When (she, her) and her mother went shopping, they met her dad for lunch.

7. I hoped it was (she, her) who called to invite me to the dance.

8. The supervisors and (we, us) are going out to lunch today.

9. Glenn and (I, me) will change the goldfish's water.

10. I answered the phone by saying "This is (she, her)," when someone asked for me.

11. Ed and (I, me) want to get a paper route to earn extra money.

12. The umpire and (we, us) disagreed on several major calls.

13. I can't believe it was (he, him) who caused that fight at work.

14. Only Evan and (I, me) have been to Yosemite.

15. It had to be (they, them) who planned that surprise party at the office.

16. The neighbors and (we, us) are planning a Fourth of July barbecue.

17. David is confident that the winner will be (he, him).

18. The Endicotts and (we, us) always have a Christmas dinner together.

19. Shannon and (he, him) are good friends.

20. It was (we, us) you heard coming in late last night.

Practical English: A Complete Course

NAME: _____

Worksheet 27B: PRONOUN CASES: DATE: _____
NOMINATIVE EXERCISE

Select a subject pronoun from those given below to complete each of the following sentences.

I, he, she, we, they

21. Brandon and _____ prepared the campers' breakfast.

22. Was it _____ you took to the Giants' game?

23. Devin is sure that the Employee of the Month will be _____ .

24. That might be _____ at the door now.

25. It was _____ who mailed the anonymous letter.

26. Margie and _____ plan to go to Paris Beauty College in the fall.

27. Saturday Armond and _____ looked for summer jobs.

28. We and _____ have a hard time balancing school, sports, and work.

29. Addie and _____ belong to the Cleveland Dramateurs.

30. It must have been _____ who called about the kitten.

Worksheet 28A: PRONOUN CASES: DATE: _____
OBJECTIVE EXPLANATION

OBJECT PRONOUNS

When a pronoun is used as an object in a sentence, it must be in the objective case.

That coyote startled *me*.
(Direct object of verb)   Startled whom? *Me*

My dad sent *us* some money.
(Indicate object of verb)   Sent to whom? *Us*

Give that book to *her*.
(Object of preposition)   To whom? *Her*

When a pronoun by itself is an object in a sentence, you do not usually have a problem choosing the proper form. These are the objective pronouns to use when the pronoun is a direct object, an indirect object, or an object of a preposition:

ME, YOU, HIM, HER, IT, US, YOU, THEM

COMPOUND OBJECTS WITH PRONOUNS

When an object is compound and consists of a noun and a pronoun or several pronouns, you must use the objective form for the object pronoun. One way to be sure is to say the sentence with only the pronoun as the object.

1. I hired Tom and *her* yesterday.
    (I hired *her* yesterday.)

2. Mother needed Jackie and *me* to help.
    (Mother needed *me* to help.)

3. The teacher checked the paper for Adrian and *him*.
    (The teacher checked the paper for *him*.)

Practical English: A Complete Course

NAME: _____

Worksheet 28B: PRONOUN CASES: OBJECTIVE EXPLANATION

DATE: _____

ORAL DRILL

Say aloud the following sentences; they are all correct. (Unlike the nominative case, the objective case pronouns usually will sound correct to your ear.)

1. Between you and me, this job is a piece of cake.
2. I don't want to race against him.
3. The *Elfquest* books give my friends and me a fantasy world to talk about.
4. Sharon gladly lets me do the dishes.
5. The teacher wants Tom and him to do that assignment.
6. Our buddies sent us that gag gift.
7. Usually we deliver pizza to Joan and them in the evening.
8. I mailed that invitation to Jack and her last week.
9. The job teaches Suzanne and us about the many ways of dealing with the public.
10. Our uncles took Hermie and him with us on the rafting trip.

Worksheet 29A: PRONOUN CASES: DATE: _____
OBJECTIVE EXERCISE

Select an object pronoun from the list below for each blank in the following sentences.

me, her, him, us, them

1. Did you see her and _____ at the movies?

2. The elephant liked _____ to spray water on him.

3. Will you please leave _____ a message?

4. A counselor named Barbara gave _____ a five-week-old kitten.

5. I named _____ Boo-Kay after my counselors, Boo (Barbara) and Kay.

6. When I saw _____ in the jars of formaldehyde, the two-headed creatures frightened me.

7. He shared his secret with _____ and _____ .

8. Leave Elaine and _____ alone.

9. That dress fits both Ginger and _____ .

10. I remember _____ and _____ very well.

Underline the correct pronoun in each sentence.

11. Don't tell mother and (he, him) your surprise.

12, 13. Please share with Peter and (she, her) that story you told (I, me).

14. Ask Erica and (she, her) all your questions about the car.

15, 16. Should mother offer (he, him) and (I, me) any more dessert?

17. Give your father and (I, me) a fair chance.

18. Mrs. Harrison's interview panel included Jerry and (I, me).

19. Mayor Feinstein presented the astronaut and (she, her) keys to the City of San Francisco.

20. You ought to check with the Sakeleris family and (they, them) before you all arrive for a swim.

21. Don't tell Gary and (I, me) we're too late!

Practical English: A Complete Course

NAME: _____ 183

Worksheet 29B: PRONOUN CASES: DATE: _____
OBJECTIVE EXERCISE

22. The trees towered above the children and (he, him).

23. I received letters from Aunt Louise and (she, her) last week.

24. Place your confidence in the president and (he, him).

25. The reward will be divided among the boys and (we, us.)

26. The guitarist sat down between Tony and (I, me) at the table.

27. The principal had special awards for (we, us) and (they, them).

28. For (he, him) you spent all that money?

29. The menu was chosen by all of (we, us) campers.

30. Mrs. Surges doesn't live far from the Millers and (they, them).

NAME: _____ 184

Worksheet 30: PRONOUN CASES:
DATE: _____
POSSESSIVE EXPLANATION & EXERCISE

POSSESSIVE PRONOUNS

When a pronoun is used to show ownership, it must be a possessive pronoun.

Pronouns that are used as adjectives to modify nouns are:

> my, you, his, her, its, our, your, their

(Notice that *its*, as in *its collar*, has no apostrophe.)

> I gave you *my* collection.

> The priest ate at *our* house.

Pronouns that are used as subjects of verbs, as objects of verbs, as objects of prepositions, or as words in the predicate are:

> MINE, YOURS, HIS, HERS, ITS, OURS, YOURS, THEIRS

(Notice that none of these pronouns have an apostrophe.)

> *Mine* has only three tires. (Subject of verb)

> Dad created *his* from scrap metal. (Object of verb)

> I mailed my book with *hers*. (Object of preposition)

> I'm sure this is *yours*. (Word in predicate, Predicate adjective)

Underline the correct pronoun in each of the following sentences.

1. This model must be (yours, your, your's).
2. Who destroyed (its, it's) tunnel?
3. I know this is (her, hers, her's) novel from English class.
4. She found his paper with (theirs, their's, they'res).
5. I destroyed (your's, yours, your) very carelessly.
6. (Mine and hers, Mine and her's) were the ones Mrs. Iversen chose.
7. It seemed that (their's, theirs, they'res) were the sloppiest projects.
8. She denied (his and her, his and hers) charges of stealing.
9. Something is wrong with (ours, our's, our).
10. (Theirs and ours, Their's and our's) are the closest to the originals.

Practical English: A Complete Course

Worksheet 31A: PRONOUN CASES EDITING EXERCISE

Correct any pronoun errors you find in the passage below.

Truckers have a variety of physical problems due to there job. Consider a typical trucker's day: driving for ten hours; eating greasy eggs and home fries; smoking cigarettes, maybe a couple of packs; lifting heavy boxes onto and off the truck. This professional lifestyle contributes to the chronic backache, pulled muscles, and heart disease of it's rank. Most truckers say at least one of these problems is their's.

Lucky are them now, because Gijs VanOort of the Biokinetics Research Laboratory at Temple University has designed the first individualized fitness program for truckers. My brother and me know a few truckers for Pepperidge Farm, and an uncle of our's is going to join them soon. The drivers and him found out that they will be testing the program on the job. The plant managers and them will evaluate the exercise program according to its merits.

The truckers and their employers say, "An exercise program is already our." One trucker said when the guys and her unload the truck, they get as much exercise as a player in a nine-inning ball game. And, she added, none of the equipment she uses is her's.

But VanOort has seen that the cycle of long, sedentary hours of driving followed by it's opposite spell of strenuous and sudden exertion is the problem. VanOort's program was devised carefully by a team of drivers and he. The truckers receive barbells, an exercise mat, and a log book. It must be them that they use in their brisk walking, stretching, and strength-building exercises.

Practical English: A Complete Course

Worksheet 31B: PRONOUN CASES
EDITING EXERCISE

I went with my uncle to talk to some drivers about the program. My uncle and them exercised in the trailer and in the parking lot. "Where is your nephew?" one of the guys asked.

"This is him," my uncle said, pointing at me. "Him and me are both going to be truckers, and it looks like more than a job will be our's. It might be him that needs this job more than I do," he teased, pointing at my bulging stomach.

This job could be healthier for the truckers than I thought. VanOort intends to help the managers and they combat heart disease by adding smoking cessation, stress management, and nutrition counseling to his plan. It's value is obvious and has a lot of appeal to my uncle and I. I keep wondering about why VanOort chose Pepperidge Farm to work with. Was it them who snacked on "goldfish" too often, or were the heaviest loads of little treats their's?

**Worksheet 32: PRONOUN CASES
UNIT QUIZ**

Underline the correct pronoun in each sentence.

1. Bill and (I, me) sing in the church choir.
2, 3. Last summer my teacher took (he, him) and (I, me) out to lunch.
4. We mailed Elizabeth and (she, her) some candy.
5. Mary Ellen and (he, him) were the first teenagers I knew.
6. I don't think that Cheryl and (she, her) will go to the ranch.
7. Set it down beside Dan and (he, him).
8, 9. I wrote (he, him) and (she, her) a long and dramatic letter.
10. That hamburger and fries are (ours, our's).
11, 12. The new police officers are (he, him) and (she, her).
13. It must have been (they, them) who followed us.
14. Paul and (we, us) are going out to dinner.
15. It could have been Carson, Gary, Darin, or (he, him).
16, 17. That hat isn't (hers, her's); (hers, her's) is an Orioles hat.
18. I assumed it was (he, him) who took her to the movie.
19, 20. It should be Zac and (she, her), but it might've been Josh and (he, him).

Use the following groups of pronouns correctly in sentences. Write the sentences on the back of this page. Mark **D.O.** if the group is the object of the verb, **I.O.** if the group is the indirect object of the verb (to whom or for whom), and **O.P.** if the group is the object of a preposition. Mark **S** if the group is the subject or a nominative pronoun in the predicate. Use at least one of each (**D.O., I.O., O.P., S, S in Pred.**)

1. Jason and me
2. Mother and I
3. the teacher and her
4. the leaders and me
5. Mylo and he
6. the explorers and them
7. him and her
8. Cindy or he
9. the directors and they
10. my friend and me

Worksheet 33A: PRONOUN CASES   DATE: _____
EDITING TEST

The following passage contains pronouns in the nominative, objective, and possessive cases. Some are used correctly; some are not. Make corrections where they are necessary.

Verna held several jobs as a teenager, but there was one in particular that she will never forget. It must have been the ad that beckoned her friend and her to call. "The opportunity of a lifetime is your's," read the small print. "Individual advancement. No experience necessary."

Just the job for Sharon and I, thought Verna, as she called her friend. "It must be us they are looking for!" announced Verna.

"Well, if it's a loser, its all your's!" replied Sharon.

Sharon waited for Verna to come by; then Verna and her drove together to investigate this job of a lifetime. The building was a big conglomeration of offices; it's elevator took the girls to the tenth floor. A receptionist rather sourly greeted some other girls and they and told them they could see the personnel director in a few minutes.

It was actually a group interview with questions directed at the other young people and they. "I think the personnel director *and* the business owner are her. And I think she is going to hire her, her, him, and we," whispered Verna to Sharon.

"Just think," Sharon replied, "my co-workers will be her, her, him, and you!"

NAME: _____ 189

**Worksheet 33B: PRONOUN CASES
EDITING TEST**

DATE: _____

"Remember, kids, when you hear a voice on the phone, ask if it is Mrs. _____ .
Then she will say 'Yes, this is her.' And then you can present you're sales pitch for the
magazines."

"Sharon and me will really do well at this job. I hope it is her who gets the phone next
to mine! Please give the first section of phonebook pages to Sharon and I!"

After the first call, the thrill was gone for Verna. The realization came to Sharon and
she at about the same time; they were calling people at their homes and interrupting
there days to try to sell magaines. The rudeness of the customers settled the girls' minds;
this was no way to earn some spending money. At least, it wasn't theirs.

"Between you and I," whispered Verna on the way out the door at there noon break,
"some other workers and me aren't coming back this afternoon."

"But what about giving two weeks' notice? asked Sharon, who wasn't sure she could
go along with Verna and they on walking out.

"As far as I'm concerned, no one told me I was going to be invading people's privacy
in this job. I'm happy to have made my last call!"

Practical English: A Complete Course

Worksheet 34A: OTHER PRONOUN PROBLEMS—EXPLANATION

REFLEXIVE PRONOUNS

A reflexive pronoun is a form of a personal pronoun with **-self** or **-selves** added to it. These are the reflexive pronouns we use in English:

muself	ourselves	yourselves
herself	himself	themselves
itself		

**Notice there is no reflexive pronoun HISSELF; nor is there THEIRSELVES. These are not accepted as standard usage.

USAGE OF REFLEXIVE PRONOUNS

Reflexive pronouns have two uses:

1. Use the reflexive pronoun to show action that reflects back on someone or something.

    She hurt *herself* with the new pruning shears.

    The puppy hurt *himself* on the fence.

2. Use the reflexive pronoun to place emphasis on someone's action.

    I *myself* wrote that speech I delivered.

    I want them to do it *themselves*.

**Never use the reflexive case as a subject or an object. Use the nominative and objective cases, as we have learned.

> Send the bill to Dad and me.
> (NOT—Send the bill to Dad and myself.)
>
> Barbara and I were among the delegates to the student government convention.
> (NOT—Barbara and myself were . . .)

WHO AND WHOM

In our usage of English, WHOM seems to be casually vanishing. There is still, however, a very recognizable difference between the uses of WHO and WHOM. In writing, the correct standard usage is definitely observed. Concentrate on this.

1. WHO and WHOM are question words or interrogative pronouns. Substitute HE for WHO or WHOEVER. Substitute HIM for WHOM or WHOMEVER. Say the sentence, changing the word order to form a statement where necessary.

Practical English: A Complete Course

Worksheet 34B: OTHER PRONOUN PROBLEMS—EXPLANATION

(Who, Whom) is she going with?
(He, Him) is she going with?

She is going with (he, him).
She is going with him.
Whom is she going with?

(Who, whom) is our new class president?
(He, Him) is our new class president.
He is our new class president.
Who is our new class president?

2. WHO and WHOM as relative pronouns. Relative pronouns tie together the main sentence with other related clauses. (A clause has a subject and a verb, but a dependent clause needs to be attached to an independent clause or sentence.) The case of a relative pronoun is determined by its usage in the clause it begins.

    James is a boy *who* can tell a good joke. (WHO is the subject of CAN TELL, so the nominative pronoun HE is the right choice.

    He can tell a good joke. = Who can tell a good joke.

    I saw *who* she really was.

    (WHO is a pronoun in the predicate of its clause following a verb of being, an intransitive verb.)

    She really was *she*.
    Remember: She = she (not HER)

    She = who
    I saw *who* she really was.

    Linda is the teacher's aide *whom* I just hired.

    (WHOM is the object of the verb hired in its clause. I just hired her. (not SHE)

    Her = Whom (Because he = she and him = her)
    Linda is the teacher's aide *whom* I just hired.

    Mr. Barry, *whom* I recently talked to, is evaluating my qualifications.
    (*Whom* is the object of the preposition to in its clause.)

    I recently talked to him. (not *he*) him = whom

Worksheet 34C: OTHER PRONOUN PROBLEMS—EXPLANATION

Mr. Barry, *whom* I recently talked to, is evaluating my qualifications.

**If this WHO and WHOM section seems confusing, you might need to study the subject and object pronoun explanation again.

PRONOUNS IN COMPARISONS

In English, we usually omit words in the parts of sentences with a comparison. When a pronoun is used, this creates a problem. Consider these two sentences:

My brother punches the bag harder than (he punches) me.

My brother punches the bag harder than I (do).

See how the meaning of the whole sentence is changed by the case of the pronoun? Be sure to mentally add the omitted words, and you'll come up with the correct pronoun every time. This also holds true with AS sentences.

I am just as happy as he (is).

Practical English: A Complete Course

NAME: _____

Worksheet 35A: OTHER PRONOUN PROBLEMS—EXERCISE

DATE: _____

Underline the correct pronoun in each of the following sentences below. Be ready to explain your choice.

1. Dan Lee can't do the whole job (himself, hisself).

2. Annabelle will never forgive (herself, her self).

3. Please let me know (who, whom) votes for me.

4. Share this reward with (whoever, whomever) helped you rescue Brandy.

5. They can't believe they eliminated (theirselves, themselves) from the competition by their poor attitude.

6. Sharon swings the golf club much better than (I, me).

7. Can you scale that tree faster than (he, him)?

8. Leslie is as strong as (she, her).

9. I like anyone (who, whom) laughs at my jokes.

10, 11. Someone (who, whom) takes (himself, hisself) too seriously is Mr. Clarence.

12. That man has absolute authority over everyone (who, whom) works in his department.

13. Can you show me (who, whom) she is?

14. I love to be with a baby (who, whom) laughs.

15. Mr. Edwards nearly lost (himself, hisself) in his project last year.

16. I can't remember (who, whom) I sent the check to.

17. (Who, Whom) are you recommending for the supervisory position?

18. (Who, Whom) do you think he will appoint?

19. I'm more uncoordinated and awkward than (she, her).

20. To type as well as (they, them) is my ambition.

Practical English: A Complete Course

Worksheet 35B: OTHER PRONOUN   DATE: _____
PROBLEMS—EXERCISE

Choose from the following pronouns to correctly complete the phrases below:

I, me, myself   we, us, ourselves

she, her, herself   they, them, themselves

he, him, himself   who, whom

21. I brought m _____ a bicycle.

22. to w_____ you wrote

23. W_____ left you here alone?

24. I sang more loudly than h_____ .

25. She cried h_____ to sleep.

26. w_____ you were waiting for

27. Jack wrote the letter all by h_____ .

28. for w_____ you designed the dress

29. She kicks the ball harder than h_____ .

30. Mother bakes cakes much better than h_____ .

Practical English: A Complete Course

Worksheet 36: OTHER PRONOUN PROBLEMS—EDITING EXERCISE

Correct any errors you find in the use of reflexive pronouns WHO and WHOM and pronouns in comparison structures.

Starting a new job is a bit like going back to school the first day each year. I can remember how my brother and myself used to look forward to the posting of the class lists on the office windows the Friday before Labor Day. He could read those lists faster than me, but I would be right behind. Now I find me wondering who will be working in my new office. I wonder who my new co-workers will be; who will be the ones I'll talk to?

Discovering who the teacher was used to be important; now I feel that whomever is my supervisor will determine a lot about my job. If he's someone who basically likes hisself, he'll be easier to work for than an unsure, unconfident person. My brother always had an adjustment problem, no matter who the teacher was. I seemed to adapt better than him regardless of whomever the teacher was.

Wondering how much I had forgotten over the summer was another worry, and I seem to find myself worrying about my job skills now. I know I am a person who can get the job done, no matter what it is, but knowing whom will evaluate your success helps to lighten the concern. My brother said he worried hisself sick over his qualifications and abilities the night before his job started, but his supervisor said no one could tell whom the new employee was by his performance.

He told me to look forward to meeting whoever I will work with, to enjoy figuring out whoever my new supervisor is, and to show whoever is interested just how qualified I really am for this new position. I wish he had given me all that advice before the first day of school—any year!

Practical English: A Complete Course

Worksheet 37A: OTHER PRONOUN   DATE: _____
PROBLEMS—UNIT QUIZ

Underline the correct pronoun that reflects standard usage in each of the sentences below.

1. Allen, (who, whom) I selected, will be the new pizza delivery person.

2. She respects anyone (who, whom) can explain his position politely.

3. He covered (himself, hisself) with tattoos.

4. I can take dictation as well as (she, her).

5. The coach says you can swing the bat harder than (he, him).

6. I knew the answer as well as (she, her).

7. (Who, Whom) is to have the final say on the matter?

8. (Who, Whom) do you think should be chosen to represent our business on the council?

9. Kathy and (I, myself) will go to the store for you.

10. I injured (me, myself) when I fell through the rickety stairs.

11, 12. Tom is taller than (I, me), but I weigh more than (he, him).

13, 14. I can eat as much pizza as (she, her) but I am more sensible than (she, her).

15. For (who, whom) are you waiting?

16. I will call (whoever, whomever) is to blame into my office.

17. Mr. Mayer can't tell (who, whom) enjoys his stories more, the parents or their children.

18. The clerk can't be sure (who, whom) the security police pointed out to watch.

19. The bike worked harder at climbing the road than (I, me).

20. The last chairman of the board, (who, whom) I introduced you to, wants to be invited to the awards ceremony.

Practical English: A Complete Course

Worksheet 37B: OTHER PRONOUN PROBLEMS—UNIT QUIZ

Complete the following sentences with a standard usage pronoun.

21. I know I can dive better than _____ .

22. Mrs. Lanier bakes pies as well as _____ .

23. Adam hurt _____ while he was carving the soapstone.

24. _____ do you think will take his place over vacation?

25. Richie, _____ I remember from the sixth grade, has just returned from Saudi Arabia.

26. Ian is confident that he is a better swimmer than _____ .

27   Josh shoots those marbles more accurately than _____ .

28. I have confidence in _____ that I can complete the job.

29. The checker _____ I like best always remembers my name.

30. The shopper _____ is pleased with our service always returns.

©1987 J. Weston Walch, Publisher

Practical English: A Complete Course

Worksheet 38A:
SENTENCE ERRORS—UNIT TEST

Make any corrections needed in the passage below:

Yosemite National Park is really a wonderful family vacation spot. There is facilities for every travel style. Even folks not wanting to be inconvenienced by nature is exposed to the beauty of all that surrounds them. The hotel visitor, as well as the camper, have several dining facilities and some is very affordable.

Accommodations for every vacationer is to be found there. Both the Ahwahnee Hotel and the Yosemite Lodge offer comfortable rooms and a pleasant dining room. For those used to travelling in style and with a minimum of discomfort. An older person who don't want to sleep on the ground or be out in cold weather chilling themselves find the hotel or lodge very comfortable. If neither the hotel nor the tent style sound right, then a vacationer may try housekeeping camp. Which is a compromise between the two extremes. What's the facilities that are considered "in between?" The group of housekeeping campers prefer a kind of open hut with bench beds and a cement floor. More adventurous campers in the valley selects from a half dozen campgrounds within the park and several on the road into the park, there is even a group camp area. One reason Yosemite is so ideal. The vacationers having choices.

Just as mumps are inescapable for most people, so is nature for the Yosemite vacationer. Only not nearly as painful. The comfortable visitor may ride the shuttle buses around the park their shorts is their clothing in summer their pants and ski jackets in winter.

Practical English: A Complete Course

Worksheet 38B:
SENTENCE ERRORS—UNIT TEST

When the bus stops at a scenic area, each visitor decides for themselves whether to continue their ride or whether to get out and take a look around. About three-fourths of the riders choose to walk to see the nearby site. Because someone whom can walk one-third of a mile and back can see Lower Yosemite Falls. Just a trickle in the summer but a full waterfall in the spring. Mirror Lake and Vernal Falls is only one mile down the hiking trail from the shuttle bus stop. Buses coming every ten to fifteen minutes to let out and pick up passengers. One family I know feels the shuttle don't quite accommodate all its individual styles. The grandparents take the Yosemite bus tour to see Half Dome, El Capitan, Bridalveil Fall, and more, there's even a Glacier Point Tour. The parents ride the shuttle, sometimes the grandparents and them ride together.

The daughter Kim and the son Keith travel by foot or horseback. It's usually them that are leading the hikers or riders in their nature discovery. In fact, one summer when Keith couldn't go, Kim was hired as a guide. It was her who you might have had as a horseback guide on you're two-hour trail ride to beautiful Mirror Lake. As you can see, nature is inescapable, you can work for it or enjoy it in comfort.

Every camper can find their kind of place to eat at Yosemite, a restaurant offering prime rib and a fast-food place for pizza. Keith and Kim's family are my dining experts, because they are a family whom I've seen eat in every place or style. Grandma and Grandpa prefer their dinner at the hotel, but him and her occasionally eats a croissant sandwich at the deli. To Grandpa and she, good food and good service still very important on vacation.

Practical English: A Complete Course

Worksheet 38C:
SENTENCE ERRORS—UNIT TEST

Keith and Kim have a different perspective on dining, they consider a hamburger or a large frosty cone a gourmet lunch. Because them kids are used to cooking on there Coleman. Keith cooks Dinty Moore Beef Stew better than her, but Kim fixes Hormel's Chili as well as him. They assure me that you can eat the way you want to in Yosemite.

There is few drawbacks to Yosemite as a vacation spot, but preparation, in addition to common sense, help. Be sure to make reservations well in advance, unless you are a gambler, if you are, you might find Reno or Tahoe more the spot for you.

Chapter Twelve

CORRECTING
WORD-USAGE ERRORS

Chapter Twelve attacks problems in common word-usage errors, adjective-usage errors, and adverb-usage errors. The sequence of explanation, exercise, and quiz worksheets begun in Chapter Eleven is continued.

Worksheet 1A: COMMON WORD-USAGE ERRORS—EXPLANATION

This section is concerned with common errors made with a number of sets of words. Following each set of confusing words is an explanation and some examples. Although some of the word-usage errors are "passable" in conversation among friends, none of them are standard English. Since STANDARD ENGLISH is the usage that is appropriate at all times and in all places, it should definitely be used in writing.

ACCEPT/EXCEPT

To ACCEPT something is to agree to something or to willingly receive something. To EXCEPT is to leave out or exclude. EXCEPT is also used as a preposition meaning "but" or "excluding."

Adam Hacket will *accept* the award for the writing contest.

Everyone *except* John Williams was invited.

No one will be *excepted*; even last year's entrants are invited.

ADVICE/ADVISE

ADVICE is an opinion or a suggestion; it is a noun. To ADVISE is to give an opinion. In other words, ADVISE is what you do, and ADVICE is what you give.

Why doesn't anyone take my *advice*?

I'd like to *advise* you on some personal matters.

AFFECT/EFFECT

AFFECT is a verb meaning "to influence." EFFECT is a noun meaning "the result." EFFECT can also be used as a verb meaning "to bring about change or to cause to happen."

Tom doesn't allow his job to *affect* his grades.

What is the *effect* of that overtime on your salary?

I believe I can *effect* the changes you desire in the payroll department.

ALL READY/ALREADY

ALREADY means "before now." ALL READY means "completely ready."

Frank is *already* finished with the addition.

My brother's den is *all ready* to perform its skit.

Worksheet 1B: COMMON-WORD USAGE ERRORS—EXPLANATION

ALL RIGHT/ALRIGHT

Always write ALL RIGHT as two words. Never write the one word combination ALRIGHT.

It is *all right* with Mom if you sleep over tonight.

ALL TOGETHER, ALTOGETHER

ALL TOGETHER means that all the parts of a group are considered as one whole. ALTOGETHER means "entirely or on the whole."

The fourth graders sang the songs of the Old West *all together.*

That woman is *altogether* too nervous and high-strung to care for young children.

ALLUSION, ILLUSION, DELUSION

An ALLUSION is a reference to something; it can be found in speaking, writing, even in a film. An ILLUSION is a mistaken image or impression, something that appears to be other than it really is. A DELUSION is a belief in something that is definitely not so; usually a delusion involves self-deception.

The novel *Darkangel* by Meredith Ann Pierce contains *allusions* to Icarus of Greek mythology.

My mother had the *illusion* that she was in charge of scheduling my summer.

The birch leaves falling gave the *illusion* of a light snowfall.

The man was institutionalized because he suffers from a *delusion* of absolute power over his family.

ALUMNA, ALUMNUS

An ALUMNA is one female graduate. ALUMNAE are female graduates (plural). An ALUMNUS is a male graduate. ALUMNI are male graduates or male and female graduates considered together.

My sister is an *alumna* of Vassar College.

The *alumnae* of Miss Prudence's charm school are gathering for a social.

Who in this room is an *alumnus* or *alumna* of a state certified school for auto mechanics?

The *alumni* of North Miami High School's Class of 1966 met for their twenty-year reunion.

Worksheet 1C: COMMON-WORD USAGE ERRORS—EXPLANATION

AMONG/BETWEEN

AMONG means "together with" or "in the company of others;" use it when three or more persons or things are involved. BETWEEN refers to sharing or separation involving only two persons or things.

Susan is *among* the student workers chosen to landscape the new atrium.

Divide this ice cream equally *between* your brother and you.

AMOUNT/NUMBER

Use AMOUNT when you mean "a quantity thought of as one unit." Use NUMBER when you mean "a quantity thought of as several things."

A large *amount* of rain fell yesterday.

A *number* of assignments are missing.

Worksheet 2A: COMMON-WORD USAGE ERRORS—EXERCISE

Underline the correct word, the one that is considered standard English usage for each sentence below.

1. Philip will (accept, except) the prize for his brother.

2. Please (advice, advise) us on the best venture to start for Junior Achievement.

3. The rising cost of a permanent and a hair coloring treatment have had a serious (affect, effect) on my mother's beauty salon business.

4. The Concert Choir members were (all ready, already) to make their first appearance by the end of September.

5. "(All right, Alright)," she responded. "I'm coming as fast as I can."

6. The neighborhood boys worked (all together, altogether) to save money for the go-cart.

7. There are many (allusions, illusions, delusions) to the Bible in literature.

8. Ninety percent of the (alumna, alumnae, alumni) of the women's college are in attendance.

9. Jackie and Barr strolled (among, between) the pigeons at the park.

10. I've never seen Mr. Barsuglia so (angry at, angry with) his supervisors before.

11. How do you plan to (affect, effect) any changes in a department with all old employees and no young blood?

12. The first group seems to be (all ready, already) finished with their term projects.

13. The steam from the teakettle gave the (allusion, illusion, delusion) that we were at the foggy coast.

14. How much (advice, advise) do you think I need on a job I've already done before?

15. My mother shouted, "This is (all together, altogether) too late to be coming home on a school night!"

16. The two brothers divided the inheritance from their parents equally (among, between) them.

17. I have noticed a large (amount, number) of errors in your typing this week.

18. How can you think of (accepting, excepting) Ben from the party and inviting all his best friends?

19. He forced his (allusion, illusion, delusion) of authority upon his co-workers until he was judged incompetent to hold his position.

20. Is that boy an (alumna, alumnae, alumnus) of a community college or a technical school?

Fill in each blank with one of the confusing words from the sentences above.

1. No one e_____ her high-school friends really knew the kind of person she was.

2. We are a_____ too late to enter the concert now.

3. This touched-up photograph gives my complexion the i_____ of being lovely.

4. When I dyed my hair last month, the last e_____ I expected was green!

5. In this company is there not one a_____ of Marina Technical Institute?

6. There was a huge n_____ of soccer players on the field.

7. I cannot a_____ the reward money for doing something I had to do.

8. Mrs. Sorensen wants us to e_____ that change in the operating procedure immediately.

9. What e_____ can the new foreman possibly have on your raise?

10. My father is a_____ too tense and too much a perfectionist to ever coach a young team.

         Practical English: A Complete Course

Worksheet 3A: COMMON WORD-USAGE ERRORS—EXPLANATION

BESIDE, BESIDES

BESIDE means "next to." BESIDES can be a preposition meaning "in addition to" or an adverb meaning "moreover or furthermore."

Come sit in the car *beside* me.

There are so many others *besides* you that I don't have to worry.

I'm going to have to cancel that interview. *Besides*, the job didn't sound very interesting.

BROKE, BROKEN

BROKE is the past tense of "break;" it is not used as an adjective. BROKEN is part of the verb "to break" that is used as an adjective.

That welder in the maintenance shop is *broken*.

(NOT—That welder in the maintenance shop is broke.)

BURST, BUST

BURST means "to break open." BUST used as a verb has only slang meanings (to catch someone doing wrong, to break out of prison, etc.) and should not be used as standard English.

That little boy *burst* my birthday balloon.

(NOT—That little boy *busted* my birthday balloon.)

CAN, MAY

You remember learning this. Just practice it! CAN means "to be able." MAY means "to have permission."

Can I hold my breath for one minute underwater?

Elsa *may* come home with you girls tonight.

CAN HARDLY, CAN'T HARDLY

I CAN HARDLY means I "can barely." Since "hardly" and "barely" are considered negative words in English (like "no," "not," "none," etc.) do not use CAN'T HARDLY. Standard English never uses a double negative.

I *can hardly* see you in the shadows.

(NOT—I *can't hardly* see you in the shadows.)

*The same usage problem occurs with "could hardly" and "couldn't hardly." Never use "couldn't hardly."

Practical English: A Complete Course

Worksheet 3B: COMMON WORD-
USAGE ERRORS—EXPLANATION

COULD HAVE, (COULD OF), COULD'VE

COULD'VE is the contraction for COULD HAVE. When you say it, it sounds like COULD OF. Never write COULD OF.

Use either COULD HAVE or COULD'VE.

*This also holds true for SHOULD'VE, WOULD'VE, etc.

Cheryl *could have* won that typing contest.

Cheryl *could've* won that typing contest.

(NOT—Cheryl *could of* won that typing contest.)

(DROWNDED), DROWNED

DROWN means "to suffocate in liquid, especially in water." The past tense of DROWN is DROWN*ED*, not DROWN*DED*."

When their puppy *drowned,* the whole family was very upset.

(NOT—When their puppy *drownded,* . . .)

HANGED, HUNG

Criminals used to be HANGED. Paintings and photographs are *HUNG*.

The state has not *hanged* anyone in years.

Mr. Wigginton *hung* the class picture on the front wall of the classroom.

IMPLY, INFER

To IMPLY is "to suggest." To INFER is "to conclude from evidence given." Person A IMPLIES something to Person B. Person B then INFERS something from the information Person A gives him.

The salesman IMPLIED that we had better decide tonight or else the car would be gone tomorrow.

My father INFERRED from his comments that someone else was seriously considering buying the car.

Worksheet 3C: COMMON WORD-USAGE ERRORS—EXPLANATION

LEAVE, LET

To LEAVE is "to go away" or "to not take away." To LET is to "allow."

My children and I will *leave* for Miami on Saturday.

Do not *leave* your gym uniform here another weekend.

Let that child be by himself for awhile.

(NOT—*Leave* that child be by himself for awhile.)

FEWER/LESS

FEWER means "not so many separate items." LESS means "a smaller amount of a substance."

This class has *fewer* students sent to the office than the other classes.

(NOT—This class has *less* students sent to the office than the other classes.)

The artist used *less* paint on his canvas than his student did.

There are *fewer* apples on our trees this year.

Mother always uses *less* sugar than the recipe calls for.

Chapter Twelve

Worksheet 4A: COMMON WORD-USAGE ERRORS—EXERCISE

Underline the correct word, the one that is considered standard English usage, for each sentence below.

1. The kitten is sleeping (beside, besides) the basket of pears.

2. The baked potato (burst, busted) when we cooked it in the microwave oven.

3. The generator in the hydroelectric plant is (broke, broken).

4. Baby Brendan (can hardly, can't hardly) climb up on the couch.

5. (Can, May) I invite a guest to your party?

6. He (could of, could've) finished the marathon if he had paced himself better.

7. I wish I had (hanged, hung) those pictures by myself.

8. The farmer said his new calf (drownded, drowned) in the flash flood.

9. How dare you (imply, infer) that I cheated?

10. That (broke, broken) old lawn mower is all I have to work with.

11. Sharon must (leave, let) home early to take her sisters to day care.

12. You certainly (can, may) walk well on those stilts after practicing.

13. The teacher (implied, inferred) from the boy's short story that he had a drug problem.

14. Close the gate before you (leave, let) the colt out of the corral.

15. Three men were (hanged, hung) from this tree on April 13, 1880.

     Practical English: A Complete Course

NAME: _____

Worksheet 4B: COMMON WORD-USAGE ERRORS—EXERCISE

DATE: _____

Fill in each blank with one of the confusing words or groups of words from the sentences on the previous page.

1. B_____ me, there are nineteen girls coming to the slumber party.

2. That Vista Cruiser is b_____ again; this time it's a head gasket.

3. Don't b_____ my paper bag; it has my model rocket in it.

4. You m_____ audition at a convenient time, even if it is not on the regular schedule.

5. The boys c_____ h_____ wait until their Uncle Bill arrives from Florida.

6. She c_____ swum across Lake Tahoe if she had coated her body with Vaseline for warmth.

7. I could tell right away that my dad h_____ the new light, because it wasn't centered.

8. How could you i_____ such a negative meaning from what your father said?

9. L_____ me in the movies with my cousins.

10. No Boy Scouts d_____ this summer at any of their local summer camps.

11. Come place the baby b_____ me on the couch.

12. You c_____ stay awake until dawn, but do you really want to?

13. Wyoming h_____ all of its convicted criminals in the old Western days.

14. The newspaper article i_____ that Northgate caused the riot at the Ygnacio game.

15. Only those who were at the game could i_____ that the newspaper was definitely biased in its coverage of the riot at the ball game.

16. There were f_____ kindergarten students last year than this year.

17. Our family used l_____ gas and electricity this winter because of our wood-burning stove.

Practical English: A Complete Course

Worksheet 5A: COMMON WORD-USAGE ERRORS—EXERCISE

ITS, IT'S

ITS is a possessive pronoun, one word, that shows ownership of something. IT'S is a contraction for "it is" usually; sometimes it is a contraction for "it has."

My car has lost *its* power.

It's a well known fact that the police in this town do not accept bribes. (It's = It is)

Even though *it's* been years since they met, they are still close friends. (It's = It has)

LAY, LIE

LAY means "to put something down." LIE has two meanings. No one gets confused with LIE when it means "to tell an untruth" or "an untruth." The other meaning of LIE is "to rest or recline." This is the confusing one. It is also confusing because the past tense of lie (down) is LAY.

Please *lay* that package on the table.
(lay = put)

Children must never *lie* to their parents.
(lie = tell untruth)

I feel that I need to *lie* down and rest this afternoon.
(lie = rest)

Yesterday I *lay* in the shade under the pear tree for an hour.
(lay = past tense of lie)

LIKE, AS, AS IF

Most people use LIKE when they are making comparisons. LIKE should be used when only a noun or pronoun follows in the comparison. AS or AS IF should be used when a verb follows the noun in the comparison.

Read these several times:

I danced *like* my sister.

I dance *as* my sister does.

(NOT—I dance *like* my sister does.)

John sounded *as if* he had been really frightened.

(NOT—John sounded *like* he had been really frightened.)

She reads *like* her brother.

She reads *as* her brother does.

She reads *as if* her teacher is listening.

*Can you find the verb in the comparison part of the *as* and *as if* sentences above?

Practical English: A Complete Course

Worksheet 5B: COMMON WORD-USAGE ERRORS—EXPLANATION

SET, SIT

To SET is to put or place something. To SIT is to be seated.

Why can't you *set* those glasses on the table carefully?

Jeff needs to *sit* down so the people behind him can see.

THEIR, THERE, THEY'RE

As homonyms, these three words sound alike, but you learned long ago they have different meanings and different usage. THEIR is a possessive pronoun meaning "belonging to them." THERE is an adverb that tells a place. THEY'RE is the contraction formed by "they" plus "are."

The Hendersons invited me to *their* restaurant.

Jane went with me over *there* last night.

They're such a nice family.

THIS, THIS HERE, THAT, THAT THERE, THESE, THESE HERE, THOSE, THEM THERE

Use only THIS when you are indicating something. Also use only THAT and THESE and THOSE. "Them" does not take the place of "those," because it is not used in the same pronoun case. "Here and "there" should never be used following these pronouns.

This is the best book I've read this year.

(NOT—This here book is the best book I've read this year.)

I asked you to hand me *that* tool.

Have you seen *these* bracelets on my sister before?

No, but she wore *those* earrings last night.

TO, TOO, TWO

Confusion with these homonyns occurs often in writing. TO is a preposition indicating direction. TOO is an adverb meaning "also" or "more than enough." TWO is the sum of one plus one. If you concentrate on the differences, you should not use them incorrectly again.

Take this package *to* the post office.

You can mail my letters *too*.

I have *too* much to do today.

Why should *two* people make the same trip?

Worksheet 5C: COMMON WORD-USAGE ERRORS—EXPLANATION

WEATHER, WHETHER

WEATHER is the climate conditions. WHETHER means "if."

> The *weather* conditions have been very strange this summer.

> I don't know *whether* Gymboree is Thursday or Friday.

WHO'S, WHOSE

WHO'S, is the contraction of "who" plus "is." WHOSE means "belonging to whom."

> Charlie isn't sure *who's* taking her to the dance.

> Andy doesn't know *whose* pen he picked up at work.

YOU'RE, YOUR

YOU'RE is the contraction of "you" plus "are." YOUR is the possessive pronoun meaning "belonging to you."

> I know *you're* going to be angry with me for not having any ice cream in the freezer.

> *Your* birthday is exactly three months after mine.

Practical English: A Complete Course

Worksheet 6A: COMMON WORD-USAGE ERRORS—EDITING EXERCISE

The following letter contains several common word-usage errors. Some of the words we studied are used correctly. Correct the errors above the words.

June 1, 1987

Dear Brian,

I can't hardly wait to see you, and it's going to be alright to stay with your family all summer. I hope your looking forward to it as much as I am. I'll let you know whether I'm arriving on Saturday or Sunday as soon as I can.

Who's room are we going to sleep in? I don't care as long as I can lay down and sleep somewhere. Can I borrow your brother's bike, or does he let anyone use it? I feel like I could of asked you all this stuff on the phone, but my mother was already angry at me for the to long conversation.

Do you really think we should take your dad's advice and not go job hunting together? I don't mean to imply that he's not wise, but we've always shared things among just ourselves and I don't think looking for a job together will effect our chances that much. Alright, the worst that could happen is that we won't find a job for either of us; but we won't be drowned in our sorrow. We'll convince one of them there business owners

to hire us, even if it's just to fix equipment that's broke. Besides, I'm suffering from no

delusions about summer work. It is all together possible we'll do something we never

ever dreamed of; my cousin hanged wallpaper one summer. And now he's an alumni of

Georgia Tech.

Sit this letter somewhere you will remember, so you'll answer it.

Your buddy,

Joe

Worksheet 7A: COMMON WORD-USAGE ERRORS
UNIT QUIZ

Underline the correct choice of the standard English usage in each of the following sentences below.

1. My friend Ed is studying the (affect, effect) of aspirin on the nervous system.

2. (Can, May) we buy our lunch at Lawrence Hall of Science?

3. Shirley doesn't want to (advice, advise) me concerning the separation.

4. I remember the (allusion, illusion, delusion) that the revolving light on the metal Christmas tree produced.

5. One of the graduation speeches really (affected, effected) me.

6. There is no one (accept, except) Andrew who would return the empty ice cream carton to the freezer.

7. The mythological (allusions, illusions) in poetry are numerous.

8. My aunt is an (alumna, alumnus) of Bryn Mawr.

9. The mirrors were (hanged, hung) on the walls of the living room.

10. The counselor (implied, inferred) that I was not community college material.

11. What could you (imply, infer) from the teacher's notes on your child's behavior?

12. How many outlaws were (hanged, hung) without a trial?

13. His shirt looks (like, as) an old cleaning cloth.

14. Will you (leave, let) me go to Day on the Green?

15. (Let, Leave) go of my kitten now.

16. I shouted (like, as if) my life depended on it.

17. I packed the camping equipment (all together, altogether) in the garage.

18. Is it (all right, alright) if I ride to school with Ray tomorrow?

19. The patient had (delusions, illusions) that he would die of germs if someone touched him.

Worksheet 7B: COMMON WORD-USAGE ERRORS
UNIT QUIZ

20. The ring bearer should stand (beside, besides) the flower girl.

21. There are (fewer, less) applicants for this position this time.

22. Daniel is an (alumnus, alumni) of two state technical schools.

23. Everyone gave the new boys (advice, advise) on the first day of school.

24. "(Whose, Who's) your new friend?" my father asked.

25. (Among, Between) the two of us, we ought to be able to get the job done.

26. I found the engine for the go-cart (between, among) the many items for sale in the classified section.

27. (Beside, Besides) my brother, there is not one worthwhile mechanic in the class.

28. She (can hardly, can't hardly) get out of bed by 7:30 every morning to get to her 8:00 class.

29. Briana (could have, could of) come to the luncheon if she had wanted to.

30. My mother (drownded, drowned) her sorrows in a cup of coffee.

31. What do you have to say about (this, this here) broken lamp?

32. The birthday boy cried when his balloon (busted, burst).

33. I could (lay, lie) in the sun for hours if you'd leave me alone.

34. Mrs. Erickson didn't know (weather, whether) to believe him or not.

35. How can you (set, sit) here all night and watch television?

36. (Their, They're) the ones I saw entering the building last night.

37, 38. Go (to, too) the doctor's office before it's (to, two, too) late.

39. I know *Annie* was (your, you're) favorite musical play.

40. I don't believe I have a (broke, broken) steering wheel.

**Worksheet 8A: COMMON WORD-USAGE ERRORS
EDITING TEST**

The following passage contains many common word-usage errors. Some of the words in this unit are used correctly. Correct the errors above the word.

Barbara couldn't hardly wait to attend her ten-year high-school reunion. At first, it was hard for her to accept the fact that she was now an alumnus of ten years. She still looked as if she could of graduated just last year. In fact, when people saw her and her children altogether, they often asked her whose children she was babysitting.

She wondered weather the alumni attending would include most of her best friends. Beside Judy, she hadn't been in touch with most of her high-school friends. In fact, those letters between Judy and her had had to many months in between this year. She determined not to just let those letters set on her desk anymore. Friends sometimes became angry with each other over a misunderstanding not cleared up or an unanswered question. She also wondered about that special guy she didn't marry. Would her heart be broke when she saw him with someone else?

How would it effect her life to be with all her best friends again? Would being all together present the allusion of being carefree? This here daydreaming would accomplish nothing, Barbara thought to herself. I'm acting like a teenager, whether I am one or not.

Worksheet 8B: COMMON WORD-USAGE ERRORS
EDITING TEST

The Friday night of Reunion Weekend soon arrived, although Barbara thought she would of busted open if it had taken any longer. "Alright, everyone, welcome to the Class Class of '77's ten-year reunion!" greeted there class president, Jim Guenther. "Who's going to have a good time?" "We are!" yelled almost everyone.

"Alright!" responded Jim, "Your in for music like you used to know it. I'd advise you to take advantage of the good weather and swim. I don't want any of my friends drownded at this reunion, so use your good sense and your bound to have a great time! I don't mean to infer that you'd use anything but good sense, of course. Let's just leave each other have a good time, and I won't need to lay down any rules."

"Whew!" said Barbara, who's conversation between her friends Judy, Karen, and Linda, had been minus illusions and full of friendship renewed. "To think of all those pictures of Jim I hung on my bedroom wall eleven years ago. I can honestly say now that I made the right decision ten years ago. I could not of been sure unless I'd seen him again!"

NAME: _____

Worksheet 9A: ADJECTIVE USAGE EXPLANATION

DATE: _____

ADJECTIVE USAGE

An adjective modifies a noun or a pronoun.

COMPARISONS

There are three forms of adjectives: Positive, Comparative, and Superlative. See the list below:

Positive	*Comparative*	*Superlative*
large	larger	largest
nice	nicer	nicest
short	shorter	shortest

Comparative Form

Use the comparative form to compare only two things. Form the comparative by adding "-er" or by placing "more" before the word. Usually one-syllable adjectives and many two-syllable adjectives form the comparison by adding "-er." Some two-syllable words, however, use more.

| angry | angrier | (angriest) |
| precious | more precious | (most precious) |

Words that end in "-full," "-ous," and "-ish" form the comparative and the superlative with "more" and "most."

Superlative Form

Use the superlative form to compare three or more things. Form the superlative by adding "-est" or by placing "most" before the word. For deciding whether to use "-est" or "most," see the comparative explanation.

*Avoid double comparisons. Do not use "-er" and "more" at the same time. Do not use "-est" and "most" at the same time.

Practical English: A Complete Course

Worksheet 9B: ADJECTIVE USAGE EXPLANATION

Irregular Comparisons

In English, there are several adjectives which change completely in the comparative and superlative forms.

Positive	*Comparative*	*Superlative*
good	better	best
bad	worse	worst
much	more	most
far	farther	farthest

ADJECTIVE USAGE PROBLEMS

DOUBLE NEGATIVE

1. In English one negative word makes the sentence meaning negative. If you use more than one, you are using a double negative. Avoid using a double negative at all times. The negative words we use most often are "no," "not," "none," "nothing," and "never." Some other negative words to remember are "barely," "hardly," and "scarcely."

   Incorrect: Sharon *can't* do *no* more typing today.

   Correct: Sharon *can't* do any more typing today.

   Incorrect: I *don't hardly* have any money left.

   Correct: I *don't* have much money left.

"FEWER" AND "LESS"

2. Use FEWER for two or more things that can be counted. A plural noun should always follow FEWER. Use LESS for something that is measured, but not for things that can be counted. A singular noun should always follow LESS.

   Incorrect: There are *less* middle management people in this company.

   Correct: There are *fewer* middle management people in this company.

   Correct: There is *less* friction in our office since Mary left.

   *LESS if often used when FEWER should be used, but FEWER is rarely used when LESS should be.

Practical English: A Complete Course

Worksheet 9C: ADJECTIVE USAGE EXPLANATION

THIS, THAT, THESE, THEM AND THOSE

THIS and THAT describe singular nouns when they are used as adjectives. THIS and THAT may also be pronouns. Use THIS or THAT before "kind," "short," and "type." THESE and THOSE describe plural nouns. THESE and THOSE may also be used as pronouns. THEM is *never* an adjective and *never* describes a noun. THEM is always an object pronoun.

This kind of chocolates is my favorite. (Not—These kind. . .)

That type of machinery is being shipped to you.

This type of glasses is a prize at Burger King. (Not—These type . . .)

I have typed all of *those* letters. (adjective)

Give me *those* to mail. (pronoun)

Suzanne sent *them* to me. (pronoun)

Note: Since THIS refers to an object right *here* and THAT refers to an object over *there* , it is incorrect to say "this here" and "that there."

Incorrect: This here book is hers.
Correct: *This* book is hers.

Incorrect: That there child hit me.
Correct: *That* child hit me.

NAME: _____ 224

Worksheet 10A: ADJECTIVE USAGE EXERCISE

DATE: _____

Write the comparative and superlative forms of the adjectives given below:

		Comparative	*Superlative*
1.	simple	_____	_____
2.	lonely	_____	_____
3.	short	_____	_____
4.	angry	_____	_____
5.	calm	_____	_____
6.	beautiful	_____	_____
7.	magnificent	_____	_____
8.	awful	_____	_____
9.	generous	_____	_____
10.	childish	_____	_____

Indicate a correctly written sentence with a **C** and an incorrectly written sentence with an **I**. Circle the error(s) in the incorrect ones. Write above the sentence any needed word(s).

_____ 11. Katie can't hardly type with that sprained wrist.

_____ 12. Don't you have no time left?

_____ 13. This here lunch break is too short.

_____ 14. I asked for that there piece of spice cake.

_____ 15. I will hardly finish before the supervisor checks my progress.

_____ 16. Is working at the bank more harder than working for the store?

_____ 17. Do you like Coke or Pepsi better?

_____ 18. These kind of assignments really drive me crazy.

_____ 19. Of the two dinner specials, I like the salmon with potatoes and peas better.

Worksheet 10B: ADJECTIVE USAGE DATE: ＿＿＿＿＿＿＿＿＿＿＿＿＿
EXPLANATION

_____ 20. That is the most calmest baby I have ever seen.

Underline the correct word in each sentence.

_____ 21. Have you seen (those, them) children?

_____ 22. I wish you'd send (those, them) boys to the office.

_____ 23. Kyle didn't say (anything, nothing) about his surgery.

_____ 24. I (will, won't) hardly make it to work on time.

_____ 25. Of my two cousins, Lynne is the (better, best) swimmer.

_____ 26. (That, That There) book is the one I've been looking for.

_____ 27. (This kind, These kind) of directions is impossible to comprehend.

_____ 28. Give me (that, that there, them, those) paychecks.

_____ 29. She swears she told (anyone, no one) the answers.

_____ 30. I didn't see (anyone, no one) come home after 10:00 p.m.

_____ 31. Jackie is the (more athletic, most athletic) of the two sisters.

　　　　　　　　　　　　　　　　Practical English: A Complete Course

Worksheet 11A: ADVERB USAGE EXPLANATION

ADVERB USAGE

An adverb is a word that modifies a verb, an adjective, or another adverb. When an adverb modifies a VERB, it answers the question HOW, WHEN, WHERE or TO WHAT EXTENT.

How	When	Where	To What Extent
noisily	now	there	always
busily	then	away	nearly

How?	Karen played *noisily*.
When?	Michael can drive *then*.
Where?	The boy threw the Frisbee *there*.
To What Extent?	Adam has *nearly* finished his homework.

When an adverb modifies an ADJECTIVE, it usually appears right before the adjective. When an adverb modifies another ADVERB, it usually appears right before it.

almost	nearly	so
just	not	somewhat
more	quite	too
most	rather	very

She is *almost* ready.

He ran *very* quickly.

ADJECTIVE OR ADVERB USAGE

When you cannot tell whether to use an adjective or an adverb, try to figure it out this way:

1. Does the word modify a noun or a pronoun? Does it tell which one, what kind, or how many? If so, then use an adjective.

2. Does the word modify a verb, an adjective, or an adverb? Does it tell how, when, where, or to what extent? If so, then use an adverb.

Practical English: A Complete Course

Worksheet 11B: ADVERB USAGE EXPLANATION

ADVERB COMPARISONS

The comparison of adverbs is accomplished very much like the comparison of adjectives. Some adverbs add "-er" and "-est" to form the comparative and the superlative.

soon   sooner   soonest

Most adverbs that end in "-ly" use "more" and "most" in front of them.

rapidly   more rapidly   most rapidly

ADVERB USAGE PROBLEMS

ADVERBS AND PREDICATE ADJECTIVES

When a description word follows a linking verb (a verb of being and not one of action), then an adjective is used. Remember: AM, IS, ARE, WAS, WERE, BE, BEING, BEEN, SEEM are linking verbs. Caution: FEEL, LOOK, SMELL, and SOUND may be linking verbs or action verbs, depending upon how they are used.

She *seems* gentle. (linking verb *seems*)

She __ __ __ gentle (use adjective to describe *she*)

Jamie looks angry. (linking verb *looks*)

Jamie __ __ __ angry (Use adjective to describe Jamie.)

Jamie looked angrily at me. (action verb *looked*.)

How did he look? angrily (Use adverb to describe how he looked.)

Practical English: A Complete Course

Worksheet 11C: ADVERB USAGE EXPLANATION

When a descriptive word follows an action verb and modifies the verb or an adjective or another adverb, then an adverb is needed.

He dove briskly into the water.

How did he dive? (Use adverb to describe how he dove.)

The coach felt my wrist carefully.

How did he feel it? (Use adverb to describe action verb "felt.")

That police dog smells horribly when he has a cold.

How does he smell with his nose? (Use adverb to describe action verb "smells.")

GOOD AND WELL

This may be the number one usage error in the English language, but it is a simple one to correct. If you want to say how someone does an action, you need to use WELL. GOOD is an adjective; it should describe a noun or a pronoun, not tell how someone does something.

Incorrect: My mom cooks so *good*.

Correct: My mom cooks so *well*.

Correct: My mom is a *good* cook.

*WELL can be used as an adjective also. WELL means "healthy."

My brother isn't feeling *well*.

BAD AND BADLY

This is probably the number two usage error in the English language. Like GOOD, BAD is an adjective and describes a noun or a pronoun. It tells which one or what kind. Like WELL, BADLY is an adverb that describes how someone does an action.

Incorrect: The team played *bad*.

Correct: The team played *badly*.

Correct: The team played a *bad* game.

Practical English: A Complete Course

Worksheet 11D: ADVERB USAGE EXPLANATION

REAL AND REALLY

You guessed it. This is possibly the number three usage error in English. REAL, like GOOD and BAD, is an adjective. REAL means "genuine or authentic." REALLY, like WELL and BADLY, is an adverb. REAL means "very" and is used to describe an adjective or another adverb (really pretty, really casually).

Incorrect: Mrs. Mallonee is *real* nice.

Correct: Mrs. Mallonee is *really* nice.

Correct: Mrs. Mallonee is a *really* nice teacher.

Worksheet 12A: ADVERB USAGE EXERCISE

Write the comparative and superlative forms of the adverbs given below:

	Comparative	*Superlative*
1. soon	_____	_____
2. late	_____	_____
3. early	_____	_____
4. quickly	_____	_____
5. slowly	_____	_____

Indicate a correctly written sentence with a **C** and an incorrectly written sentence with an **I**. Circle the error(s) in the incorrect ones. Write above the error(s) the correct form(s).

_____ 6. Janine looks angry with her mother.

_____ 7. Sharon stared jealously at her boyfriend and the strange girl.

_____ 8. Those rotten apples smell horrible.

_____ 9. My police dog smells so horrible he can't search for missing people anymore.

_____ 10. My dad barbecues so good I entered his name in a chef's contest.

_____ 11. I am not feeling very well at the moment.

_____ 12. She answered the phone so well I thought she was an older person.

_____ 13. My brother punts bad.

_____ 14. Gary passes so badly that the captain changed his position.

_____ 15. Mickey is a real friend.

Worksheet 12B: ADVERB USAGE EXERCISE

——— 16. I asked Shana to come over because she is real nice to me at school.

——— 17. This is a really friendly kitten.

——— 18. She came in last because she ran so slow.

——— 19. We finished that job easy in ten minutes.

——— 20. The garlic smelled so strongly I had to cover my nose.

Indicate whether the adjective or the adverb is the correct choice in the following sentences. Underline the correct one; then write **ADJ**. or **ADV**. in the blank. Be ready to explain your choice.

——— 21. Joyce looks (beautiful, beautifully) with her new glasses.

——— 22. Your eye is swelling (bad, badly).

——— 23. I helped her as (good, well) as I could.

——— 24. My grandmother is (real, really) special to me.

——— 25. Of the two men, John swam (more quickly, most quickly).

Worksheet 13: ADJECTIVE AND ADVERB USAGE EDITING EXERCISE

Make any necessary corrections in the letter that appears below.

August 31, 1987

Dear Paul,

School is starting real soon, and I just have to tell you about my river rafting trip this summer. Usually these kind of active vacations sound a little too rough for me, but this here one was perfect.

You hit the waves and go down real fast, like a roller coaster, and you can't hardly believe you will live to tell about it! I'd better back up. I want to write it so bad; I'm going too quick.

My dad, brother, two uncles, and I rafted down the San Juan River in southeastern Utah this summer. It was much more scarier than our usual packing through the mountains vacation, but it wasn't barely any less exhausting or challenging.

I forgot to mention that one of my uncles is a river guide for these sort of rafting trips. He'd tell us what to do in rough water, like to paddle left side only or right side only, really good directions when you can't think clear and are overwhelmed. Most of the time we were real wet. In fact, there were less dry times than wet times, but the sun dried our clothes out good. When things weren't too rough, we'd jump out quick and go bobbing. There were less complaints and less boredom on this trip than ever before.

After we all began to feel less awkward about handling our rafts, we relaxed and really enjoyed ourselves.

Hope to see you soon.

Your buddy,

Frank

Practical English: A Complete Course

Worksheet 14A: ADJECTIVE AND ADVERB USAGE EDITING TEST

Make any necessary corrections in the letter that appears below.

September 15, 1987

Dear Frank,

I was real excited to hear from you after so long and to read about how good you handled your raft on the San Juan River. I was even more excited because I wanted to go rafting so bad this summer, but my dad had another vacation in mind that wasn't hardly rafting but was great!

He had planned a business trip to Australia, and he was really happy when he found out he could take me along. I don't have to tell you I looked eager when he asked me. In fact, I remember I wasn't feeling good that day, but his invitation sounded perfectly to my sluggish body. I perked up real quick and began to ask questions right away. I can't hardly remember whether my dad mentioned exploring the Great Barrier Reef, or whether I did. I do remember that he said if all went good for him on this trip, we'd try to dive at the reef.

Wow! Of the two of us, I can't say who was the most excited, Dad or I. We talked easy about the trip, unlike most of our talks lately. This here adventure could do more for me than expand my horizons; I began to think positive about being with my dad.

Worksheet 14A: ADJECTIVE AND ADVERB USAGE EDITING TEST

There were less problems than Dan expected in Sydney, so we left more earlier for the reef than we had planned. I can't barely describe how beautiful the 1,250-mile-long reef is. Of course, I took this trip very serious and learned how the little corals are tiny animals, some of which produce a limy substance that forms a skeleton strangely outside their bodies. When the corals die, the skeletons remain and other corals attach naturally to them. It is the most interesting and usefulest use of a skeleton you've ever imagined!

We dove and swam and photographed together, Dad and I, and we understand and respect each other more better than we did before the trip.

Your pal,

Paul

Worksheet 15A: COMMON WORD-USAGE ERRORS
CUMULATIVE TEST

The following passage contains errors in adjective usage, adverb usage, and confusing word usage. Correct all errors so that the passage is written in standard English.

DAVID FINLEY EXCEPTS WEBELOS LEADERSHIP

MARTINEZ—David Finley, alumni of University of California, Berkeley, has accepted the position of Webelos leader for Den 1 of Martinez. The den includes five Webelos scouts, who will meet altogether with Finley once a week. The scoutmaster of Pack 12 adviced the council to approach Finley with the request, as he is all ready serving the pack very good as assistant scoutmaster. "When I was deciding between the four or five available men who are qualified, I could of asked David right away. But since his son is in a younger den, I didn't know weather he would except. Most people wouldn't hardly consider a request to lead a den without there own son in it. Besides, David works like a full-time cubmaster does now. I don't want to infer that it might be to much for him, but whose to say? I had to leave him make his own decision. I wanted to influence him real bad, but I'm happy to say my wants didn't effect him in his decision."

Although David's den is more smaller than others in the pack, less boys doesn't mean the den will have less activities. In fact, Finley's illusions to past scouting activities that he is planning real soon for this here den led me to an investigation. The scouting office has scrapbooks and records of each local pack and it's achievements, and I found

Worksheet 15B: COMMON WORD-
USAGE ERRORS
CUMULATIVE TEST

David Finley listed as an Eagle Scout. His former scoutmaster had written, "David works real hard and does every job real good. I've never known a colorfuler scout; he's involved in many activities but he hasn't drownded himself with to much." Then I noticed that the offfice had hung pictures and articles of the local Eagle Scouts, and I searched real good until I found David.

I guess you folks in Martinez can set back and relax, knowing that David Finley can do the job with those Webelos. If you find yourself getting a little angry at yourself for not volunteering, contact Finley to find out how you can help.

Chapter Thirteen

CORRECTING PUNCTUATION ERRORS

Chapter Thirteen covers the most comon rules of punctuation. The sequence of explanation, exercise, and quiz worksheets continues.

Worksheet 1A: CAPITALIZATION EXPLANATION

FIRST WORDS OF SENTENCES

Capitalize the first word of any sentence.

*T*he first day of school is always a social event.

*B*asketball season can't end too soon for me.

PROPER NOUNS

As you may already know, there are two kinds of words that name persons, places, and things: proper nouns and common nouns. PROPER NOUNS, which are the names of specific persons, places, or things, are capitalized, and COMMON NOUNS are not. This rule seems easy, but the hard part is telling common from proper nouns. Here are some examples. Study them.

COMMON NOUNS	PROPER NOUNS
student	Lori Jameson
police officer	Officer Claire
high school	Northgate High School
mountain	Mount Diablo
city	Portland
park	Yellowstone National Park
motorcycle	Honda
a winding road	Highway 127
a news magazine	*Newsweek*
history class	Modern History 2

Notice that in these lists, the proper nouns refer to a single, specific person, place, or thing. There are only one *Lori Jameson*, one *Officer Claire*, one *Northgate High School*, one brand of *Honda* motorcycle, one course called *Modern History 2*, and so on. The common nouns, however, may refer to any of a class of persons, places, or things. Anyone who goes to school or who enforces the law may be called a *student* or a *police officer*. There are many places called *high schools* and many vehicles called *motorcycles*. The question to ask yourself when deciding whether a noun is common or proper is this: Could this word be used to refer to many things or just one? If it refers to just one, the noun is proper; otherwise it is common.

Practical English: A Complete Course

Worksheet 1B: CAPITALIZATION EXPLANATION

ADJECTIVES

Capitalize adjectives (words that describe nouns and usually come before them) if they are formed proper nouns. Never capitalize them otherwise.

> He climbed on his *H*onda motorcycle and headed down a *l*ong, *h*illy road to Highway 80.

> Maggie was a *N*orthgate student who worked mornings as a *Gazette* newspaper carrier.

TITLES

Capitalize the titles of books, magazines, movies, songs, and albums, but don't capitalize the short words in these titles (such as *the, a, an, of, by, in, with, and, but, or*) unless they are the first word of a title.

> *Gone with the Wind* is my favorite book, but the little-known movie *In the Heat of the Night* is my favorite film.

SCHOOL SUBJECTS

School subjects are not capitalized unless they are languages or are specific courses followed by a number.

> This semester I am taking *E*nglish, *T*yping 2, *S*panish, *m*ath, *b*iology, and *g*ym.

SEASONS AND POINTS OF THE COMPASS

The names of the seasons (spring, summer, winter, fall) are never capitalized, and the points of the compass are capitalized only if they refer to geographical areas rather than directions.

> I am going to the *E*ast (a place, part of the United States) this *s*pring.

> It is strange that most of the real American *W*est (a place) now lies *e*ast (a direction) of California.

Practical English: A Complete Course

Worksheet 2A: CAPITALIZATION EXERCISE

Copy over the phrases below, adding capitals as needed. Refer to the rules on Worksheet 51 for help with each section.

PROPER NOUNS AND COMMON NOUNS

1. next to st. mark's church

2. a baptist church

3. a big street downtown

4. the corner of elm street

5. taft high school and its rivals

6. the u s. senate and the house of representatives

7. at the lincoln memorial

1. _____

2. _____

3. _____

4. _____

5. _____

6. _____

7. _____

ADJECTIVES

8. a panasonic stereo

9. a toyota pickup

10. her new french sunglasses

11. the new subway line

8. _____

9. _____

10. _____

11. _____

SCHOOL SUBJECTS

12. my chemistry class

13. my print shop 3 teacher

14. his english and math books

15. the history assignment

12. _____

13. _____

14. _____

15. _____

NAME: _____ 241

Worksheet 2B: CAPITALIZATION EXERCISE

DATE: _____

TITLES

16. the movie *return of the jedi*   16. _____

17. singing "jingle bells"   17. _____

SEASONS AND POINTS OF THE COMPASS

18. flying to the south in winter   18. _____

19. turning east on main street   19. _____

20. yosemite national park in autumn   20. _____

21. going to school in the west   21. _____

ADD CAPITALS AS NEEDED IN THESE SENTENCES.

21. his mustang convertible and his apartment on lake street are his symbols of independence.

22. she works in the masterson building on the street north of the park.

23. while you're at safeway, get me a loaf of bread, some wheaties, a quart of nonfat milk, a copy of *good housekeeping*, and a small bottle of tylenol.

24. this fall my history class is studying the revolutionary war and the declaration of independence.

25. did you know that reno, nevada, is actually west of los angeles, california?

Worksheet 3: CAPITALIZATION EDITING EXERCISE

The passage below contains many errors in capitalization. Some words that are capitalized should not be, and some words that are not capitalized should be. Correct any errors you find.

When Susan moved to san jose, California, she faced some real problems getting settled. For a while she lived with her Aunt, but since she was allergic to the Wool in her Aunt's imported persian carpets, she wanted to get her own place quickly. She bought a copy of the *mercury-news* and searched the ads for an inexpensive apartment. The first place she looked at was too far east of town, but the second was conveniently located on Page boulevard and fully furnished with a general electric refrigerator, a tappan gas range, and a wonderful air conditioner. The price was right, so she grabbed the place.

Her next task was finding Work. She was trained as a Computer Programmer, and she hoped to find a position in nearby Silicon valley. Again she scoured the Newspaper. She spent days on the phone and driving her ford escort to interviews, carefully dressed in her only Business Suit. Finally she landed a job with Executron enterprises on Twelfth street in santa clara. It was a growing Company that specialized in Software for accounting firms. The pay was good, the benefits excellent, and she liked the people she met there, especially one handsome, young vice-president with a porsche. Things were definitely looking up for Susan.

Worksheet 4A: CAPITALIZATION
UNIT QUIZ

Copy over the phrases below, adding capitals as needed.

1. paris in the spring   1. _____

2. winter in florida   2. _____

3. the bill of rights   3. _____

4. driving south on highway 99   4. _____

5. her spanish and science homework   5. _____

6. a spielberg film   6. _____

7. next to the supermarket   7. _____

8. where elm street crosses king way   8. _____

9. st. mary's catholic church   9. _____

10. a cold root beer float   10. _____

11. visiting the american west   11. _____

12. a pair of lee's jeans   12. _____

Add capitals as needed in these sentences.

13. she loves to whiz down the freeway in her porsche convertible with her blaupunkt

     stereo blasting.

14. my grandmother lives near kingman, arizona, not far from the grand canyon.

15. i need to make a trip to the hardware store to buy some g.e. bulbs, a stanley wrench,

     some nails, and a can of paint.

16. next spring my biology class is reading *a whale for the killing.*

**Worksheet 4B: CAPITALIZATION
UNIT QUIZ**

Correct any capitalization errors you find in the passage below.

Preparing for school by shopping for School Supplies is serious business. You'll need the usual notebooks, pencils, and bic pens. But it's also important to have new Nike Tennis Shoes and a couple of pairs of levi's jeans. Stock your kitchen for after-school snacks and late-night study sessions, too. Have a good supply of fruit juice and skippy peanut butter on hand.

Practical English: A Complete Course

Worksheet 5A: ENDMARKS EXPLANATION

Endmarks are the three punctuation marks that end sentences: the period, the question mark, and the exclamation mark. The purpose of the sentence, not the words in the sentence, determine which punctuation mark will end it.

PERIODS

If the purpose of a sentence is to make a statement, the sentence ends in a period.

> The resort is located in the Rocky Mountains near Denver.
>
> Roosevelt was elected to four terms.

Use a period even if the statement made is about a question.

> Ellen asked where the resort is located.
>
> The teacher asked how many times Roosevelt was elected.
>
> The old man asked if I'd ever been stung by a dead bee.

QUESTION MARKS

If the purpose of a sentence is to ask a question that expects an answer, the sentence ends in a question mark.

> Where is the resort located?
>
> How many times was Roosevelt elected?
>
> Could I be stung by a dead bee?

Use a question mark in a sentence with the purpose of asking a question, even if the words are not in the normal order for a question.

> Roosevelt was elected to four terms?
>
> I could be stung by a dead bee?

EXCLAMATION MARKS

If the purpose of a sentence is to show strong feeling, it ends in an exclamation mark. Do not overuse exclamation marks, however, since they quickly lose their effect.

> Look out!
>
> That game was the most incredible thing I've ever seen!
>
> What do you think of that!

Practical English: A Complete Course

**Worksheet 5B: ENDMARKS
EXPLANATION**

PERIODS IN ABBREVIATIONS

Periods follow most abbreviations.

> Dr. Thomas Grant received a C.O.D. package from Vienna yesterday at four A.M.

Abbreviations for corporations, organizations, and government or international agencies often omit periods.

> Last night I saw a *CBS* documentary on *UN* and *CARE* agricultural aid to developing countries.

**Worksheet 6A: ENDMARKS
EXERCISE**

Supply endmarks in the sentences below.

1. Is it time to leave yet

2. For the third time in ten minutes the student asked the teacher what time it was

3. How long can a nuclear submarine remain under water

4. A flute is easier for a small child to play than a piano

5. Her mother asked if a flute would be easier to play than a piano

6. Watch out for that truck

7. Although she had a bad start, Julie easily won the race

8. Is there an easy way to tell the age of a horse

9. Ask the guide if the Senate is in session

10. How dare you say something like that

11. I've never been so insulted in all my life

12. Has he finished yet

13. Ask him if he has finished yet

14. Hasn't he finished yet

15. Did he say when he would be finished

Add periods to the abbreviations below that *always* need them.

16. CBS	21. Dr	26. GM
17. BC	22. Ave	27. Ms
18. COD	23. Feb	28. RCA
19. bldg	24. mph	29. DC
20. Ph D	25. Jr	30. J R Tompkins

Practical English: A Complete Course

Worksheet 6B: ENDMARKS EXERCISE

Write six sentences below. Each should end in the punctuation mark indicated next to the number.

31. (Period) _____

_____

32. (Period) _____

_____

33. (Question Mark) _____

_____

34. (Question Mark) _____

_____

35. (Exclamation Mark) _____

_____

36. (Exclamation Mark) _____

_____

**Worksheet 7: ENDMARKS
EDITING EXERCISE**

The passage below contains many errors in the use of endmarks. Sometimes the wrong punctuation marks are used, and sometimes they are omitted, but some sentences are correct. Correct any errors you find.

Anyone who can drive a car can parallel park! It just requires a little practice, coordination, and a set of eyes in the back of your head!

Ask someone who has been driving for a while if he or she will come along as a teacher. And ask someone where there is a good place to practice? A quiet street with straight curbs and little traffic is perfect

Pick the space you want to park in and pull up to the left of the car in front of the space. Are you two or three feet away. You should be! Are the backs of the two cars even? They should be. Next shift into reverse and swing the back of your car into the space No, no. That will never do. Turn the steering wheel clockwise, and back in at a forty-five degree angle to the curb! When the right front bumper of your car has passed the left rear bumper of the car ahead, start turning the wheel counterclockwise.

Doesn't that slip your car neatly into the space and parallel to the curb. If not, ask the teacher you brought along what you did wrong? Ask if you were too close or far from the car next to you when you began. Were the backs of the two cars even. Did you turn clockwise or counterclockwise too soon. Did you turn too far? Perhaps you reversed the way you were turning the wheel too early or too late?

Keep practicing, and you shouldn't have any problem! In no time you'll be parking like a New York taxi driver!

Worksheet 8: ENDMARKS
UNIT QUIZ

Supply needed endmark and abbreviation punctuation in the sentences below.

1. What a book

2. What is the name of that book

3. I asked her the name of that book

4. Do you know that England was last successfully invaded in A D 1066

5. Athens was a major city long before the birth of Christ

6. Please explain why Elvis Presley made such good music and such bad films

7. What a pest she can be

8. How can I find out whether NBC is a division of RCA

9. Boy, did I feel like a jerk

10. Ask him how long it takes to get a B A degree

11. I have a package for Mr T C Wellington at this address

12. Is the car ready

13. Ask him if the car is ready

14. Wasn't three P M when the car was supposed to be ready

15. Look out You're going to fall

16. My mother never asked me what grade I received

17. What is the difference between an L P record and a compact disk

18. How homely he is

20. Used car prices have soared since 1980

21. Dr and Mrs C M Antonio cordially invite you to dinner at seven P M on Wednesday, January 23 Please RSVP

22. How long are you willing to put up with this state of affairs

Correct any errors in endmark punctuation in the passage below.

No matter how long you have been in school, the first day in the fall can be full of surprises! It is an obvious chance to size up new teachers. Ask around to find out their reputations? Find out which have a good sense of humor, and which don't? Who are the easiest to talk to. Who are most readily available to give extra help. Study the school class schedule to find out which teachers fit best into your program. Can't good teachers go a long way toward making a good year.

Practical English: A Complete Course

Worksheet 9A: ENDMARKS
CUMULATIVE TEST

Correct the capitalization, abbreviation, and endmark errors in the passage below.

What a horrible nightmare. That was what Lulu thought as she left the guidance office. She longed for a class that would help her land a job as a salesclerk at the summit, the most exclusive boutique at Alpine Valley mall What better way to spend the Summer than surrounded by the latest Fashions. And what about that thirty-percent employee discount? Didn't happiness begin with the right clothes. She would return to Alpine high in the fall as popular as the latest designer labels. How could she know that her dreams of a jammed closet and an endless string of exciting Saturday nights would be so quickly shattered.

She had asked Mr. Tweedy, her counselor, if the school offered classes in Retail Sales or Small Business Management? But there wasn't one. As usual, Lulu was a little late signing up for classes The only remaining electives were auto shop 2 and ornamental horticulture. Spark plugs and roses were all dear old Valley Union high school district had to offer.

How could she face such a drab summer. It was going to be long days in the office of her father's fertilizer plant and long nights with her pet goldfish, Buster Crabbe She would be lucky if one of her brother's creepy friends asked her out to the Drive-In. Ugh!

But as she walked back to her spanish class, Lance Steele, the irresistible captain of the Football team, ran up Lulu's father had just hired him for the summer as an assistant fertilizer processor. He asked her if she didn't think it would be great to see one another every day? Lulu beamed. Yes, it would be very nice.

As she continued to class, Lulu wondered if Lance had an interest in roses.

Worksheet 10A: COMMA EXPLANATION

Commas are important marks of punctuation that have a variety of uses. The most common errors, however, are made in compound sentences, in series, in addresses and dates, in separating nonessential elements of sentences, and in sentences with introductory clauses.

IN COMPOUND SENTENCES

Commas are used with conjunctions (usually AND, OR, BUT, or YET) to combine two sentences into a single compound sentence unless the two sentences being combined are extremely short.

> My sister washed the car. Then my father polished it.
> My sister washed the car, and then my father polished it.

> We work hard during the week, but we relax on weekends.
> Write down the assignment, or you're sure to forget it.

> She walked. I drove
> She walked but I drove. (No comma is used to combine these short sentences.)

IN A SERIES

Commas are used to separate the parts of a series. The items in the series may be single words or groups of words.

> Loni, David, and Craig headed the dance committee.
> The national colors of both France and the United States are red, white, and blue.
> He looked down, saw the snake, and screamed in terror.
> For lunch I ate a sandwich, fruit, and milk.
> For lunch I ate a cheeseburger with onions and pickles, a juicy apple, and a carton of cold milk.

These series are almost like lists, but remember that it takes at least three items to make a series.

> Wolves_ and hyenas always travel in packs. (Two words, no comma.)
> Wolves, hyenas, and cheerleaders always travel in packs.

> I washed_ and dried every dish. (Two items in series, no comma.)
> I washed, dried, and put away every dish. (Three items, use a comma.)

Use commas in series of adjectives (descriptive words) before a noun only if the adjectives are of equal importance. The importance of adjectives can be checked by changing their order. If the order is changed and the adjectives sound awkward, the adjectives are *not* of equal importance and do not need commas between them.

> We saw *two old Hitchcock* films. (*Old Hitchcock two films* sounds very strange. No commas in this series.)

Practical English: A Complete Course

Worksheet 10B: COMMA EXPLANATION

We saw an *exciting, fast-paced, new* movie. (These adjectives may be moved around. *New, exciting, fast-paced movie* sounds fine. The series needs commas.)

ADDRESSES AND DATES

Commas separate the parts of addresses and dates in much the same way they separate items in a series. Notice, however, that although a comma is not used at the end of a series, it is used at the end of an address or a date.

On Thursday, June 14, 1986, vacation for Fritz, Willie, and Scott will begin. (Comma after date, no comma after series.)

On July 4, 1776, the Declaration of Independence was adopted in Philadelphia, Pennsylvania.

Her address as of Monday, September 10, will be 1243 Winton Avenue, Las Vegas, Nevada.

SEPARATING NON-ESSENTIAL PARTS OF A SENTENCE

Commas are sometims used to separate sentence parts that can be removed without destroying the sentence's meaning.

One kind of nonessential element is the name of the person to whom the sentence is spoken.

Susan, do you know the biology assignment?

When will you, you mindless slug, learn to be on time?

Do you have a date for the prom yet, Marilyn?

Another kind of nonessential element is the casual, by-the-way statement added for emphasis.

Ms. Jenkins, by the way, is my favorite teacher.

To tell the truth, I really don't care.

It was quite an assembly, wasn't it?

Practical English: A Complete Course

Worksheet 10C: COMMA EXPLANATION

Descriptive clauses and phrases are also sometimes nonessential. In these cases you must ask yourself if omitting the clause or phrase would greatly change the sentence. Look at the way the phrase *wearing cutoffs* is used in the two sentences below.

No students *wearing cutoffs* were allowed into the dance.

Ronnie, *wearing cutoffs*, was on his way to the beach.

In the first sentence the phrase is an essential part of the sentence. If the phrase is removed the sentence becomes: "No students were allowed into the dance." In the second sentence the phrase is not so necessary. The fact that Ronnie wore cutoffs is interesting, but it is not essential to the meaning of the sentence. Since the phrase is essential to the first sentence, no commas are needed. Commas *are* included in the second sentence since the phrase is not essential. Here are some more examples of essential and nonessential phrases and clauses.

Most cars *not used in years* are hard to start. (Clause needed, no commas.)

The rusty, old tractor, *not used in years*, was hauled off for scrap. (Clause unneeded, use commas.)

Students *who dislike math* should not study physics. (Clause needed, no commas.)

My brother Charles, *who dislikes math*, is a history major. (Clause unneeded, use commas.)

A movie *which I have already seen* is playing at the Bijou. (Clause needed, no commas.)

Her new projection television, *which I have already seen*, has a murky picture. (Clause unneeded, use commas.)

IN SENTENCES WITH INTRODUCTORY CLAUSES

Commas are used to separate the first parts of sentences that are introduced with certain words. The most common of these words are listed below. Learn them.

after	because	so (that)	where
although	before	though	wherever
as	every time	unless	whether
as if	if	until	while
as long as	in case	when	
as though	since	whenever	

Practical English: A Complete Course

Worksheet 10D: COMMA EXPLANATION

When a sentence begins with one of these words, listen for the place where there is a pause. This is the end of the introductory clause, and a comma is needed.

When Katie arrived, Craig began to enjoy himself even more.

While their first album was still on the charts, he left the group.

Unless I am mistaken, he graduated in 1981.

*WORDS OF WARNING: Some of these introductory words are used in places other than at the beginning of an introductory clause. Remember that a real introductory clause—one that requires a comma—always contains a subject and a verb. Be especially careful of sentences beginning with BEFORE and AFTER.

After he heard the facts, he changed his mind. (AFTER is followed by the subject and verb *he heard*. Use a comma)

After the lecture he changed his mind. (AFTER is followed by *the lecture*. No subject and verb; no comma.)

Before he left for the lake, he spent a week preparing his camping equipment. (BEFORE is followed by the subject *he* and the verb *left*. Use a comma.)

Before the trip he spent a week preparing his camping equipment. (AFTER is followed by *the trip*. No subject and verb; no comma.)

Also be sure that the words WHEN and WHERE begin introductory clauses and not questions. Sentences beginning with these words require a comma only when they are not questions.

When will the job be finished? (WHEN starts a question, not an introductory clause. No comma.)

When time allows, I'll have the job finished. (WHEN starts a sentence that is not a question. Use a comma.)

Practical English: A Complete Course

NAME: _____

Worksheet 11A: COMMA EXERCISE DATE: _____

Add commas to the sentences below according to the rules heading each section. Not all of the sentences require more punctuation.

COMMAS IN COMPOUND SENTENCES

1. Susan tuned the old Chevrolet but I drove it away afterwards.
2. Either she will be finished or we'll have to do it for her.
3. I wanted to help Tim with his paper yet he refused aid from anyone.
4. I searched my route four times but I still couldn't find my lost ticket.
5. She drove but I flew.

COMMAS IN A SERIES

6. Who is on the committee besides Mr. Thomas Ms. Meyers and Mr. Hardy?
7. He gathered his courage took a deep breath walked up to the teacher and asked for his test.
8. A Big Mac hamburger is made with two all-beef patties special sauce lettuce cheese pickles onions and a sesame-seed bun.
9. The huge craggy ominous mountain loomed above the climbing party.
10. Mrs. Cookston and the entire class pitched in to clean up the mess.

COMMAS IN ADDRESSES AND DATES

11. She lives at 3224 Walton Circle Albany New York.
12. The meeting will he held at the Explorers' Club 9887 Dinston Boulevard Chicago Illinois on Thursday October 14.
13. Miami Florida has been my home since April 1985.

COMMAS SEPARATING NONESSENTIAL PARTS OF SENTENCES

14. Mark please tell Maria that I'm ready.
15. Dr. Rinaldi how much longer will it take?
16. To tell the truth I never dreamed you were wearing that clown costume.
17. This door on the other hand has always been stuck.
18. Larry who always mumbles his words was elected class president.
19. Teachers who always mumble their words are a real frustration.
20. Oliver amazed by the cut of her dress was speechless.
21. John who was sitting in the back seat escaped unharmed.
22. Sylvia red-faced and angry slowly stood up and left the room.

Practical English: A Complete Course

Worksheet 11B: COMMA EXERCISE DATE: _____

COMMAS IN SENTENCES WITH INTRODUCTORY CLAUSES

23. When I saw Mr. Fletcher I shouted and waved to him.

24. Before the game the team was confident and optimistic.

25. Before you leave be sure to check with the boss.

26. Because he has such a reputation I was careful from the start.

27. Whether you like it or not Joni will do as she pleases.

Add commas to the sentences below according to all the rules you have studied. Not all of the sentences require additional punctuation.

28. I told her to be on time Jim but she just didn't seem to care.

29. We met Nora and Sam and Fred gave them the assignment.

30. Before the prom he'll have to rent a tuxedo.

31. The cruise departs on Sunday January 13 doesn't it?

32. The boys hid under the garage under the hedge and behind the car.

33. The room is always cold early in the day but it warms up after lunch.

34. Ed raked the leaves but Edna put them in bags and hauled them away.

35. Edna raked the leaves put them in bags and hauled them away.

36. Ed raked the leaves and hauled them away.

37. Her old address was in Rye but of course I don't know her new address.

©1987 J. Weston Walch, Publisher

Practical English: A Complete Course

Worksheet 12: COMMA EDITING EXERCISE

The passage below contains many errors in the use of commas. Sometimes they are included where they are not needed, and sometimes they are omitted where they are needed. Correct any errors you find.

The rodent invasion of Craggy Rock High School was no laughing matter and it was not easily ended. The mice, who arrived first, stayed well-concealed behind trash and under furniture. They were seldom seen by day but after dark they emerged from their nests. They nibbled crumbs and made midnight trips to the cafeteria kitchen to feed on stray, bits of rubbery spaghetti wilted salad and rotting meatloaf.

The mice became bolder gloating over their success. Classes were occasionally interrupted by gray shadows chasing along walls, windowsills and chalktrays. One English teacher fainted and several students refused to go into the home economics room. It had become overrun with fat ugly rodents. Things had gone too far, and the principal called a faculty meeting to discuss the problem hear suggestions and take decisive action.

Saturday November 16 1986, spelled doom for the round happy furballs of Craggy Rock High. Before dawn a five-person team of exterminators wearing black jumpsuits and carrying frightening machines descended upon the building. On Monday of course there was not a mouse to be seen. The principal amazed by the efficiency of the deadly team strutted proudly about the school.

As the week passed students prepared for a grudge-match football game with the blue-and-gold team from Ziggley Valley High. The team practiced with a vengeance and pep rallies stirred school spirit but on the morning of the game came the ultimate, humiliation. Craggy Rock students were met again by hundreds of tiny "mice"—but this time each one had been dyed blue or gold and placed there as a prank, by their rivals, at Ziggley.

Practical English: A Complete Course

Worksheet 13A: COMMA
UNIT QUIZ

Supply needed comma punctuation in the sentences below.

1. His home was burglarized on Thursday October 24 wasn't it?

2. The restaurant that we ate at last night is open every day.

3. The tour departs on July 1 for England France and Germany.

4. Chris was so absentminded that someone had to tell him when school was over where his locker was and how to catch the bus.

5. Nothing is so annoying as a salesperson who is impolite.

6. Elaine ran all the way to school but she was late just the same.

7. The man whom you see is really a woman in disguise.

8. Beginning Tuesday July 30 1985 her new address will be 616 Boynton Way Salt Lake City Utah.

9. I walked up to her smiled irresistibly and got slapped in the face.

10. It has to be finished and turned in by Tuesday.

11. Whenever Jan is late to class you are aren't you?

12. When do you think Jan will finally get here?

13. John who seldom makes a mistake failed the test.

14. The stately elegant decaying Ambassador Hotel built before the turn of the century is to be torn down.

15. Miss Yee startled by my remark couldn't think of a reply.

16. When the principal tells Frank Todd will inform the rest of us.

17. We walked slowly along the winding road to the strange house and carefully entered the yard with its huge oak and brown lawn.

18. The manager came to their table asked them to leave and threatened to call the police.

19. Columbus first landed in America on October 12 1492 didn't he?

Worksheet 13B: COMMA UNIT QUIZ

20.   Mr. Arnold do you think modern teaching methods include corporal punishment?

21.   I left it under the tree last June and never saw it again.

22.   After the stereo was set up we started dancing.

Correct any errors in comma punctuation in the passage below.

Because he was the only boy in a home economics class Scott was shy nervous and self-conscious on the first day. Thirty pairs of female eyes, all seemed to be aimed squarely at him and he didn't know what to do. Time passed, and he got to know the girls. They were eager to explain the complicated workings of food processors microwave ovens and digital timers. He began to enjoy the class and sometimes even played dumb to get more attention. At semester's end he had learned more than he had ever expected and that's what school is all about isn't it?

**Worksheet 14: PUNCTUATION
CUMULATIVE TEST**

Correct comma, capitalization, endmark, and abbreviation errors in the passage below.

The v.c.r. will never replace the movie theater. A nineteen-inch television a tiny speaker and stale potato chips just aren't the same as a fifty-foot screen Dolby stereo and the array of goodies at a snack counter. *Raiders Of The Lost Ark* just isn't the same when Indiana Jones is only five inches tall.

And a lively excited eager audience adds as much to a movie as a huge screen and monster speakers. Waiting in a line on a cold Winter night and paying for tickets make you even more anxious to see a film. Then you go inside and stock up on popcorn and coke. As the lights go down and the MGM lion appears can't you sense the tension. Sometimes people cheer or boo the coming attractions. When the feature begins a hush falls over the audience. This is what they've waited in line and paid good money to see isn't it. People laugh at what's funny and scream at what's scary. At the end of the movie you can eavesdrop on other people as they comment on the film. Some people agree with you and some have no taste at all?

None of this happens at home. You just slap a cassette into the machine flop down on the couch and stare. Then the telephone ringing like a fire alarm forces you to stop the action. You have to stop again you dummy because you forgot your snacks. You pause again to go to the bathroom. There are even people, who stop in the middle of a film. They go to bed and they continue the next day. This completely destroys the pacing of a good film. Why bother watching at all.

So seeing a movie on a V.C.R. is convenient but it is second-rate. Movie theaters add big screens big sound big reactions and big fun.

©1987 J. Weston Walch, Publisher   *Practical English: A Complete Course*

Worksheet 15A: SEMICOLON EXPLANATION

The semicolon (;) has only two uses. Master them, and you will know all there is to know about semicolons.

IN COMPOUND SENTENCES

You already know that a comma and a conjunction (usually AND, OR, BUT or YET) can be used to combine two sentences into a single compound sentence.

> My sister washed the car. Then my father polished it.
>
> My sister washed the car, and then my father polished it.

You can also write a compound sentence without a conjunction. To do this, use a semicolon between the two parts of the compound sentence to replace the comma and conjunction.

> My sister washed the car; then my father polished it.

Here are some more examples of compound sentences joined by a semicolon.

> Dad missed his flight; the taxi stalled on the freeway.
>
> The junior meeting was in the gym; the sophomores met in the auditorium.
>
> Sue drove, and I walked; he ran all the way.

IN A SERIES

You have also learned that commas are used to separate items in a series.

> Loni, David, and Craig headed the dance committee.

But the items in a series sometimes themselves contain commas. When this happens, it is hard to know which are being used to separate which items.

> On Brad's trip he'll visit Seattle, Washington, Vancouver, British Columbia, and San Francisco, California.

How many areas will Brad visit? It's hard to say. Will he visit Seattle and parts of Washington state or just the city of Seattle? Just Vancouver or Vancouver and other parts of British Columbia? Using semicolons, which are stronger marks of punctuation than commas, the series can be separated more understandably.

> On Brad's trip he'll visit Seattle, Washington; Vancouver, British Columbia; and San Francisco, California.

Practical English: A Complete Course

Worksheet 15B: SEMICOLON EXPLANATION

Here are some other examples of sentences containing commas within a series. Semicolons keep the series easy to understand.

The dance committee was headed by Loni, the student body president; David, the vice-president; and Craig, the senior-class president.

This year my uncle George sent a fishing reel to my father, who can't stand fishing; a box of chocolates to my mother, who is always dieting; and an overcoat to my cousin Phil, who lives in Honolulu.

Practical English: A Complete Course

Worksheet 16A: SEMICOLON EXERCISE

Each compound sentence below needs either a comma or a semicolon. Supply it.

1. I weeded the garden my brother mowed the lawn.

2. I weeded the garden but my brother mowed the lawn.

3. The radio had been left on all day and the batteries were dead.

4. I didn't care about her problems I had plenty of my own to keep me busy.

5. You may not fish here with your state license you need to buy a special permit.

6. I did my best to explain the grade to my parents they didn't buy it.

7. I went to the store at the address you gave me if they sell running shoes there, they do it in a vacant gas station.

8. Some people say the old mine is haunted but most scoff at the idea.

9. He watches the door with one eye he watches the class with the other.

10. She did all the talking she was the only one who spoke Spanish.

Add commas and semicolons in the compound sentences and series below.

11. An hour later the roof collapsed the earthquake had weakened it.

12. The earthquake cracked the foundation and the roof collapsed.

13. Susan arrived in class soaking wet she had changed a tire in the rain.

14. The members of the team couldn't stand him he was always complaining about something.

15. The winning teams were from Springfield Ohio Princeton Wisconsin and Bloomingdale Indiana.

16. Two club members had to leave early they had paper routes.

17. The travel agent advised Stan to take the late plane it would save him money.

Practical English: A Complete Course

Worksheet 16B: SEMICOLON EXERCISE

18. The review committee consists of Mr. Luxley who is principal Ms. Shanna who is a counselor and Tony Garcia who is student body president.

19. The Sterns' new house has a family room with a stereo a fireplace and a projection T.V. a kitchen with a built-in food processor a microwave oven and two dishwashers and a back yard equipped with a swimming pool a tennis court and a hot tub.

20. Laurel was expected to answer the phone for Mr. Post Mr. Lowrey and the rest of the sales staff take dictation for Mrs. Isaacson and do typing bookkeeping and payroll for the entire office.

On the lines below write a compound sentence requiring a semicolon.

21. _____

    _____

On the lines below write a sentence with a series requiring semicolons.

22. _____

    _____

Practical English: A Complete Course

Worksheet 17: SEMICOLON EDITING EXERCISE

The passage below contains many errors in the use of commas and semicolons. Sometimes the wrong punctuation marks are used, and sometimes they are omitted. Some sentences are correct. Correct any errors you find.

Disneyland has a private face in addition to the public one its millions of visitors have seen. Disneylanders which is what park employees are called see a side to the Magic Kingdom hidden from the view of visitors from St. Louis, Missouri, London, England, and Canton, China.

Workers pass daily through locker rooms where mountain climbers, astronauts, and turn-of-the-century popcorn boys, suit up side by side. They even catch occasional glimpses of a Mickey Goofy or Donald without a rubber head.

The park itself is wonderfully quiet before the public gates open. Gardeners put finishing touches on flowerbeds, ride operators run the Matterhorn bobsled safety check, and fry cooks ride the raft to Tom Sawyer's Island to deliver the day's supply of hot dogs.

Then thousands of tourists descend upon the place, but employees are provided with restful break areas away from the crowds that they must serve with unvarying safety courtesy and speed. Behind Main Street, where visitors shop for souvenirs; adjacent to Adventureland, where steamers challenge jungle rivers and near Autopia, where youngsters develop driving habits they will later perfect on California freeways, employees sip Cokes away from the noise; crowds; and heat.

Many say Disneyland is prettiest at night, but its prettiest time of night is when it is empty. When workers wander out of the park; the recorded music still plays; and the lights still twinkle, reflected now on freshly washed sidewalks.

Practical English: A Complete Course

**Worksheet 18A: SEMICOLON
UNIT QUIZ**

Supply needed comma and semicolon punctuation in the sentences below.

1. The subway was slow but Mr. Kimura made his appointment on time.

2. The plane was delayed she missed her connection.

3. The three members of the committee were Mrs. Reynolds the principal Mr. De Rue the vice principal and Mrs. Elmore the chairperson of the English department.

4. A century ago most Americans worked on farms today most live and work in cities.

5. Our neighborhood basketball team consists of Jerry the center Bob and Rick the forwards and Sue and Elizabeth the guards.

6. From now on there will be no more monkey business today begins a new regime.

7. The South High *Tiger* specializes in stories on student activities school sports and administrative foul-ups.

8. We got to the dock at dawn but we waited until nine o'clock before the wind tide and weather permitted us to sail.

9. What small colleges lack in reputation they often make up for in instructor-student ratio.

10. Our English teacher always allows us time to think plan write and revise before we turn in our papers.

11. During the week I'm usually in bed by ten on weekends I stay up much later.

12. Would you rather spend a winter vacation in Miami Florida Phoenix Arizona or Honolulu Hawaii?

13. I remember where I read the article it was in *Time* last spring.

14. Thick gloves are a help for any heavy work.

15. Kitty had lost her engagement ring and immediately everyone started furiously searching the furniture floor and wastebaskets.

Practical English: A Complete Course

Worksheet 18B: SEMICOLON
UNIT QUIZ

Correct any errors in comma or semicolon punctuation in the passage below.

The substitute's arrival was very exciting, it meant Mr. Tremble's wife had had her baby. The students immediately wanted to know the sex, size, and time of delivery but the poor substitute knew nothing. She had received a brief phone call, from the school; a substitute was required there was no other word. The class settled down, to work. Halfway through the period Mr. Tremble entered the room, smiled, sat down and announced the birth of triplets. There was Michael, weighing five pounds, James, weighing five and a half, and William, weighing four and three-quarters. His wife was very tired.

Worksheet 19: SEMICOLON CUMULATIVE TEST

Correct semicolon, comma, endmark, capitalization, and abbreviation errors in the passage below.

Spending Summers as a cook, in a fast-food restaurant can be hard work. The heat is high, the pressure is high, and the wages are usually low.

Few things are hotter than a hamburger grill in August. Hour after hour you lay rows of patties on the blackened steel; wait for them to fry; and flip them over. The only real entertainment is asking yourself how many need cheese? An occasional Dr. Pepper helps avoid dehydration, but soon your head, arms, and back are soaked with sweat, and a film of hamburger grease.

At breakfast, which comes between seven and ten, lunch, which comes between noon and three, and dinner, which comes between six and eight, the pressure is on. Waitresses scream for orders; food flies in all directions; and, of course, the manager supervises your every move, and tries to spot any inefficiency. If anyone fails to do his or her part there could be a disaster. It is possible to run out of ice, hot Fries, or even thawed patties. What if a Soft Drink machine breaks down. That means unhappy customers, lower sales, and an angry boss.

And what do you get paid for this agony? To tell the truth you get minimum wage, and rarely, do you get more. Tips are unheard of in fast-food chains. If you don't like the pay scores of other unemployed teenagers are waiting to take your job.

Don't you think it's a tough way to make money. If you can't stand the heat you should stay out of the kitchen.

Practical English: A Complete Course

Worksheet 20A: APOSTROPHE EXPLANATION

The apostrophe (') is used to replace missing letters in contractions, to show possession, and in a few unusual cases to show plurals.

CONTRACTIONS

Often we make one word of two. We say, "I'll go," instead of "I will go." These shortened words are called *contractions*, and an apostrophe is used in them to replace missing letters. Here is a list of common contractions.

any name (Al + is = Al's)	must + have = must've
(Al + has = Al's)	should + have = should've
are + not = aren't	that + is = that's
can + not = can't	they + are = they're*
does + not = doesn't	were + not = weren't
had + not = hadn't	we + had = we'd
I + am = I'm	where + is = where's
is + not = isn't	who + is = who's*
it + is = it's*	who + will = who'll
let + us = let's	you + are = you're*

Two irregular contractions:	shall + not = shan't
	will + not = won't

*A WORD OF WARNING: Do not confuse the possessive pronouns ITS, THEIR, WHOSE, and YOUR with the contractions IT'S, THEY'RE, WHO'S and YOU'RE.

POSSESSION

Apostrophes are also used to show ownership or *possession*, such as *the girl's belt*. Follow three steps to form the possessive form of any noun: (1) Write the noun; (2) Add an apostrophe; and (3) Add an S if there is not already one before the apostrophe.

Imagine you are writing a sentence about injuries to a boy, some men, and some dogs. First write the sentence with the possessive nouns but with no apostrophes or S's.

A *boy* hand, the *men* feet, and some *dogs* paws were injured.

Practical English: A Complete Course

Worksheet 20B: APOSTROPHE EXPLANATION

Add an apostrophe after each possessive noun.

    A *boy'* hand, the *men'* feet, and some *dogs'* paw were injured.

Then add an *S* if one does not preceed the apostrophe.

    A *boy's* hand, the *men's* feet, and some *dogs'* paws were injured.

Using this system, you cannot fail.

PLURALS OF LETTERS, NUMBERS, AND SYMBOLS

The plurals of letters, numbers, and symbols are formed by adding an apostrophe and S. This is the only case where an apostrophe indicates plural.

    He used @'s, #'s, &'s and *'s, in place of the profanity.

    Be sure your capital T's don't look like capital F's.

Practical English: A Complete Course

Worksheet 21A: APOSTROPHE EXERCISE

The underlined item in each of the following groups tells what is owned. The second item (the possessive noun) tells the name of the owner or owners. To the right of each set of words, write the correct form of possessive noun followed by the name of the thing owned.

Example: <u>clock</u> Kelly   Kelly's clock _____

1. <u>house</u> the dog   1. _____

2. <u>house</u> the dogs   2. _____

3. <u>department</u> the girls   3. _____

4. <u>department</u> the men   4. _____

5. <u>purse</u> the lady   5. _____

6. <u>purses</u> the ladies   6. _____

7. <u>turn</u> Sam Jones   7. _____

8. <u>pickup</u> the Joneses   8. _____

9. <u>tools</u> the repairmen   9. _____

10. <u>gifts</u> his friends   10. _____

11. <u>conference</u> the teachers   11. _____

12. <u>visit</u> my brother-in-law   12. _____

13. <u>kids</u> my brothers-in-law   13. _____

14. <u>hats</u> the team   14. _____

Write the contracted form of the words below.

15. it is   _____   19. shall not   _____

16. they are   _____   20. who is   _____

17. will not   _____   21. Tom is   _____

18. you are   _____   22. must have   _____

          _____   _____

     Practical English: A Complete Course

Worksheet 21B: APOSTROPHE EXERCISE

Supply apostrophes as needed in the sentences below.

23. Its under Johns geometry textbook.

24. Bobs going, but he shouldnt.

25. Its the Millers fence thats too high.

26. That ladys dogs collar isnt too uncomfortable, is it?

27. There were seven 2s on the home teams scoreboard.

28. Didnt Phil say hed wait until ten oclock?

29. You shouldnt interrupt him when hes talking.

**Worksheet 22: APOSTROPHE
EDITING EXERCISE**

The passage below contains many errors in the use of apostrophes. Sometimes apostrophes are included where they are not needed, and sometimes they are omitted. Some sentences are correct. Correct any errors you find.

Some days you just shouldnt get out of bed. Last Wednesday was a day like that for Jim Taylor. The more the day wore on, the worse it got.

Day's start early for Jim. The alarm's buzz jarred him out of bed before seven. He was able to shower, grab a bite, and be to school in time to do some last minute homework before classes' began. First period he faced a metal shop quiz; second it was a biology lab with a partner who's idea of helping was minding his own *P*s and *Q*s, and third it was a lesson on apostrophe's. Lunch should've been a pleasant break, but it wasn't. Jim waited in line twenty minutes for a chance to battle other students for the cafeterias' lousy food. The cook's idea of a hamburger was a chewy bit of ground crud on a stale bun. Jims lunch conversation with two friends was the highlight of the day. They talked about car's, record's, and last Saturday's basketball game. Then it was back to class. Mr. Thomas' surprise fourth period was the announcement of a math exam later in the week. Fifth period Jim got the sad results of last week's business test, and sixth period there was no hot water in the gyms showers.

Now you'd think he'd have a chance to go home and enjoy a nice snack of his moms' cooking, but the minute he walked in the door, his boss called for him to come down to the gas station. One of Jim's co-worker's had called in sick. When he got back home, it was after ten. There was just enough time to study and fall into bed.

As he was dropping off to sleep, Jim remembered his father's words. "Jim," he had said, "these are the best year's of your life."

Practical English: A Complete Course

Worksheet 23: APOSTROPHE
UNIT QUIZ

Supply needed apostrophes in the sentences below.

1. Didnt Shannon say shed wait at Tess house?

2. Whos been fooling around with whose camera equipment?

3. He told me youd find it in the mens and boys department.

4. My mother-in-laws luggage is still at the station, isnt it?

5. The Wongs front yard is always the neighborhoods pride.

6. Mr. Langlys ties are always so colorful!

7. That ladys packages fell all over the hallway. Help her, wont you?

8. Lets put Ruths books, folders, and binder in Elaines locker.

9. The freshmens float didn't win, but it showed lots of hard work.

10. Thats the girl whose notes I borrowed.

11. Its hers and Joannas, not theirs.

12. The odometer on the Johnsons car is all *2*s.

13. Eisenhowers administration was in power during the 1950s.

14. Theyre over there with your costume.

15. Dont forget to cross your *t*s and dot your *i*s.

Correct any errors in apostrophe punctuation in the passage below.

A computer's keyboard is much like one for a typewriter, but its important to keep a few things in mind. You mustnt use capital *O*'s instead of zeros, and don't confuse *i*s and *I*s; the differences are important to a computer. There are also some computer keys that you'll never see on a typewriter. The one's marked "control" and "esc" are used with other keys to make the computer do some of its tricks. Don't touch them unless you know what your doing. But don't be afraid of a computer keyboard either. It's impossible to damage the machine by pushing any of the key's.

Practical English: A Complete Course

**Worksheet 24: APOSTROPHE
CUMULATIVE TEST**

Correct the apostrophe, semicolon, comma, endmark, capitalization, and abbreviation errors in the passage below.

When school's out and summers here, meals around our house become very informal. Other things are more important than eating during hot july weather, and Mom or Dads' cooking is usually light, fast, and easy to fix. Whose in the mood for more?

My summer breakfasts are usually hurried. I roll out of bed late, and ready to get going, and I dont like to fool around with a nutritionists idea of a well-balanced breakfast. I swallow some Cheerios, fruit, orange juice, and coffee, and I'm on my way. Lunch can be even more hurried, sometimes I skip it altogether. Occasionally I'll have one of my mothers bag lunches, but a cheeseburger, some Fries, and a diet cola from the Burger King are all I usually need to keep going through the afternoon. When dinner comes the family tries to eat together; but it is hard to get someone to cook on hot days. Dad, who is a Mexican-food fan; Mom, who always wants salad; and my sister, who loves fried chicken, have great debates about where to go for some fast food. I usually win by asking who'd like pizza?

One thing well always agree on is that the best summer meals are cooked and served outdoors. Our backyard barbecue won't produce gourmet french cuisine, but it treats good beef better than anything we can think of. Dad's favorite is rare steak, Mom's is fresh corn on the cob and I go for potatoes baked on the coals. These are the only really big meals we eat all summer. Can you think of a better way to spend a warm Summer evening.

Worksheet 25A: QUOTATION MARKS—EXPLANATION

Quotation marks (" ") are used around words someone has actually spoken and around some titles.

TITLES

The titles of short stories, magazine articles, essays, songs, poems, and chapters of books are enclosed in quotation marks. The titles of longer works like books, plays, magazines, newspapers, and feature films are set in italic print. This is indicated in longhand and typing by underlining.

"The Tell-Tale Heart" is my favorite story, but my favorite novel is *The Grapes of Wrath.*

Blue Hawaii was Elvis' best film, and his best single was "Heartbreak Hotel."

DIRECT AND INDIRECT QUOTATIONS

When writing the exact words of a speaker or writer (a *direct quotation*), put quotation marks around what is said. But if you are just using your own words to report what was written or said (an *indirect quotation*), you do not need quotation marks.

DIRECT:	"We'll be late," Lloyd warned.
INDIRECT:	Lloyd warned us that we would be late.
DIRECT:	"Do you have change for a dollar?" he inquired.
INDIRECT:	He asked me if I had change for a dollar.

PUNCTUATING DIRECT QUOTATIONS

There are five rules to keep in mind when you are punctuating direct quotations.

1. Each time a sentence with a new speaker is started, a new paragraph is also started. Begin these paragraphs by indenting.

    ⟶ "My name is Roy," he said as he approached.

    ⟶ "And I'm Dale," she replied.

2. A direct quote (the words actually spoken) begins with a capital letter whether it begins the sentence or not.

    "<u>Y</u>ou're home early," remarked Cathy.

    Norman replied, "<u>W</u>e ran out of money."

Practical English: A Complete Course

Worksheet 25B: QUOTATION MARKS—EXPLANATION

3. If a sentence is quoted in two parts, two sets of quotation marks are used, but only one capital letter is needed.

   "My grades," he announced, "are better than ever."

4. Words that tell who spoke (like *he said* or *Sue announced*) are set off by commas that always come before quotation marks.

   "Sammy's books," she said," are missing again.

5. If a quotation ends with an exclamation mark or a question mark, that mark replaces the comma before the words that tell who spoke.

   "What's wrong with Lucy?" Mr. Leonard asked.

Worksheet 26A: QUOTATION MARKS—EXERCISES

Some of the sentences below contain direct quotations and some contain indirect quotations. Put quotation marks where they are needed in the direct quotations and leave the indirect quotations unchanged.

1. I didn't touch your motorcycle, said Don.

2. Don said that he hadn't touched my motorcycle.

3. Penny explained that she couldn't stand anchovies on her pizza.

4. I can't stand anchovies on my pizza, Penny explained.

5. Do you have a pencil? Frank asked.

6. Frank asked if I had a pencil.

Supply needed quotation marks and underlining in the sentences below.

7. I have no intention of staying, he announced.

8. She told me she had just replaced her lost copy of Moby Dick.

9. Hamlet is the only play by Shakespeare I've seen, she said.

10. Bob told me that The Lottery is a frightening short story.

11. The best article in this issue of Rolling Stone is John Lennon: The Myth and the Man.

12. Whenever he walks into the room, she explained, I get nervous.

13. Why did you invite him? He's such a bore, moaned Ron.

14. He's home sick with the flu, explained his mother.

15. I know which one is the center, said Paul, but which is the quarterback?

16. No seat-saving allowed! screamed the angry bus driver.

17. Then she said that she wanted us all off the bus immediately.

18. The Chronicle is a good newspaper, but I get most of my current events from Newsweek.

19. When this ordeal is over, she sighed, I'm going to sleep for a week.

Practical English: A Complete Course

**Worksheet 26B: QUOTATION
MARKS—EXERCISES**

20. They say that the smell from the dump is overpowering.

21. Robert Redford's best film was Butch Cassidy and the Sundance Kid.

22. Ellen thinks that Robert Redford's best film was Butch Cassidy and the Sundance Kid.

23. Ellen said, Robert Redford's best film was Butch Cassidy and the Sundance Kid.

24. Do you know I'm leaving soon? he asked.

25. No, I don't. Hum a few notes and I'll fake it, she replied, sitting down at the piano.

Copy the passage below. Provide missing quotation marks and paragraphing.

Well, I finally made it, didn't I? Diane announced as she entered the room. You're half an hour late, David answered. What kept you? Oh, she said, my car's battery went dead on me again. What a nuisance, replied David. Don't you have jumper cables? Yes, I do, she sighed, but they don't do any good if they're home in the garage! Too bad. You should keep them in your trunk, he said. I've learned my lesson, Diane replied. I'll never leave home without them again.

Practical English: A Complete Course

Worksheet 27: QUOTATION MARKS—EDITING EXERCISE

Correct the passage below. Add or remove quotation marks and underlining as needed, and mark new paragraphs with a P.

"Well, how was your weekend?," Dave asked Jerry as he slumped into his desk. Mr. Madonwald was late to class, as was usual on Mondays, and it was a good time to talk over the weekend. Jerry looked up and replied, "Don't even ask!" "I worked all day Saturday and when I got home the only thing on T.V. was an old movie called Gold Diggers of 1933." "But you must have seen the Dolphins' game on Sunday afternoon, said Dave. That pass that won the game was incredible." "I'm sure it was, but I didn't see it," sighed Jerry. "Sunday morning our television went on the blink while I was reading an article about the game in the *Times*." Just then Mr. Macdonwald arrived. "Good morning, people, he said cheerfully. "Isn't it splendid to be starting a new week together?" The class groaned in unison; it was the old joke every Monday morning. "Open your books to act two of "Macbeth," he said. Jerry, will you read the part of Banquo?" "Mr. Macdonwald, I'm not feeling very well," said Jerry. "Couldn't you get someone else?" Jerry thought to himself that the last thing he needed was fifty minutes of reading Elizabethan drama. He asked himself "why he had taken this class." Christopher, the class eager-beaver, saved him. His hand shot into the air. "I'll be happy to read, if Gerald is feeling under the weather, Mr. Macdonwald," he said. "I love this play!" Jerry relaxed and slouched into his seat. "Shakespeare's not as bad as I thought it would be," Jerry whispered to Dave, "but I'm just not in the mood." "I'm never in the mood for anything on Monday morning," Dave replied. "Only five days till Friday," Jerry muttered.

           Practical English: A Complete Course

Worksheet 28: QUOTATION MARKS—UNIT QUIZ

Supply needed quotation marks and underlining in the sentences below.

1. She told me yesterday that she lost her latest issue of Time.

2. Why are you shouting? asked the coach.

3. Have you ever read Gone with the Wind? Mrs. Jenkins asked.

4. When he leaves the room, we'll sneak out, suggested Timothy.

5. My favorite musical is Cats, but I also really liked A Chorus Line.

6. I just finished an excellent Reader's Digest article called Ten Ways to Have a Good Marriage.

7. Sit down, Kate, George said. Don't move until I return.

8. I want to go! shrieked Sarah's little brother. Give me one good reason why I can't.

9. I asked him why he liked Star Wars so very much.

10. Terri moved close to Scott and whispered, Did you hear a noise?

11. Grady asked if I had an extra copy of the geometry book.

12. It's just not fair, whined Bob. You always single me out.

13. Talking to your father, complained Grandpa, is like shouting down a well.

14. The zookeeper shouted, Look out! A rabid gerbil has escaped!

15. Unquestionably the Beatles most innovative album was Sargeant Pepper's Lonely Hearts Club Band, he stated gravely.

Correct the following passage, which is adapted from Lewis Carroll's *Alice's Adventures in Wonderland.* Supply quotation marks as needed and mark places where new paragraphing should occur with a P.

Suppose we change the subject, the March Hare interrupted. I vote that young lady tells us a story. I'm afraid I don't know one, said Alice. Then the Dormouse shall, said the March Hare. Wake up, Dormouse! I wasn't asleep, said the Dormouse. I heard every word you said. Tell us a story, said the March Hare. Yes, please do! pleaded Alice, and the Mad Hatter added that he should be quick about it.

Practical English: A Complete Course

Worksheet 29: QUOTATION MARKS—CUMULATIVE TEST

Correct underlining, quotation mark, apostrophe, semicolon, comma, endmark, capitalization, and paragraphing errors in the passage below.

From the day she entered Colter high as a Freshman on September 8, 1986 Loni wanted to play basketball for the school. She loved to play the game and she loved to watch it on television. She was a sophomore now, she was eligible for the varsity squad the following year. She talked things over with her mother.

"Well" her mom said, "I'm not happy with your grade in Spanish. "I know Mom," Loni replied, "but I know I can keep it up. You saw how well I did last quarter." "And you know I need help at home" her mother sighed. "It hasn't been easy since I started work when your father and I separated."

"But, Mom," Loni pleaded, "Don't I always do my chores?"

"O.K.," her mother said. "Give it a try if it's really what you want."

And she did try. She borrowed her cousin's sweatsuit and her boyfriends' basketball, and she headed for tryouts. She really gave it her all; that's the way to win, isn't it. She never missed practice, practiced additional hours at home, and even checked a book titled "Advanced Basketball Technique" out of the library. The chapter on free throws, called Advantage Under Pressure, was particularly helpful. But the day of the final cut came closer and she wavered. She asked herself whether she was really good enough. Did she have the timing Did she have the drive?

Before the final selections were made she was depressed. She wasn't at all sure shed made it. But the new team for next year was posted during her Gym class, and she let out a squeal of joy. Her work had paid off.

Practical English: A Complete Course

Worksheet 30: COLON AND PARENTHESES—EXPLANATIONS

COLON

The three common uses for the colon (:) are before formal quotations, before some lists at the ends of sentences, and in a few special situations.

FORMAL QUOTATIONS

A colon is usually used in factual writing (essays and articles, but not stories) to introduce a quotation.

> The press secretary made the following announcement: "The President is resting well after his surgery and doctors expect a speedy recovery."

LISTS

If a list at the end of a sentence explains a noun that comes before it, use a colon between the noun and the list.

> Jenifer faced three problems: getting to school, finishing her homework, and getting back home.

> Three sophomores made the varsity team: Kevin Michaels, Larry Gomez, and Henry O'Leary.

Do not use a colon before a list that is preceded by anything but a noun.

> The three sophomores who made the varsity team were Kevin Michaels, Larry Gomez, and Henry O'Leary.

> The list of sophomores making the varsity team consists of Kevin Michaels, Larry Gomez, and Henry O'Leary.

SPECIAL SITUATIONS

Besides the salutation of a business letter (See Chapter Six), colons are also used between the hour and minute when writing time and between chapter and verse when referring to the Bible.

> The subject of the sermon next Sunday at the 10:00 service will be John 1:1.

Worksheet 30B: PARENTHESES EXPLANATION

PARENTHESES

Use parentheses to keep any extra words of explanation you add to a sentence from standing out too strongly. Use parentheses sparingly and keep two rules in mind.

If the words in parentheses form a complete sentence, begin with a capital, but use no endmark unless the sentence requires a question mark or exclamation mark.

> The boy in the corner (I don't know him_) is a doll.

> The boy in the corner (Who is he?) is a doll.

When the words in parentheses come at a place in the sentence that needs a punctuation mark, the mark comes after the parentheses.

> I don't know what to do (I seldom do), but I'll think of something.

Worksheet 31A: COLON AND PARENTHESES—EXERCISES

Supply colons, if needed, in the sentences below.

1. It's certainly a beautiful day bright sun, blue skies, and crisp autumn air.

2. His beautiful home was full of pests ants, termites, and his little sister.

3. The train leaves at either 6 30 or 6 40. I'm not sure which time.

4. Job 3 4 is always an inspiration to me.

5. Don excelled in basketball, geometry, and chess.

6. Three members of the team deserve special credit for the victory the quarterback, the center, and the manager.

7. There's a special schedule tomorrow, and I'm not sure if school is out at 3 00 or 3 30.

8. Day after day he wore the same ridiculous outfit faded jeans, a Save-the-Chocolate-Mousse T-shirt, and green sneakers.

9. Every employee has a responsibility to take short breaks, obey every company rule, and be loyal to the boss.

10. Carrie has the qualitites that make for corporate success a driving ambition, endless energy, and the ability to play scratch golf.

Some of the sentences below require a colon before their quotations; some require a comma, and some are indirect quotations that require neither. Supply what is needed.

11. The speaker quoted from *Poor Richard's Almanac* "A penny saved is a penny earned."

12. My mother said with a smile "A penny saved is a penny earned."

13. My uncle always says that a penny saved is a penny earned.

14. Mr. Van Loon opened his daily television commentary with a thought-provoking statement "Television is a bore."

15. Lenny walked into the classroom, took his seat, and announced "I'm dropping this class."

16. One film critic wrote the following after viewing the film "In the future Miss La Rue's attempts to act should be confined to the privacy of her own home."

Practical English: A Complete Course

Worksheet 31B: COLON AND PARENTHESES—EXERCISES

17. Coming out of the theater, Bill said "I certainly don't go to Lora La Rue films because I like her acting."

18. Ralph said excitedly that there was food available at the snack bar around the corner.

19. The warning on the container stated "Danger! Do not take internally."

20. James walked up to Mr. Langston and casually asked "When will you be giving the next surprise quiz?"

Supply necessary parentheses in the following sentences.

21. Tanzania formerly Tanganyika is located in East Africa.

22. The Grand Tetons a French name are an inspiring mountain range.

23. *Leave It to Beaver* Why did it ever go off the air? was an early television show that extolled the virtues of the American family.

24. I knew Kim had the money for a ticket She saved it by skipping lunches, but I don't know how Sally bought hers.

25. The chart on page 251 shows the decline in unemployment.

Worksheet 32A: COLON AND PARENTHESES—EDITING EXERCISE

The passage below contains many errors in the use of colons and parentheses. Correct any errors you find.

Good morning, class. Let's begin our review of punctuation (Where are my notes) with endmarks: periods, question marks, and exclamation marks. The endmark you use depends on your purpose, a period to make a statement, a question mark to ask a question, and an exclamation mark to show great feeling.

Next let me quote from your explanation sheet on commas: "The most common comma errors are made in: compound sentences, in series, in addresses and dates, and in separating nonessential elements of sentences." Be sure to look over these rules carefully; (Remember that a test is approaching) they can be complicated.

The semicolon has (only two) uses: in a compound sentence, where it replaces a comma and a conjunction, and in a series with elements that contain commas. Master these two rules.

Apostrophes are used to form plurals of: numbers, letters, and symbols, but they are usually used in contractions (They replace missing letters.), and in possessives. Three steps form the possessive of any noun: first, write the noun; second, add an apostropohe; and third, add an *s* if the word doesn't already end in one.

Worksheet 32B: COLON AND PARENTHESES—EDITING EXERCISE

Quotation marks are used around the titles of short works like stories, articles, poems, and songs. They are also used in direct quotations, but there are five rules (see Worksheet 25) to keep in mind.

That just leaves: colons and parentheses. The colon has four uses: in formal quotations, in lists preceded by nouns, in expressions of time between the hour and minute, and in references to the Bible between numbers for chapters and verse. Parentheses (Use them sparingly) keep any extra words of explanation you add from standing out strongly.

Worksheet 33A: COLON AND PARENTHESES—UNIT QUIZ

Supply colons and parentheses, if needed, in the sentences below.

1. I love everything about her sports car its chic styling, its good acceleration, its low gas mileage, and its owner.

2. Her new sports car has chic styling, good acceleration, and low gas mileage.

3. Two graduating seniors Max Canfield and Roy Gold are planning on spending the summer in Hawaii.

4. Two graduating seniors will be spending the summer after graduation in Hawaii Max Canfield and Roy Gold.

5. Kate ran into the room and shouted, "We've won the championship again!"

6. The man behind the counter told us at 8 30 that the 7 10 flight from Chicago wouldn't arrive before 2 00 a.m.

7. My father likes to say that kids today have it easy.

8. She quoted Song of Solomon 4 9 "Thou hast ravished my heart my sister, my spouse! How much better is thy love than wine!"

9. The new president of the class We hope it's Connie, but who knows? will have fund-raising as first priority.

10. Study the diagram figure B to understand the relationship between supply and demand.

11. The mayor's press representative made the following announcement at 2 00 p.m. "Due to unforseen circumstances the press conference has been cancelled."

12. The senator think what you want of her politics certainly uses television effectively.

13. Mrs. Lazzoli How rude! asked him how much his new house cost him.

14. Maria has unusual talents in three areas drafting, sailing, and baking chocolate-chip cookies.

15. From the back of the hall it was impossible to hear what Sam had to say, but I heard your remarks from the audience loudly and clearly.

16. He has high grades, but they're the result of good concentration, hard work, and a little luck.

**Worksheet 33B: COLON AND
PARENTHESES—UNIT QUIZ**

17. Her hard work paid off in two ways a check from her boss and a tidy sum from tips.

18. Julie shouted furiously, "The last person who did that was sorry she lived to tell about it!"

19. The lead sentence of the newspaper article was "A fire, believed to have been set by an arsonist, swept through Taylor's Hardware Store last night, doing $400,000 damage."

20. The girl in the shadows See her next to the oak tree? is the same girl I met last week at Claire's party.

21. From early in the morning until late at night I had only two things in mind staying warm and finding my way home.

22. Cragmont State Beach offers balmy temperatures, clear water, and beautiful white sand.

23. Our poetry unit covered the following concepts metaphor, simile, rhyme scheme, meter, and personification.

24. That huge guy in the third row They call him Monster Malone is the center on their team.

25. Those two teachers the ones who leave together each day at 4 00 are the most helpful in the school.

Practical English: A Complete Course

NAME: _____ 292

Worksheet 34A: COLON AND PARENTHESES—CUMULATIVE QUIZ

DATE: _____

In the letter below correct errors in the use of colons, parentheses, apostrophes, semicolons, commas, endmarks, quotations marks, abbreviations, and paragraphing.

May 14, 1987

Dear Louise,

I'm really in a fix. Do you believe (I certainly can't!) I actually have three dates for the junior prom. It's next Friday May 20, at 9 00 pm, so I need advice fast. Here's a description of the three guys: Larry, my cousin whom I asked to take me two months ago; Tom, an absolute hunk who asked me last month and Jason, a very sweet boy I'd really like to go with but who didn't get up the courage to ask me, until two weeks ago. It sounds like a soap opera doesn't it?

I just don't know how I ever said "Yes that would be wonderful!" to all three boys. My cousin is really no problem, and I can call him and explain; he's always been close, understanding and willing to help me out of a jam. Tom's not so easy. All my friend's advice is to go with him because he's so cute and has a Nissan sports car. But I really think hes' stuck on himself, to tell you the truth. And, of course, I really like Jason. You should've seen how shy he was when he asked me, (I just fell love) and he has the greatest eyes.

Practical English: A Complete Course

**Worksheet 34B: COLON AND
PARENTHESES—CUMULATIVE QUIZ**

I asked Mom (It took guts, believe me.) what to do.

"Squeekie how do you get into these things?" she asked. "Just lucky, I guess" I answered. "Well, don't expect to use your dads' charge account to buy a formal until you straighten things out," she said, and that was that.

Louise, please give me some advice. Meantime I'll just remember my favorite Scarlet O'Hara quote, "I'll think of it tomorrow."

Love,

Squeekie

Practical English: A Complete Course

**Worksheet 35A: PUNCTUATION
UNIT TEST**

Copy the phrases below, adding capitals as needed.

1. a sony television   1. _____

2. *gone with the wind*   2. _____

3. a west turn on elm street   3. _____

4. yellowstone park in spring   4. _____

5. a school in the south   5. _____

Supply endmarks in the sentences below.

6. Again he asked the boss what time it was

7. Hasn't he finished the assignment yet

8. Ask if he has finished the assignment yet

9. Watch out for that falling piano

10. Checkers is easier to learn than chess

Add periods to the abbreviations below that always
need them.

11. NBC   12. Ave   13. RCA   14. H T Stevens   15. bldg

The underlined item in each of the following groups tells what is owned. The second item (the possessive noun) tells the name of the owner or owners. To the right of each set of words, write the correct form of the possessive noun followed by the name of the thing owned.

16. locker room the boys   16. _____

17. compliments his friends   17. _____

18. car my sister-in-law   18. _____

19. uniforms the team   19. _____

20. lawn the Thomases   20. _____

Practical English: A Complete Course

**Worksheet 35B: PUNCTUATION
UNIT TEST**

21. it is   _____

22. you are   _____

23. who is   _____

24. shall not   _____

25. Leo is   _____

26. should have _____

Supply apostrophes as needed in the sentences below.

27. Its hidden behind Kerrys bicycle.

28. Youre your own worst enemy.

29. Its speedometer is its problem.

30. My social security number has five *1*s in it. Theirs have none.

31. Whose books are in rooms 103 and 105? Yours.

**Worksheet 35C: PUNCTUATION
UNIT TEST**

Correct the punctuation errors in the following passage.

Entering Smiling Sam's used-car lot, Joni remembered her conversation with her father.

"Owning a car is your first real financial responsibility," he had said. "you know you'll have to take care of your own gasoline, repairs and insurance."

"I know Dad," she had replied, "And I'm sure I can handle it.

She opened the door of the red Volkswagen convertible, slipped onto the seat, and gripped the steering wheel. This moment (she would always remember Thursday, April 6, 1987.) fulfilled years of working, planning, and dreaming. The car was perfectly equipped with an automatic transmission, soft, black vinyl seats, and a stereo with F.M., a cassette deck, and four powerful speakers. Her head filled with plans trips to football games with her girlfriends, shopping sprees whenever she wanted, and quiet drives on warm summer evenings.

But there were also misgivings. She asked herself how much it would cost to support the car? How many evenings a week would she have to work at the empire theater? And what would happen to her grades in English, Biology 2, and History.

She remembered the hours she had spent poring over "Consumer Reports" and "Car and Driver". One night she had stayed up so late reading (Almost 2 00 am) that her mother grew concerned. This was the car she wanted, she was certain.

She stepped out of the car and headed for the sales office to make the purchase.

Practical English: A Complete Course

Answer Key

Chapter Two
Worksheet 2: Passive Verbs

Exercise A

1. P 2. A 3. A 4. P 5. P 6. P 7. A

Exercise B

1. Lisner kicked the ball to the right of the goalpost.
2. The police noticed the pickpocket before he escaped.
3. A friend gave Joan and Susan free tickets.
4. Hail almost destroyed the roof of the barn.
5. After the body shop painted the car, we washed and polished it.
6. The student government has presented the principal with a petition to lengthen lunch.
7. She wore new, painful, high-heeled shoes to the prom.
8. Everyone knew and understood Mr. Tweek's class rules.
9. Many Americans fly flags on national holidays.
10. Dion solved his financial problem by getting a weekend job.
11. Mr. Arnette delivered the letter too late to include their ideas in the plan.
12. The Chinese invented fireworks long before Europeans knew about gunpowder.
13. We had cleaned the house and mowed the lawn by noon Saturday, and a long, pleasant afternoon lay ahead.
14. The nurse closed the door softly as she left the room.
15. The faculty decided to postpone the assembly until after final examinations.

Worksheet 3: False Starts

1. A boy in my biology class has a mind like a salamander.
2. From now on he will behave differently.
3. Sometimes Tina hated him for being right.
4. No practice will be held tomorrow.
5. Space travel is a waste of money.
6. I don't know very much about this.
7. The menu at this restaurant gives you a choice of Chinese, Indian, or kosher food.
8. Teachers who mumble enrage me most.
9. His mind is made up.
10. I will never understand some aspects of this problem.
11. A lot is to be said in favor of his point of view.
12. Drivers who follow too closely drive me crazy.
13. A crowd of cheering fans was outside the locker room.
14. The boys are more conscious about how they dress than the girls.
15. At times she is not as thoughtful as her brother.

Worksheet 4: Overwriting

1. Using his talented foot, Henderson kicked the ball through the goalposts.
2. I left early for a week's visit with my uncle.
3. Easily maintaining his balance, Larry glided down the snow-covered hill.
4. I put away my school books, lay down on the couch, and studied the evening newspaper.
5. I spent the afternoon shopping for records at a local music store.
6. Your own home always gives the greatest comfort after you return from foreign countries.
7. The crowd in the stadium cheered when Bottoms scored.
8. To avoid being turned down, I asked Ellen's brother about her weekend plans before asking her out to a movie.
9. My observation of human nature makes me think that the idea of human progress is a myth.
10. Turn out the lights before you leave.

Chapter Two

Worksheet 5:
UNNECESSARY WORDS

Most writers occasionally allow a few unneccessary or repetitive words to slip into their writing. Sometimes these words repeat what is being said, as in "the modern farm practices *of today*" or "*true* facts." Words may also be carelessly repeated by not keeping the entire sentence in mind while writing, as in "This school is a good *school* for electronics."

EXERCISE: Revise the sentences below by crossing out unnecessary words. If a sentence does not need revision, place a C next to it in the left margin.

1. Let me refer you ~~back~~ to the first chapter.
2. Ms. Bloom circulated the book ~~around the room~~ for the class to see.
3. The rookie shortstop shows real promise ~~for the future~~.
4. The meeting will be held Tuesday at 7:00 p.m. ~~in the evening~~.
5. Her last novel is the best ~~novel~~ she has written.

C 6. The new gymnasium is extremely large and well-equipped

7. ~~Both of the two~~ Rasston twins said they will be there
8. We watched the ~~big~~, massive clouds building over the ~~level~~ plateau.
9. The pines were outlined ~~in silhouette~~ against the red ~~and scarlet~~ of the dawn.
10. His first film won several awards and is ~~besides an~~ exciting ~~film~~ to watch.
11. Modern automobiles ~~of today~~, unlike older cars ~~of the past~~, are efficient as well as comfortable.
12. What the teacher had said was not audible ~~to my ears~~, so I asked him to repeat it ~~again~~.
13. My first experience with computers was confusing, but ~~my understanding of computers is now much improved for the better~~ *now I understand them much better.*

C 14. During her freshman year Suzanne discovered boys.

15. We thought ~~in our minds~~ about how to solve the ~~puzzling~~ problem.
16. The variety of ~~different~~ television programs offered on a ~~n ordinary and~~ typical weeknight is ~~marvelous and~~ amazing.
17. He had decided to combine ~~together~~ the two leagues to achieve ~~eventually~~ better competition ~~in the long run~~.
18. The car lay upside down at the side of the highway, ~~resting on its roof~~.
19. The ~~final~~ conclusion of the play occurred in the third act when the entire cast sang ~~the song~~ "Oklahoma!"
20. We descended ~~down~~ the cliff and approached the ~~edge of the~~ riverbank.

Chapter Three

Worksheet 1

Form the plurals of regular nouns by adding S or ES.

Add ES to nouns that end in CH, S, SH, X, Z and some that end in O. Add S to all other regular nouns

EXAMPLES:	Add S	candle, candles
		ball, balls
	Add ES	witch, witches
		brush, brushes

EXERCISE A

Write the following words in their singular and plural forms

1. ax (or axe) **axes**
2. book **books**
3. punch **punches**
4. ski **skis**
5. peach **peaches**

6. pie **pies**
7. kitten **kittens**
8. wish **wishes**
9. waltz **waltzes**
10. bus **buses**

EXERCISE B

Write five words that end in CH, S, SH, X (and Z) respectively if you can think of some. Then write five regular common nouns. Form their plurals correctly.

SINGULAR	PLURAL
1. (Answers will vary.)	_____
2. _____	_____
3. _____	_____
4. _____	_____
5. _____	_____
6. _____	_____
7. _____	_____
8. _____	_____
9. _____	_____
10. _____	_____

Chapter Three

WORKSHEET 2

Form the plurals of nouns ending in Y after a consonant by changing the Y to I and adding Es.

Form the plurals of nouns ending in Y after a vowel by adding S.

EXAMPLES:	infirmary	infirmaries
	secretary	secretaries

EXAMPLES:	toy	toys
	key	keys

EXERCISE A

Write the correct plural for each of the following nouns ending in Y.

1. passkey **passkeys**
2. canopy **canopies**
3. identity **identities**
4. buoy **buoys**
5. Monday **Mondays**

6. boy **boys**
7. entity **entities**
8. relay **relays**
9. theology **theologies**
10. peculiarity **peculiarities**

EXERCISE B

Think of five more nouns that end in Y, some with a vowel and some with a consonant before the final Y. Then form the correct plurals.

SINGULAR	PLURAL
1. (Answers will vary.)	_____
2. _____	_____
3. _____	_____
4. _____	_____
5. _____	_____

Chapter Three

Worksheet 3

PART 1

Form the plural of most nouns ending in F by adding S. Form the plural of some nouns ending in F by changing F to V and adding ES.

EXAMPLES:	belief	beliefs	thief	thieves
	creampuff	creampuffs	leaf	leaves

EXERCISE A

Write the correct plural for each of the following nouns ending in F. When you are not sure, consult a dictionary. Do not guess!

1. wife **wives**
2. chief **chiefs**
3. chef **chefs**

4. muff **muffs**
5. life **lives**

PART 2

Form the plural of nouns ending in O following a vowel by adding S. Also form the plural of most musical terms that are nouns ending in O by adding an S.

EXAMPLES:	video	videos
	patio	patios
	piano	pianos

Form the plurals of nouns ending in O following a consonant by adding ES.

EXAMPLES:	hero	heroes
	torpedo	torpedoes

EXERCISE A:

Write the correct plural form of the following nouns ending in O.

1. tomato **tomatoes**
2. soprano **sopranos**
3. potato **potatoes**
4. radio **radios**

5. alto **altos**
6. tattoo **tattoos**
7. shampoo **shampoo**
8. cameo **cameos**

EXERCISE B:

Think of other nouns that end in O. Then write them and their plural form.

Chapter Three
Worksheet 4

NAME: _____ 28
DATE: _____

Irregular nouns do not follow the rules for forming plurals in Lessons II through V.

Some irregular nouns change their spelling and some remain the same in singular and in plural. You have to learn the irregular spellings; there is no rule to cover them all. Consult the dictionary in the singular form and it will give you the plural spelling also.

EXAMPLES: woman   women
            mouse   mice
            trout   trout

EXERCISE A

Write the irregular plurals of the following words. Consult the dictionary when you are unsure.

1. tooth __teeth__
2. man __men__
3. child __children__
4. foot __feet__
5. goose __geese__

EXERCISE B

Think of other irregular nouns and be sure to spell their plurals correctly. Teach them to the class tomorrow.

Chapter Three
Worksheet 5

NAME: _____ 29
DATE: _____

PART 1

Form the plurals of most foreign words as they are formed in the foreign language. When you are not sure, check the dictionary by looking up the singular form.

EXAMPLES: index   indices or indexes
            alumnus   alumni
            alumna   alumnae

EXERCISE

Write the plurals of the following words we have adopted from foreign languages. Check the dictionary when you are not sure.

1. datum __data__
2. crisis __crises__
3. appendix __appendices__
4. matrix __matrices__

PART 2

Form the plurals of most compound words by making the main part of the word plural.

EXAMPLES: brother-in-law   brothers-in-law
            maid of honor   maids of honor

REVIEW EXERCISE

Write the plural forms of all the following nouns.

1. clock __clocks__
2. contralto __contraltos__
3. sheaf __sheeves__
4. swatch __swatches__
5. infirmary __infirmaries__
6. cherry __cherries__
7. wish __wishes__
8. editor in chief __editors in chief__
9. buoy __buoys__
10. louse __lice__

Chapter Three
Worksheet 6

NAME: _____ 30
DATE: _____

PART 1

A prefix is a letter or a group of letters added to the beginning of a word to change its meaning. Sometimes it is added to a root to help form a word. The spelling of the word remains the same when the prefixes DIS, IL, IM IN, MIS, OVER, RE, and UN are added to a word.

EXAMPLES: dis + satisfied = dissatisfied
            il + luminate = illuminate
            im + mobile = immobile

EXERCISE

Correctly spell the following new words.

1. dis + appear __disappear__
2. il + legitimate __illegitimate__
3. im + mortal __immortal__
4. in + evitable __inevitable__
5. mis + shape __misshape__
6. over + ride __override__
7. re + entry __reentry__
8. un + noticed __unnoticed__

PART 2

Form a new word by adding the suffixes NESS and LY to the word's correct spelling.

EXAMPLES: sudden + ly = suddenly
            sudden + ness = suddenness

The exceptions to this rule are as follows:

1. Words ending in **Y** usually change the Y to an I before adding a suffix.

EXAMPLES: merry + ly = merrily
            stocky + ness = stockiness

2. true + ly = truly

Chapter Three
Worksheet 7

NAME: _____ 31
DATE: _____

PART 1

Drop the final E before a suffix beginning with a vowel.

EXAMPLES: hate + ing = hating
            sincere + ity = sincerity
            dominate + ion = domination

The exceptions to this rule are as follows:

1. Keep the final E after C or G when adding A or O to keep the soft G (as in ENRAGE).

EXAMPLES: outrage + ous = outrageous
            notice + able = noticeable

2. Dye + ing = DYEING so as to separate it from DYING.

PART 2

Keep the final E before a suffix beginning with a consonant.

EXAMPLES: hate + ful = hateful
            peace + ful = peaceful
            love + ly = lovely

Some of the exceptions to this rule are:

            argue + ment = argument
            true + ly = truly

EXERCISE

Form the new words indicated.

1. dis + semble __dissemble__
2. il + legible __illegible__
3. im + modest __immodest__
4. mis + spell __misspell__
5. true + ly __truly__
6. sincere + ly __sincerely__
7. virtue + ous __virtuous__
8. revere + ent __reverent__
9. feisty + ly __feistily__
10. courage + ous __courageous__

PART 1

When adding ED, ER, or ING to a one-syllable word ending in a single consonant preceded by a single vowel, double the final consonant.

EXAMPLES: man   manning   manning
           span   spanned   spanning

When adding ED, ER, or ING to two-or more syllable words ending in a single consonant preceded by a single vowel, double the final consonant if the accent is on the last syllable.

EXAMPLES: confer   conferred   conferring
           propel   propelled   propelling

EXERCISE

Form the new words indicated.

1. propel + er   _propeller_
2. answer + ed   _answered_
3. plan + ing   _planning_
4. prefer + ed   _preferred_
5. prefer + ence _preference_

6. chin + ing   _chinning_
7. occur + ing   _occurring_
8. occur + ed   _occurred_
9. propel + ing   _propelling_
10. dispel + er   _dispeller_

PART 2

When you are adding ING to a word that ends in IE, you usually change the IE to Y.

EXAMPLES: die + ing = dying
           lie + ing = lying

When you are adding a suffix that begins with a vowel to a word ending in E, you usually omit the final E.

EXAMPLES: care + ing = caring
           grate + er = grater

When you know that a word has either IE or EI in it, here are the two rules to remember:

1. Write IE when the sound is EE except after C.

   EXAMPLES: niece, piece, conceive, receipt
   EXCEPTIONS: either, neither, leisure, seize, weird

2. Write EI when the sound is not EE and especially when it is A.

   EXAMPLES: neighbor, weigh, height
   EXCEPTIONS: friend, science

EXERCISE:

Following the two rules to help with IE or EI spellings, fill in the blanks below. Note the exceptions beneath each rule!

1. r_ei_gn
2. bel_ie_ve
3. rel_ie_f
4. p_ie_ce
5. fr_ei_ght
6. w_ei_ght
7. conc_ei_ve
8. rec_ei_pt
9. ch_ie_f
10. f_ie_rce

11. pr_ie_st
12. s_ei_ze
13. sc_ie_nce
14. _ei_ther
15. n_ei_ther
16. l_ei_sure
17. ach_ie_ve
18. c_ei_ling
19. rec_ei_ve
20. cash_ie_r

Most people go to the dictionary to check the spelling of a word or to find a word's meaning. Although you have already consulted a dictionary many times for one of these reasons, you may review some information to help you find words more quickly. What else does a dictionary offer you?

1. A vocabulary of abbreviations.
2. Biographical information on famous people.
3. A pronouncing guide to common English names.
4. A vocabulary of rhyming words.
5. A list of spelling rules.
6. Guides to punctuation, capitalization, and italicization.

While not all dictionaries offer precisely the same information, the dictionary could possibly be your most useful reference book. It's useful not only for school, but for your job as well, if it involves any writing. Lesson V will familiarize you with what your class or personal dictionary offers.

Today's lesson will also review looking up words in alphabetical order, a useful skill to practice at any age.

Open to the Table of Contents of the dictionary you will be using in class or at home. Tell in which *section* of the dictionary you would look for the following information:

1. How to pronounce **morecambe**.

   (Answers will vary by dictionary, will most often be found at entry.)

2. What the abbreviation ct stands for.

   _____

3. What the symbol ⬤ stands for.

   _____

4. Who Lysimachus was.

   _____

5. How to address a letter to a baron's son.

   _____

6. How to say Yvette and what nationality it originates from.

   _____

7. How to add the suffix **an/ ian** to geographical and personal names ending in **-a**.

   _____

8. Whether to capitalize the name of a breed of dog (airedale terrier or Airedale terrier).

   _____

9. A picture of a mordent or a mortarboard. _____

10. The origin of the word **morale**. _____

*This exercise may also be used as practice for going from the Table of Contents to the precise section and page to find the specific information.

Guide words are the words that appear at the top of each dictionary page in heavy, dark print. The word on the left tells the first word that appears on that page, and the word on the right tells the last word that appears on that page. Looking at the guide words, you can see quickly whether the word you are looking for falls somewhere between them.

Check the words that would fall on a page with the guide words **manufacture** and **mare**.

1. marjoram
2. march ✓
3. manuscript ✓
4. maritime
5. mariner

6. maraud ✓
7. maraschino ✓
8. maraca ✓
9. margrave
10. marginal

Chapter Four   NAME: _____ 47
WORKSHEET 6A: DATE: _____
CAPITALIZATION

When you look up a word in the dictionary, you will sometimes see the abbreviation *cap.* in italics before one of the definitions of the word. This means that when the word is used in this way, it must be capitalized.

EXERCISE

Look up the following words and use them in good sentences that show their meanings. If a word can be both capitalized and uncapitalized, use both forms in sentences.

1. god / *God*   4. locofoco / *Locofoco*   7. republican / *Republican* 10. finn / *f*
2. Swiss   5. son   8. spinet
3. lord / *Lord* 6. democrat / *Democrat*   9. terrier

EXAMPLE: shawnee

The Shawnee are an Algonquin tribe living in most of the states east of the Mississippi.

1. (Answers will vary.)
2.
3.
4.
5.
6.
7.
8.
9.
10.

Chapter Four   NAME: _____ 49
Worksheet 7: SYLLABICATION   DATE: _____
AND WORD FORMS

EXERCISE A Syllabication:

When you are writing or typing, it is especially helpful to know where to divide a word if you must at the end of the line. The dictionary divides the words into syllables by using dots (·). Do not confuse these with hyphens (-). Look up the following words and write them in syllables with dots in between.

1. newsworthy news·wor·thy
2. oxidation ox·i·da·tion
3. pathetic pa·thet·ic
4. reconnaissance re·con·nais·sance
5. bruise bruise
6. contradictoriness con·tra·dic·to·ri·ness
7. dragonfly drag·on·fly
8. penultimate pen·ul·ti·mate
9. syllabication syl·lab·i·ca·tion
10. journalism jour·nal·ism

EXERCISE B: Different Forms of Words:

The dictionary can be helpful when you aren't sure which form of a word to use. For example, some verbs are not as regular as WALK, WALKED, HAVE WALKED. Take the verb SWIM. If you are writing, "He has s_____ m across this lake many times," but you aren't sure which form to use, consult your dictionary under SWIM. The entry will begin with the word SWIM followed by SWAM and then SWUM. The last entry (either the second or third) is the irregular verb form you need to use with HAS or HAVE, the past participle form of the verb. English has several verbs that are misused often because of their irregular past participles. Another way the dictionary can help you is in determining the comparative and superlative forms of adjectives. Most adjectives work this way: SMALL, SMALLER, (for comparing two), SMALLEST (for comparing three or more). Some adjectives, however, are like GOOD. When you look up GOOD, you will find BETTER and BEST listed immediately after the word GOOD usually. The dictionary also provides irregular comparative and superlative forms for some adverbs like WELL (BETTER and BEST).

Chapter Four   NAME: _____ 50
Worksheet 7B: SYLLABICATION   DATE: _____
AND WORD FORMS

EXERCISE B (continued)

Look up the following word forms in your dictionary:

1. past tense of SHRINK shrank
2. superlative form of CURLY curliest
3. comparative form of BAD worse
4. superlative form of GOOD best
5. past tense of BURST burst
6. past participle of BURST burst
7. past participle of BEGIN begun
8. past participle of RING rung
9. past participle of DRINK drunk
10. past tense of KNOW knew

Chapter Ten   NAME: _____ 132
Worksheet 4: MENU WORD QUIZ   DATE: _____

Write the letter of the correct English word next to the French word that means the same thing. Not all of the English words will be used.

1. d beurre
2. g cafe
3. i chocolat
4. m escargot
5. a a la carte
6. t jambon
7. p fromage
8. j creme
9. bb saute
10. ff vin rouge
11. w oeuf
12. y poisson
13. aa poulet
14. k dessert
15. o filet
16. r glace
17. b agneau
18. h champignon
19. x oignon
20. y legume
21. l entree
22. f boeuf
23. e bifteck
24. c aperitif
25. ee vin blanc
26. z potage
27. q gateau
28. cc veau
29. dd viande
30. s haricot

ENGLISH WORDS

a. separate price for each menu item
b. lamb
c. appetizer
d. butter
e. steak
f. beef
g. coffee
h. mushroom
i. chocolate
j. cream
k. dessert
l. main dish of a meal
m. snail
n. turkey
o. slice of meat with bone removed
p. cheese
q. cake
r. ice cream
s. bean
t. ham
u. potato
v. vegetable
w. egg
x. onion
y. fish
z. soup
aa. chicken
bb. fry in sauce
cc. veal
dd. meat
ee. white wine
ff. red wine

Chapter Eleven

Worksheet 2B: SENTENCE FRAGMENTS—EXERCISE

NAME: _____ 137

DATE: _____

9. Since Phil was my father's boss at the plant.

_____

_____

10. Although I had never written a resume before.

_____

_____

Indicate whether the following are sentences (**S**) or fragments (**F**).

__S__ 11. I might attend a community college.

__F__ 12. While I am working full-time.

__F__ 13. My friend doing both at the same time.

__F__ 14. If I decide to go on to a four-year college

__S__ 15. All my community college credits will be credited.

Chapter Eleven

Worksheet 3: SENTENCE FRAGMENTS—EDITING EXERCISE

NAME: _____ 138

DATE: _____

(Correction of fragments will vary)

The passage below contains both complete sentences and sentence fragments. Correct any sentence fragments that you find by making them into complete sentences. You may attach fragments to complete sentences (if the new sentence makes sense), add words to fragments, omit words in fragments, or change verb forms in fragments

(F) The new County Community Services Department is hiring this month. Weatherization engineers, crew foremen, designers, installers. When I heard about the new positions, I went down to the department for some information.

(F) Sending me out to watch a weatherization crew at work **(F)** Seemed to be a good way to "tell" me about the job. One worker was having a time **(F)** The front door, which was rotting at the bottom. Another one added aluminum siding to cover cracks in the wall. Because the team also caulked the edges of doors and windows I could tell that this would cut down on heating costs. I could see the value of learning this kind of work.

(F) My junior-high camp buddy, Joe, replacing a broken window on one side of the house

(F) When he told me he was learning a lot by working with his crew everyday.

As I looked in the window, I saw a worker covering the water heater with a blanket A fairly simple way to conserve heat and therefore, money

(F) As I heard the crew foreman talking to the owner of the house I realized that this was being done as a county service. **(F)** Being done free for someone who couldn't afford to weatherize his home.

I made my decision that afternoon. **(F)** Definitely the job for me right now. **(F)** Earning money, learning useful skills, and helping people who can't help themselves.

Chapter Eleven

Worksheet 4A: SENTENCE FRAGMENTS—UNIT QUIZ

NAME: _____ 139

DATE: _____

Indicate **S** for sentence or **F** for fragment.

__S__ 1. The students enjoyed the speaker.

__F__ 2. Since the apples are not ripe.

__F__ 3. Her horse loping around the ring.

__F__ 4. Because they made me feel welcome.

__S__ 5. When I had to go, they didn't try to stop me.

__S__ 6. She was strapping her skis to the van.

__F__ 7. Then Dan shouting angrily at her.

__F__ 8. A $75.00 pair of running shoes.

__F__ 9. Spaghetti and ravioli with meatballs.

__S__ 10. Running on foggy or rainy days is great.

Convert each fragment below into a complete sentence. Use each method at least once: add a part needed, omit a word or words, or change a verb form.

1. The dog barking wildly at the fire engine.

_____(Student responses will vary.)_____

2. The eerie midnight call of the foghorn.

_____

_____

3. When the pine tree crashed through our garage roof.

_____

_____

4. The red wagon wheels lending themselves to the new go-cart.

_____

_____

Chapter Eleven

Worksheet 6: RUN-ONS EXERCISE

NAME: _____ 143

DATE: _____

(student responses will vary.)

Correct the following RUN-ONS by changing them into well-structured sentences by one of the four methods explained on Worksheet 5. Use each method at least once.

1. I was the main witness, I saw the car drive through the store window.

_____

_____

2. I've got a new job after school it's helping me to organize my time.

_____

_____

3. We planted a vegetable garden the first five years we lived here, we haven't had one in two years because of the baby.

_____

_____

4. Mark is a very intelligent young man he hides his intelligence from his co-workers

_____

_____

5. My grandfather swears like a sailor my dad never says a swear word.

_____

_____

Indicate **S** for sentence and **RO** for run-on.

__S__ 6. The Rodgers' old Jeep doesn't run the way it used to

__RO__ 7. Reed's handwriting is illegible, I advised him to buy a typewriter or a printer for his computer.

__RO__ 8. That job has a lot of appeal for me the wages, the working conditions, and the vacations are fine

__S__ 9. Because he used to be my boyfriend we are still good friends

__S__ 10. Although he used to be my boyfriend we are still good friends

Worksheet 7: RUN-ONS
EDITING EXERCISE

Chapter Eleven   NAME: _____ 111   DATE: _____

(Student answers will vary.)

The passage below contains many run-ons. Convert them into well-constructed sentences using the four methods from Worksheet 5.

(RO) Terry laughed at herself all the way home from her first afternoon at work, the ad had said, "Advancement depends on individual skill, and speed. Many opportunities. Call now." There certainly had been many opportunities, but her speed and skill hadn't exactly made her a prime candidate for advancement.

(RO) What a chuckle her family would have over her first job she had found the ad, answered it, interviewed, been hired, and worked an afternoon. She'd done all that in two days, (RO) forty-eight hours. What exactly was she doing to earn her tuition for beauty school she knew her family would ask her.

(RO) Would you believe tying flies for a fish-and-tackle shop? Gray Gnat and Royal Coachman and Yellow Humpy were her specialties today, who knows what tomorrow will bring?

(RO) Maybe this job would be useful after all, she was still chuckling as she envisioned the hairdo of the future, complete with Gray Gnat and Royal Coachman and Yellow Humpy on top.

Worksheet 8B: RUN-ONS
UNIT QUIZ

Chapter Eleven   NAME: _____ 146   DATE: _____

(Student answers will vary.)

Correct any RUN-ONS in the passage below. Use several different methods of converting them into good sentences.

(RO) The use of computer technology is rapidly changing the movie industry, the coming of sound to the movies was an earlier and equally significant technological advancement.

(RO) In 1926 Warner Brothers produced *Don Juan*, a silent film with accompanying musical score on records the picture used a device called a Vitaphone. But talking pictures really started in 1927 when Warner Brothers used the Vitaphone to produce *The Jazz Singer*, (RO) starring Al Jolson. This picture revolutionized the movie industry, just think, someday we'll read about how films like *Star Wars* and *Tron* were early examples of an equally significant movie revolution. Since I missed the "talking revolution," this is a revolution I want to be a part of.

Worksheet 9: RUN-ONS
CUMULATIVE TEST

Chapter Eleven   NAME: _____ 147   DATE: _____

(Student answers will vary.)

Correct the sentence fragments and run-ons in the passage below. Then rewrite the passage, making sure that your version is composed of well-constructed sentences.

Teenagers have an interesting diet. It seems to fall into four main food categories: french (F) fries, Whoppers or Big Macs, nachos, and large Cokes. Large Cokes being the basic liquid (F) in the teenager's diet. Injected intravenously when they are hospitalized or their growth will be stunted.

(F) In addition to large Cokes, which are ingested at any time during the day or night with or (RO) without solid food. The french fries are the main solid staple in the teenager's diet without this one element of especially greasy potato strips the meal or snack is incomplete in nourishment.

The Big Mac or Whopper is a dessert, added whenever the spending money allows. The (RO) Big Mac or Whopper is most often a snack, eaten between "meals" which Mom prepares these super burgers supply the real vitamins and minerals to counteract the ones Mom (F) thinks are in the eggplant parmagiana. And the fresh spinach and mushroom salad.

(F) Nachos supplying the finishing touch to any meal or snack with their tantalizing (RO) prepared-weeks-in-advance cheese sauce. A substitute may be made when warm nachos and cheese are not a possibility nacho chips or Doritos sometimes sour cream (F) and onion potato chips. To add vegetables and dairy foods and make the folks happy.

There's no doubt about it. When you question a teenager about his diet, you can be sure (F) that it will cover fully the four basic food groups. Large Cokes, Big Macs or Whoppers, french fries, and nachos.

Worksheet 11A: SUBJECT-VERB
AGREEMENT—STANDARD AGREEMENT
& COMPOUND SUBJECTS EXERCISE

Chapter Eleven   NAME: _____ 150   DATE: _____

Underline the verb that agrees with the subject.

1. The leaves on the birch tree (is, <u>are</u>) falling.
2. My allowance, together with my birthday money, (<u>is</u>, are) enough for these new Nikes.
3. Either Barbara or Elaine (<u>is</u>, are) going to be elected president of the club.
4. Our scout den and our leader (is, <u>are</u>) going to attend Scout Jamboree.
5. Almost all the sailboats in the race (has, <u>have</u>) capsized at least once before.
6. Neither the bing cherry tree nor the peach trees (bears, <u>bear</u>) fruit anymore.
7. The teacher, as well as the principal, (<u>attends</u>, attend) every student-parent conference.
8. Sardines or cheese (<u>is</u>, are) an excellent source of calcium.
9. Running or Jazzercising (<u>is</u>, are) going to be my daily exercise during the school year.
10. Whoppers or Big Macs (fills, <u>fill</u>) me up at lunchtime.

Complete the following sentences using only *present* tense verbs. Remember to make the verb agree with the subject. Make the sentence at least *ten* words long. Use no past tense verbs.

1. Jackie and Barr *(Student answers will vary.)*
2. Baseball or football
3. My dad, as well as my uncles,
4. Either Shannon or Gina

Worksheet 11B: SUBJECT-VERB   DATE: _____
AGREEMENT—STANDARD AGREEMENT
& COMPOUND SUBJECTS EXERCISE

(Student answers will vary.)

5. The majority of the voters _____

_____

6. That photo of my fourth-grade classmates _____

_____

7. Neither my record nor my tapes _____

_____

8. The coaches or the managers _____

_____

9. Neither the losers nor the winner of the race _____

_____

10. Ralph, together with Carmen and Kathy. _____

_____

Underline the verb that agrees with the subject

1. I wish that you (was, <u>were</u>) my partner

2. We (was, <u>were</u>) swimming when he arrived.

3. He said that you (is, <u>are</u>) going with him.

4. They (was, <u>were</u>) witnesses to the crime

5. John answered the doorbell that they (was, <u>were</u>) ringing

Worksheet 13A: SUBJECT-VERB   DATE: _____
AGREEMENT—INDEFINITE PRONOUNS
EXERCISE

Underline the verb that agrees with its subject in number. Remember that singular verbs end in S (unlike singular nouns).

1. Each of the players (<u>receives</u>, receive) his own uniform before the season begins.

2. All of the Pirates (is, <u>are</u>) in Mrs. Garfield's second-grade class.

3. Both of my cousins (serves, <u>serve</u>) the ball like a pro.

4. Many of the applicants (has, <u>have</u>) years of working experience.

5. It occurred to the manager that one of his employees (<u>was</u>, were) failing to lock up his station at night.

6. Some of the luggage (<u>seems</u>, seem) to be missing from the ship.

7. How could it be that nobody (<u>wants</u>, want) to chair the committee for the dance?

8. None of the apples (was, <u>were</u>) damaged in packing.

9. Few of the magicians (performs, <u>perform</u>) as dramatically as Adam does.

10. One of the worst situations (<u>was</u>, were) created by both girlfriends appearing at the dance.

11. Every bike and skateboard (<u>is</u>, are) to be locked up in the storage room during the meeting.

12. Everyone in the family album (<u>looks</u>, look) like my grandfather.

13. Somebody in that supermarket (<u>was</u>, were) yelling for assistance

14. I found that neither of the boys (<u>laughs</u>, laugh) loudly enough for that part in the play

15. I'll bet that anyone in this crowd (<u>cheers</u>, cheer) with more enthusiasm than he does.

Worksheet 15A: SUBJECT-VERB   DATE: _____
AGREEMENT—SUBJECT FOLLOWING
VERB EXERCISE

Underline the verb that agrees with its subject in number. Remember to look ahead to find the singular or plural subject (when it is not at the beginning), and make the verb agree with it.

1. The boys on the soccer team (does, <u>do</u>) need a physical examination before the season begins.

2. It (<u>doesn't</u>, don't) look like rain

3. Here (is, <u>are</u>) the problems I created for the math quiz

4. (Who's, <u>Who are</u>) your favorite runners of the marathon?

5. All of us (does, <u>do</u>) the selecting of the team name.

6. Why (is, <u>are</u>) Casey and Chad on the same team?

7. Onto the field (<u>runs</u>, run) my little brother whenever he can

8. There (seems, <u>seem</u>) to be several under-14's without a team this season.

9. Not one of the players (<u>kicks</u>, kick) with her left foot on this team

10. How (does, <u>do</u>) those coaches make it to a 5:00 practice?

11. When (is, <u>are</u>) the trophies going to be awarded?

12. In the bleachers (<u>sits</u>, sit) my former junior-high coach

13. (Here's, <u>Here are</u>) my fiancee and her parents.

14. Why (<u>does</u>, do) he insist on protesting every call in his team's baseball games?

15. There (<u>happens</u>, happen) to be one very qualified referee for this soccer game

Worksheet 15B: SUBJECT-VERB   DATE: _____
AGREEMENT—SUBJECT FOLLOWING
VERB EXERCISE

Read the following sentences carefully. If the subject and verb are in agreement, write C for correct in the space provided. If the subject and verb are not in agreement, write I for incorrect. Then change the verb to agree with its singular or plural subject.

___C___ 1. Below the old bridge waits a hungry troll.

___I___ 2. There's the golden eggs the goose laid.

___I___ 3. Here are my favorite book of fairy tales.

___C___ 4. Why does the fairy tale always have magic in it?

___C___ 5. There is neither a handsome prince nor an ugly frog in this tale

___I___ 6. What are the story "Snow White and the Seven Dwarves" about?

___I___ 7. There's many reasons why I still read fairy tales and folk tales.

___C___ 8. Why do those children watch cartoons instead of reading a book?

___I___ 9. On my bookshelf wait my favorite collection of Grimm's fairy tales

___I___ 10. Here's the story and the song of "Puff, the Magic Dragon."

Chapter Eleven

Worksheet 17A: SUBJECT-VERB AGREEMENT—SPECIAL SUBJECTS EXERCISE

NAME: _____ 160

DATE: _____

Each sentence below contains a collective noun. Write the collective noun in the space provided. Then write whether it is singular or plural in that sentence—**S** or **P**.

1. _**assembly**_ _S_ The assembly seems to be really enjoying the magician's performance.

2. _**mob**_ _P_ The mob behave as totally different people than they are in a different situation.

3. _**jury**_ _S_ The jury is giving its unanimous verdict at this time.

4. _**committee**_ _S_ I want to know when the committee reaches its final step in the process.

5. _**cast**_ _P_ Do you think the cast are practicing their parts when they are not at rehearsal?

6. _**flock**_ _S_ The flock is heading south, flying directly over my valley.

7. _**class**_ _S_ Mrs. MacLellan said this class was the liveliest junior class she had ever taught.

8. _**herd**_ _P_ Why are the herd scattering wildly in so many different directions?

9. _**crowd**_ _S_ The crowd is moving toward the front of the school.

10. _**team**_ _S_ The team is practicing with a visiting Canadian team today.

Chapter Eleven

Worksheet 17B: SUBJECT-VERB AGREEMENT—SPECIAL SUBJECTS EXERCISE

NAME: _____ 161

DATE: _____

Underline the correct form of the verb. Remember these are special subjects!

1. Physics (<u>uses</u>, use) all the knowledge and concentration that I have

2. My scissors (cuts, <u>cut</u>) very badly since you trimmed your dog's hair

3. *The Three Musketeers* (<u>was</u>, were) the book I reported on to the class.

4. Do you think economics (<u>helps</u>, help) you make financial decisions that will affect your career?

5. She can't believe that mathematics (<u>stretches</u>, stretch) her ability to figure things out.

6. The new pants nearly (falls, <u>fall</u>) off me when I take a breath.

7. Dad's pliers (is, <u>are</u>) supposed to be in his toolbox.

8. My father even said that *The Adventures of Buckaroo Bonzai* (<u>was</u>, were) a hilarious and entertaining film.

9. These tweezers (needs, <u>need</u>) to be replaced

10. "Those shorts (looks, <u>look</u>) like something the cat dragged in," said my mother.

Chapter Eleven

Worksheet 19A: SUBJECT-VERB AGREEMENT—EDITING EXERCISE

NAME: _____ 164

DATE: _____

The passage below contains many errors in subject and verb agreement. In the space above the words correct any errors in agreement that you find. Only correct the verb forms. Only use the present tense of the verb.

Greta would never forget ther first experience with summer camp. She arrived a day late. The camp for advanced Girl Scouts ~~were~~ **was** a mistake in the first place. She had only joined the scout troup a month ago, and the troup ~~was~~ **were** not serious scouts. Peaches and Mary Lou ~~was~~ **were** her best buddies in the den, but neither Peaches nor Mary Lou were able to come to Camp Chickaronda.

"You girls ~~is~~ **are** really going to like it here," promised the Camp Director, "and here ~~is~~ **are** fun plus learning for all!"

Inwardly Greta groaned. "Why ~~don't~~ **doesn't** my mother ever involve me in these decisions?" she asked herself. "Oh, well!" she picked herself up. "Some of this experience ~~have~~ **has** to be fun!"

"This morning each of you girls ~~select~~ **selects** a buddy," announced Mrs. Chirpini "Greta, one Treetopper or two Pathfinders ~~is~~ **are** still available for your buddy. How ~~do~~ **does** one of these girls look to you?"

Greta grimaced as she selected Treetopper Tina. Trying to make conversation later, she asked Tina, "~~What's~~ **What are** your favorite songs?"

Chapter Eleven

Worksheet 19B: SUBJECT VERB AGREEMENT— EDITING EXERCISE

NAME: _____ 165

DATE: _____

Tina quickly replied, "Anchors Aweigh" ~~are~~ **is** my all-time favorite! Every girl in my troop back home ~~know~~ **knows** all the words. In fact, anyone who ~~don't~~ **doesn't** can't join the troop."

Greta grunted that she couldn't believe everyone in the troop ~~love~~ **loves** that song. Then she added to be friendly, "Both the scouts and your counselors ~~is~~ **are** very good at singing."

That evening after the Treetoppers sang their rendition of "Anchors Aweigh," Greta delighted them all with "The One-Eyed-One-Horned-Flying-Purple-People-Eater." Thirty Girl Scouts are all very impressed with Greta's historical knowledge of the Fifties.

306   Practical English: A Complete Course

Worksheet 20A: SUBJECT-VERB AGREEMENT—UNIT QUIZ

Chapter Eleven   NAME: _____ 166   DATE: _____

Read the following sentences carefully. Write **C** for correct if the subject and verb are in agreement. Write **I** for incorrect if the verb does not agree with its singular or plural subject. Then write the correct form of the verb in the *present* tense above the existing verb.

C 1. Sports interest Adam much more than mathematics does.
I 2. The senior class has decided on their various costumes for Homecoming Week.
C 3. *Star Wars* was my favorite film for a long time.
I 4. *Raiders of the Lost Ark* are at the top of my list too.
C 5. Either he or his sisters are supposed to cook the dinner.
I 6. Where's the bicycles?
C 7. Neither the students nor the teacher knows the answer to that one.
I 8. *Aesop's Fables* are on my bookshelf.
I 9. Through the pine trees blow a lovely breeze.
C 10. Every fork, and spoon is washed
C 11. The family are going to take turns having Grandma come to visit.
C 12. The counselor, as well as the psychologist, is evaluating the boy's problem.
I 13. Is there first-class seats on this plane?
C 14. The flock were attacking each other.
I 15. A bike with hand brakes are what I want for my birthday.
C 16. No one in my club wants to be the president.
C 17. Brandon and Stephen fight all the time.
I 18. Some of the vegetables is rotten.
C 19. Few of the dockworkers support the drive to strike.
I 20. The dresses on the top rack is beautiful.

Worksheet 20B: SUBJECT-VERB AGREEMENT—UNIT QUIZ

Chapter Eleven   NAME: _____ 167   DATE: _____

Read the following passage. Correct any errors in subject and verb agreement that you find.

Greta grinned as she read the entries in her journal from Camp Chickaronda:

"A shower to these campers ~~are~~ **is** a tin can with holes in it and a pitcher of water."

"~~There's~~ **There are** buddy burners to cook on and sit-upons to sit on."

"'Smiles' or 'Hiking Along' ~~are~~ **is** the tune for each day."

"Each girl in the different troops ~~have~~ **has** to carry a compass at all times."

"Neither the mosquitoes nor the cabin's yellowjacket ~~have~~ **has** any resting time."

"The book I brought to read, *Favorite Ghost Stories,* ~~are~~ **is** really scary."

"Mumps ~~are~~ **is** going around Cabin 3 like wildfire."

"The Kirby family ~~takes~~ **take** turns writing letters to Kelly so she won't be homesick."

"My mother ~~don't~~ **doesn't** have any idea what she has gotten me into here. I wish you was here, Mom, so I could show you."

"Neither my Treetopper buddy nor my Trailblazer swimming buddy ~~have~~ **has** ever been away to camp before."

"All of the girls in Tina's troop do know the words to a weird song."

"I can't wait till my mother asks me, '~~Who's~~ **Who are** your new friends from Camp Chickaronda?'"

"Under my bed ~~is~~ **are** so many spiders and ants I check my shoes each morning."

"~~Here's~~ **Here are** a couple of drawings I made after the nature hike."

"My tweezers are my most valuable possession here. They've removed most of the cabin floor from my feet."

"Two weeks ~~seem~~ **seems** like a long time to be at camp but it's passing quickly. I think I might come back next year."

Worksheet 21: SUBJECT-VERB AGREEMENT—CUMULATIVE TEST

Chapter Eleven   NAME: _____ 168   DATE: _____

Directions: Read the following passage. Correct any errors in subject and verb agreement that you find.

I have to drive too, and the posters along the freeway ~~is~~ **are** making it a bit difficult for me to concentrate these days. ~~Who's~~ **Who are** all these beautiful girls telling me to drink milk and listen to the radio and come to Tahoe? Even mumps ~~have~~ **has** a billboard pushing for the MMR vaccination. All of these ideas are great if you don't mind being blasted all the time with visual images.

I think television advertising must be getting too expensive. *Hill Street Blues* ~~are~~ **is** attracting a lot of viewers, and the stations are charging a lot for commercial spots. Companies are getting smart. An ad in the church bulletin or a mini-poster on a parking meter is reaching many people for less money. Advertisers may be trying new forms of advertising, but two-thirds of the advertising is still done on prime-time television.

Worksheet 23B: PRONOUN-ANTECEDENT AGREEMENT—EXERCISE

Chapter Eleven   NAME: _____ 171   DATE: _____

Indicate proper agreement of pronoun and antecedent by underlining the correct choice in each of the following sentences.

1. Any man who climbs that mountain is risking (<u>his</u>, their) life foolishly.
2. Several women at my dad's trucking company handle (her, <u>their</u>) rigs better than many of the men.
3. A superior student, such as you have described, would not jeopardize (<u>his</u>, their) future by cheating on a final exam.
4. Someone in Sharon's P.E. class left (<u>her</u>, their) shoes on the court.
5. Either of the boys might have held (<u>his</u>, their) breath for another minute.
6. Everyone at baseball camp agreed to send (<u>his</u>, their) buddy a school picture in the fall.
7. I find no one who has tattooed (<u>himself</u>, themselves) in here.
8, 9, 10. Each bulb in my garden surprises me as (<u>it</u>, they) (produce, <u>produces</u>) (<u>its</u>, their) own special surprises.

Construct from the following phrases sentences with at least ten words. Be sure that the sentence contains at least one pronoun that refers to the antecedent given. (Remember that verbs in the present tense must also agree with their subject.)

EXAMPLE: A few of the boys
          A few of the boys forgot *their* towels

11. Either Mary or Sylvia
12. Both of my best friends
13. No one in this dormitory
14. Every person that I talk to
15. Anyone who wants to

(Student responses will vary.)

Chapter Eleven   NAME: _____ 172
Worksheet 24A: DATE: _____
PRONOUN-ANTECEDENT AGREEMENT
EDITING EXERCISE

The passage below contains many errors in pronoun-antecedent agreement. Some sentences are completely correct. Make any corrections that you believe are necessary to make the pronoun agree with its antecedent.

Koko, a 230-pound female gorilla, is learning to communicate with people and other animals. Both of Koko's parents came from Cameroon in West Africa, and their daughter is now a Californian. No one in ~~their~~ *his* right mind would believe Koko can actually talk but maybe one could allow ~~themself~~ *himself* to believe that Koko can communicate.

Dr. Francis Patterson is a psychologist who has been working with Koko for thirteen years. A psychologist is a person who concentrates ~~their~~ *his* study on why people behave as they do. Dr. Patterson, however, works with Koko and several other animals instead of with people. For the past thirteen years, Dr. Patterson has been teaching Koko American Sign Language, a system of hand and body movements to help someone who is deaf communicate ~~their~~ *his* feelings. Everybody who "talks" this way is expressing ~~their~~ *his* ideas by "signing."

One day Koko signed that she wanted a cat. Dr. Patterson gave Koko a cat picture and a toy cat, but neither did ~~their~~ *its* job of making Koko happy. Koko had someone else in mind, and she knew ~~them~~ *him* when she saw ~~them~~ *him*. Dr. Patterson gave Koko a little tailless kitten, whom Koko named All Ball. Every day held ~~their~~ *its* special times when Koko would hold All Ball, petting him and signing "Soft good cat." When All Ball was killed by a car, Dr. Patterson told Koko. Both of them shared their silent sorrow, and then Koko made a crying sound.

Chapter Eleven   NAME: _____ 173
Worksheet 24B: PRONOUN-   DATE: _____
ANTECEDENT AGREEMENT
EDITING EXERCISE

Soon after, Koko received a new kitten she named Lips. Anyone can see for ~~themselves~~ *himself* how Koko loves Lips, as she cradles him and signs "Love, love, love."

Each of Koko's visitors comes away with ~~their~~ *his* own personal amazement. Some say Koko is smart because she lived at Stanford University for awhile and learned from ~~their~~ *its* doctors. Some sign their own messages to Koko, and she signs back. But everyone agrees that in ~~their~~ *his* mind, Koko is a most unusual gorilla.

Chapter Eleven   NAME: _____ 174
Worksheet 25A: SENTENCE   DATE: _____
FRAGMENT, RUN-ON, SUBJECT-VERB
AGREEMENT, AND PRONOUN-ANTECEDENT
CUMULATIVE TEST

Correct the sentence fragments and run-ons; add words where necessary. Correct the subject and verb agreement, being sure to keep the verb in the *present* tense. Correct the pronoun and antecedent agreement.

Have you played any Trivial Pursuit games lately? If you have, you know the topics that ~~makes~~ *make* (F) people test their knowledge of sports records. The most pinch hits by a (F) lefthander. The most errors by a short stop in a nine-inning game. The fewest assists by a (F) catcher in a full season.

Some records are really important. (F) Like Roger Maris' sixty-one home runs in 1961 and Hank Aaron's 755 career homers. Joe DiMaggio's fifty-six game hitting streak in 1941 ~~are~~ *is* the toughest record to break. In major league baseball's 109-year history, no one of the batters ~~have~~ *has* hit safely in more than forty-four games.

Either Joe DiMaggio of the New York Yankees's sports clips or Joe DiMaggio of the coffeemaker commercial ~~are~~ *is* the strong batter and centerfielder. (RO) He was thirteen years in the majors, Joe rarely struck out. Joe, as well as his fans, ~~are~~ *is* still amazed at his 361 home runs and only 369 strikeouts. We ~~was~~ *were* all Joe's fans in the forties.

(RO) Every one of your parents ~~remember~~ *remembers* Joe's fifty-six game hitting streak, it began on May 15, 1941, with a single. There ~~was~~ *were* lots of good hitters with a twenty-game hitting streak. ~~Who's~~ *Who are* the hitters whose streaks went higher?

Chapter Eleven   NAME: _____ 175
Worksheet 25B: SENTENCE   DATE: _____
FRAGMENT, RUN-ON, SUBJECT-VERB
AGREEMENT, AND PRONOUN-ANTECEDENT
CUMULATIVE TEST

Wee Willie Keeler of the Baltimore Orioles held the record at forty-four games in 1897. Joe's team in 1941 also remember their individual reactions when Joe broke the record.

Mathematics ~~are~~ *is* really important when it comes to recordkeeping. Fifty-six games is the record, no one has matched it yet. (RO) When DiMaggio singled and doubled against the Cleveland Indians. (F) The end came the next night against Cleveland. The third-baseman throwing him out twice. Nobody in ~~their~~ *his* right mind wanted to see Joe stop hitting safely. Someone I know said that he saw Joe go zero for three, with a walk that night.

Each number in the record books ~~are~~ *is* impressive for Joe DiMaggio. During the streak Joe batted .408 and hit fifteen home runs, he batted in fifty-five. (F) For the full season he hit .357 with thirty homers and 125 RBI. The Yankees winning the pennant easily.

Maybe someday a player will break Joe's record, but don't hold your breath for ~~them~~ *him* to appear.

Chapter Eleven   NAME: _____ 178
Worksheet 27A: PRONOUN CASES: DATE: _____
NOMINATIVE EXERCISE

Underline the correct pronoun in each sentence.

1. My brother and (I, me) rode our dirt bikes to the creek.
2. (They, Them) and my grandparents drove a camper out to San Francisco.
3. Frank and (he, him) play golf every Saturday morning.
4. It was either Gina or (she, her) who interviewed the applicants.
5. The new secretary in our office must be (he, him).
6. When (she, her) and her mother went shopping, they met her dad for lunch.
7. I hoped it was (she, her) who called to invite me to the dance.
8. The supervisors and (we, us) are going out to lunch today.
9. Glenn and (I, me) will change the goldfish's water.
10. I answered the phone by saying "This is (she, her)," when someone asked for me.
11. Ed and (I, me) want to get a paper route to earn extra money.
12. The umpire and (we, us) disagreed on several major calls.
13. I can't believe it was (he, him) who caused that fight at work.
14. Only Evan and (I, me) have been to Yosemite.
15. It had to be (they, them) who planned that surprise party at the office.
16. The neighbors and (we, us) are planning a Fourth of July barbecue.
17. David is confident that the winner will be (he, him).
18. The Endicotts and (we, us) always have a Christmas dinner together.
19. Shannon and (he, him) are good friends.
20. It was (we, us) you heard coming in late last night.

Chapter Eleven   NAME: _____ 182
Worksheet 29A: PRONOUN CASES: DATE: _____
OBJECTIVE EXERCISE

Select an object pronoun from the list below for each blank in the following sentences.

me, her, him, us, them   **(Student responses will vary.)**

1. Did you see her and _____ at the movies?
2. The elephant liked _____ to spray water on him.
3. Will you please leave _____ a message?
4. A counselor named Barbara gave _____ a five-week-old kitten.
5. I named _____ Boo-Kay after my counselors, Boo (Barbara) and Kay.
6. When I saw _____ in the jars of formaldehyde, the two-headed creatures frightened me.
7. He shared his secret with _____ and _____.
8. Leave Elaine and _____ alone.
9. That dress fits both Ginger and _____ .
10. I remember _____ and _____ very well.

Underline the correct pronoun in each sentence.

11. Don't tell mother and (he, him) your surprise.
12, 13. Please share with Peter and (she, her) that story you told (I, me).
14. Ask Erica and (she, her) all your questions about the car.
15, 16. Should mother offer (he, him) and (I, me) any more dessert?
17. Give your father and (I, me) a fair chance.
18. Mrs. Harrison's interview panel included Jerry and (I, me).
19. Mayor Feinstein presented the astronaut and (she, her) keys to the City of San Francisco.
20. You ought to check with the Sakeleris family and (they, them) before you all arrive for a swim.
21. Don't tell Gary and (I, me) we're too late!

©1987 J. Weston Walch, Publisher   *Practical English: A Complete Course*

Chapter Eleven   NAME: _____ 183
Worksheet 29B: PRONOUN CASES: DATE: _____
OBJECTIVE EXERCISE

22. The trees towered above the children and (he, him).
23. I received letters from Aunt Louise and (she, her) last week.
24. Place your confidence in the president and (he, him).
25. The reward will be divided among the boys and (we, us).
26. The guitarist sat down between Tony and (I, me) at the table.
27. The principal had special awards for (we, us) and (they, them).
28. For (he, him) you spent all that money?
29. The menu was chosen by all of (we, us) campers.
30. Mrs. Surges doesn't live far from the Millers and (they, them).

Chapter Eleven   NAME: _____ 184
Worksheet 30: PRONOUN CASES: DATE: _____
POSSESSIVE EXPLANATION & EXERCISE

POSSESSIVE PRONOUNS

When a pronoun is used to show ownership, it must be a possessive pronoun.

Pronouns that are used as adjectives to modify nouns are:

my, you, his, her, its, our, your, their

(Notice that *its*, as in *its collar*, has no apostrophe.)

I gave you *my* collection.
The priest ate at *our* house.

Pronouns that are used as subjects of verbs, as objects of verbs, as objects of prepositions, or as words in the predicate are:

MINE, YOURS, HIS, HERS, ITS, OURS, YOURS, THEIRS

(Notice that none of these pronouns have an apostrophe.)

Mine has only three tires. (Subject of verb)
Dad created *his* from scrap metal. (Object of verb)
I mailed my book with *hers*. (Object of preposition)
I'm sure this is *yours*. (Word in predicate, Predicate adjective)

Underline the correct pronoun in each of the following sentences.

1. This model must be (yours, your, your's).
2. Who destroyed (its, it's) tunnel?
3. I know this is (her, hers, her's) novel from English class.
4. She found his paper with (theirs, their's, they'res).
5. I destroyed (your's, yours, your) very carelessly.
6. (Mine and hers, Mine and her's) were the ones Mrs. Iversen chose.
7. It seemed that (their's, theirs, they'res) were the sloppiest projects.
8. She denied (his and her, his and hers) charges of stealing.
9. Something is wrong with (ours, our's, our).
10. (Theirs and ours, Their's and our's) are the closest to the originals.

Worksheet 31A: PRONOUN CASES
EDITING EXERCISE
NAME: _____ 185
DATE: _____

Correct any pronoun errors you find in the passage below.

their
Truckers have a variety of physical problems due to ~~there~~ job. Consider a typical trucker's day: driving for ten hours; eating greasy eggs and home fries; smoking cigarettes, maybe a couple of packs; lifting heavy boxes onto and off the truck. This professional lifestyle contributes to the chronic backache, pulled muscles, and heart disease of ~~it's~~ *Its* rank. Most truckers say at least one of these problems is ~~their's~~ *theirs*.

they
Lucky are ~~them~~ now, because Gijs VanOort of the Biokinetics Research Laboratory at Temple University has designed the first individualized fitness program for truckers. *I* My brother and ~~me~~ know a few truckers for Pepperidge Farm, and an uncle of ~~our's~~ *ours* is going to join them soon. The drivers and ~~him~~ *he* found out that they will be testing the program on the job. The plant managers and ~~them~~ *they* will evaluate the exercise program according to its merits.

ours
The truckers and their employers say, "An exercise program is already ~~our~~." One *she* trucker said when the guys and ~~her~~ unload the truck, they get as much exercise as a player in a nine-inning ball game. And, she added, none of the equipment she uses is *hers* ~~her's~~.

its
But VanOort has seen that the cycle of long, sedentary hours of driving followed by ~~it's~~ opposite spell of strenuous and sudden exertion is the problem. VanOort's program *him* was devised carefully by a team of drivers and ~~he~~. The truckers receive barbells, an *these* exercise mat, and a log book. It must be ~~them~~ that they use in their brisk walking, stretching, and strength-building exercises.

Worksheet 31B: PRONOUN CASES
EDITING EXERCISE
NAME: _____ 186
DATE: _____

they
I went with my uncle to talk to some drivers about the program. My uncle and ~~them~~ exercised in the trailer and in the parking lot. "Where is your nephew?" one of the guys asked

he   *He*   *I*
"This is ~~him~~," my uncle said, pointing at me. "~~Him~~ and ~~me~~ are both going to be *ours*   *he* truckers, and it looks like more than a job will be ~~our's~~. It might be ~~him~~ that needs this job more than I do," he teased, pointing at my bulging stomach.

them
This job could be healthier for the truckers than I thought. VanOort intends to help the managers and ~~they~~ combat heart disease by adding smoking cessation, stress *Its* management, and nutrition counseling to his plan. ~~It's~~ value is obvious and has a lot of *me* appeal to my uncle and ~~I~~. I keep wondering about why VanOort chose Pepperidge Farm *they* to work with. Was it ~~them~~ who snacked on "goldfish" too often, or were the heaviest *theirs* loads of little treats ~~their's~~?

Worksheet 32: PRONOUN CASES
UNIT QUIZ
NAME: _____ 187
DATE: _____

Underline the correct pronoun in each sentence.

1. Bill and (<u>I</u>, me) sing in the church choir.
2, 3. Last summer my teacher took (he, <u>him</u>) and (<u>I</u>, me) out to lunch.
4. We mailed Elizabeth and (she, <u>her</u>) some candy.
5. Mary Ellen and (<u>he</u>, him) were the first teenagers I knew.
6. I don't think that Cheryl and (<u>she</u>, her) will go to the ranch.
7. Set it down beside Dan and (he, <u>him</u>).
8, 9. I wrote (he, <u>him</u>) and (she, <u>her</u>) a long and dramatic letter.
10. That hamburger and fries are (<u>ours</u>, our's).
11, 12. The new police officers are (<u>he</u>, him) and (<u>she</u>, her).
13. It must have been (<u>they</u>, them) who followed us.
14. Paul and (<u>we</u>, us) are going out to dinner.
15. It could have been Carson, Gary, Darin, or (<u>he</u>, him).
16, 17. That hat isn't (<u>hers</u>, her's); (<u>hers</u>, her's) is an Orioles hat.
18. I assumed it was (<u>he</u>, him) who took her to the movie.
19, 20. It should be Zac and (<u>she</u>, her), but it might've been Josh and (<u>he</u>, him)

Use the following groups of pronouns correctly in sentences. Write the sentences on the back of this page. Mark **D.O.** if the group is the object of the verb, **I.O.** if the group is the indirect object of the verb (to whom or for whom), and **O.P.** if the group is the object of a preposition. Mark **S** if the group is the subject or a nominative pronoun in the predicate. Use at least one of each (**D.O., I.O., O.P., S, S in Pred.**)

1. Jason and me	6. the explorers and them
2. Mother and I	7. him and her
3. the teacher and her	8. Cindy or he
4. the leaders and me	9. the directors and they
5. Mylo and he	10. my friend and me

(Student responses will vary.)

Worksheet 33A: PRONOUN CASES
EDITING TEST
NAME: _____ 188
DATE: _____

The following passage contains pronouns in the nominative, objective, and possessive cases. Some are used correctly; some are not. Make corrections where they are necessary.

Verna held several jobs as a teenager, but there was one in particular that she will never forget. It must have been the ad that beckoned her friend and her to call. "The *yours* opportunity of a lifetime is ~~your's~~," read the small print "Individual advancement. No experience necessary."

me   *we*
Just the job for Sharon and ~~I~~ thought Verna, as she called her friend. "It must be ~~us~~ they are looking for!" announced Verna

it's yours
"Well, if it's a loser, ~~its~~ all ~~your's~~!" replied Sharon.

she
Sharon waited for Verna to come by; then Verna and ~~her~~ drove together to *its* investigate this job of a lifetime. The building was a big conglomeration of offices; ~~it's~~ elevator took the girls to the tenth floor. A receptionist rather sourly greeted some other *them* girls and ~~they~~ and told them they could see the personnel director in a few minutes.

It was actually a group interview with questions directed at the other young people *them*   *she* and ~~they~~. "I think the personnel director *and* the business owner are ~~her~~. And I think she *us* is going to hire her, her, him, and ~~we~~," whispered Verna to Sharon.

she she he
"Just think." Sharon replied, "my co-workers will be ~~her, her, him,~~ and you!"

Worksheet 33B: PRONOUN CASES　DATE: _____
EDITING TEST

"Remember, kids, when you hear a voice on the phone, ask if it is Mrs. _____ .
she
Then she will say 'Yes, this is ~~her~~.' And then you can present ~~you're~~ sales pitch for the
your
magazines."

I
"Sharon and ~~me~~ will really do well at this job. I hope it is ~~her~~ who gets the phone next
she
me
to mine! Please give the first section of phonebook pages to Sharon and ~~I~~!"

After the first call, the thrill was gone for Verna. The realization came to Sharon and
her
~~she~~ at about the same time; they were calling people at their homes and interrupting
their
~~there~~ days to try to sell magaines. The rudeness of the customers settled the girls' minds;
this was no way to earn some spending money. At least, it wasn't theirs.

me
"Between you and ~~I~~," whispered Verna on the way out the door at there noon break,
I
"some other workers and ~~me~~ aren't coming back this afternoon."

"But what about giving two weeks' notice?" asked Sharon, who wasn't sure she could
them
go along with Verna and ~~they~~ on walking out.

"As far as I'm concerned, no one told me I was going to be invading people's privacy
in this job. I'm happy to have made my last call!"

Worksheet 35A: OTHER PRONOUN　DATE: _____
PROBLEMS—EXERCISE

Underline the correct pronoun in each of the following sentences below. Be ready to
explain your choice.

1. Dan Lee can't do the whole job (<u>himself</u>, hisself).
2. Annabelle will never forgive (<u>herself</u>, her self).
3. Please let me know (<u>who</u>, whom) votes for me.
4. Share this reward with (<u>whoever</u>, whomever) helped you rescue Brandy.
5. They can't believe they eliminated (theirselves, <u>themselves</u>) from the competition by their poor attitude.
6. Sharon swings the golf club much better than (<u>I</u>, me).
7. Can you scale that tree faster than (<u>he</u>, him)?
8. Leslie is as strong as (<u>she</u>, her).
9. I like anyone (<u>who</u>, whom) laughs at my jokes.
10, 11. Someone (<u>who</u>, whom) takes (<u>himself</u>, hisself) too seriously is Mr. Clarence.
12. That man has absolute authority over everyone (<u>who</u>, whom) works in his department.
13. Can you show me (<u>who</u>, whom) she is?
14. I love to be with a baby (<u>who</u>, whom) laughs.
15. Mr. Edwards nearly lost (<u>himself</u>, hisself) in his project last year.
16. I can't remember (who, <u>whom</u>) I sent the check to.
17. (Who, <u>Whom</u>) are you recommending for the supervisory position?
18. (Who, <u>Whom</u>) do you think he will appoint?
19. I'm more uncoordinated and awkward than (<u>she</u>, her).
20. To type as well as (<u>they</u>, them) is my ambition.

Worksheet 35B: OTHER PRONOUN　DATE: _____
PROBLEMS—EXERCISE

Choose from the following pronouns to correctly complete the phrases below:

I, me, myself　　　　　　　　we, us, ourselves
she, her, herself　　　　　　they, them, themselves
he, him, himself　　　　　　who, whom

21. I brought m**yself** a bicycle
22. to w**hom** you wrote
23. **Who** left you here alone?
24. I sang more loudly than he____
25. She cried h**erself** to sleep.
26. w**hom** you were waiting for
27. Jack wrote the letter all by h**imself**
28. for w**hom** you designed the dress
29. She kicks the ball harder than he____.
30. Mother bakes cakes much better than he____.

Worksheet 36: OTHER PRONOUN　DATE: _____
PROBLEMS—EDITING EXERCISE

Correct any errors you find in the use of reflexive pronouns WHO and WHOM and
pronouns in comparison structures.

Starting a new job is a bit like going back to school the first day each year. I can
I
remember how my brother and ~~myself~~ used to look forward to the posting of the class
lists on the office windows the Friday before Labor Day. He could read those lists faster
I   myself
than ~~me~~, but I would be right behind. Now I find ~~me~~ wondering who will be working in my
new office. I wonder who my new co-workers will be; who will be the ones I'll talk to?

whoever
Discovering who the teacher was used to be important; now I feel that ~~whomever~~ is
my supervisor will determine a lot about my job. If he's someone who basically likes
himself
~~hisself~~, he'll be easier to work for than an unsure, unconfident person. My brother always
had an adjustment problem, no matter who the teacher was. I seemed to adapt better
he   whoever
than ~~him~~ regardless of ~~whomever~~ the teacher was.

Wondering how much I had forgotten over the summer was another worry, and I
seem to find myself worrying about my job skills now. I know I am a person who can get
who
the job done, no matter what it is, but knowing ~~whom~~ will evaluate your success helps to
himself
lighten the concern. My brother said he worried ~~hisself~~ sick over his qualifications and
who
abilities the night before his job started, but his supervisor said no one could tell ~~whom~~
the new employee was by his performance.

whomever
He told me to look forward to meeting ~~whoever~~ I will work with, to enjoy figuring out
whoever my new supervisor is, and to show whoever is interested just how qualified I
really am for this new position. I wish he had given me all that advice before the first day
of school—any year!

Chapter Eleven   NAME: _____ 196
Worksheet 37A: OTHER PRONOUN DATE: _____
PROBLEMS—UNIT QUIZ

Underline the correct pronoun that reflects standard usage in each of the sentences below.

1. Allen, (who, <u>whom</u>) I selected, will be the new pizza delivery person.

2. She respects anyone (<u>who</u>, whom) can explain his position politely.

3. He covered (<u>himself</u>, hisself) with tattoos.

4. I can take dictation as well as (<u>she</u>, her).

5. The coach says you can swing the bat harder than (<u>he</u>, him).

6. I knew the answer as well as (<u>she</u>, her).

7. (<u>Who</u>, Whom) is to have the final say on the matter?

8. (<u>Who</u>, Whom) do you think should be chosen to represent our business on the council?

9. Kathy and (<u>I</u>, myself) will go to the store for you.

10. I injured (<u>me</u>, myself) when I fell through the rickety stairs.

11, 12. Tom is taller than (<u>I</u>, me), but I weigh more than (<u>he</u>, him).

13, 14. I can eat as much pizza as (<u>she</u>, her) but I am more sensible than (<u>she</u>, her).

15. For (who, <u>whom</u>) are you waiting?

16. I will call (<u>whoever</u>, whomever) is to blame into my office.

17. Mr. Mayer can't tell (<u>who</u>, whom) enjoys his stories more, the parents or their children.

18. The clerk can't be sure (who, <u>whom</u>) the security police pointed out to watch.

19. The bike worked harder at climbing the road than (<u>I</u>, me).

20. The last chairman of the board, (who, <u>whom</u>) I introduced you to, wants to be invited to the awards ceremony.

Chapter Eleven   NAME: _____ 197
Worksheet 37B: OTHER PRONOUN DATE: _____
PROBLEMS—UNIT QUIZ

(Student responses will vary.)

Complete the following sentences with a standard usage pronoun.

21. I know I can dive better than _____ **(nom.)**

22. Mrs. Lanier bakes pies as well as _____ **(nom.)**

23. Adam hurt **(reflex.)** while he was carving the soapstone.

24. **(nom.)** do you think will take his place over vacation?

25. Richie, **whom** I remember from the sixth grade, has just returned from Saudi Arabia

26. Ian is confident that he is a better swimmer than _____ **(nom.)**

27. Josh shoots those marbles more accurately than _____ **(nom.)**

28. I have confidence in **(reflex.)** that I can complete the job.

29. The checker **whom** I like best always remembers my name.

30. The shopper **who** is pleased with our service always returns.

Chapter Eleven   NAME: _____ 198
Worksheet 38A: DATE: _____
SENTENCE ERRORS—UNIT TEST

Make any corrections needed in the passage below:

                                                  are
Yosemite National Park is really a wonderful family vacation spot. There ~~is~~ facilities
                                                                     are
for every travel style. Even folks not wanting to be inconvenienced by nature ~~is~~ exposed
                                                                          has
to the beauty of all that surrounds them. The hotel visitor, as well as the camper, ~~have~~
                               are
several dining facilities and some ~~is~~ very affordable.

                                           are
Accommodations for every vacationer ~~is~~ to be found there. Both the Ahwahnee
                                                                    (F)
Hotel and the Yosemite Lodge offer comfortable rooms and a pleasant dining room. For

those used to travelling in style and with a minimum of discomfort. An older person who
doesn't   **himself finds**
~~don't~~ want to sleep on the ground or be out in cold weather chilling ~~themselves find~~ the
                                                              sounds
hotel or lodge very comfortable. If neither the hotel nor the tent style ~~sound~~ right, then a
                                                            (F)
vacationer may try housekeeping camp. Which is a compromise between the two
              What are
extremes. ~~What's~~ the facilities that are considered "in between?" The group of

housekeeping campers prefer a kind of open hut with bench beds and a cement floor
(RO)   **select**
More adventurous campers in the valley ~~selects~~ from a half dozen campgrounds within
                                                     (F)
the park and several on the road into the park, there is even a group camp area. One
                                              (F)
reason Yosemite is so ideal. The vacationers having choices.

              is
Just as mumps ~~are~~ inescapable for most people, so is nature for the Yosemite
                 (F)
vacationer. Only not nearly as painful. The comfortable visitor may ride the shuttle buses
                his   **his**   **his**
around the park ~~their~~ shorts ~~is~~ ~~their~~ clothing in summer ~~their~~ pants and ski jackets in
winter.

Chapter Eleven   NAME _____ 199
Worksheet 38B: DATE: _____
SENTENCE ERRORS—UNIT TEST

                                                                        himself
When the bus stops at a scenic area, each visitor decides for ~~themselves~~ whether to
        his
continue ~~their~~ ride or whether to get out and take a look around. About three-fourths of
                                                                (F)
the riders choose to walk to see the nearby site. Because someone whom can walk
                                                            (F)
one-third of a mile and back can see Lower Yosemite Falls. Just a trickle in the summer
                                                          are
but a full waterfall in the spring. Mirror Lake and Vernal Falls ~~is~~ only one mile down the
                                                      (F)
hiking trail from the shuttle bus stop. Buses coming every ten to fifteen minutes to let out
                                                      doesn't
and pick up passengers. One family I know feels the shuttle ~~don't~~ quite accommodate all
their   (RO)
~~its~~ individual styles. The grandparents take the Yosemite bus tour to see Half Dome, El
                                                        (RO)
Capitan, Bridalveil Fall, and more, there's even a Glacier Point Tour. The parents ride the

shuttle, sometimes the grandparents and them ride together.

The daughter Kim and the son Keith travel by foot or horseback. It's usually them

that are leading the hikers or riders in their nature discovery. In fact, one summer when
                                                       she whom
Keith couldn't go, Kim was hired as a guide. It was ~~her who~~ you might have had as a
        your   (RO)
horseback guide on ~~you're~~ two-hour trail ride to beautiful Mirror Lake. As you can see.

nature is inescapable, you can work for it or enjoy it in comfort

                           his
(RO) Every camper can find ~~their~~ kind of place to eat at Yosemite, a restaurant offering

prime rib and a fast-food place for pizza. Keith and Kim's family are my dining experts,

because they are a family whom I've seen eat in every place or style. Grandma and
                                                       he **she**   **eat**
Grandpa prefer their dinner at the hotel, but ~~him~~ and ~~her~~ occasionally ~~eats~~ a croissant
                                              (F)
                                     her
sandwich at the deli. To Grandpa and ~~she~~, good food and good service still very

important on vacation

Chapter Eleven

NAME: _____ 200

Worksheet 38C:
SENTENCE ERRORS—UNIT TEST

DATE: _____

(20) Keith and Kim have a different perspective on dining, they consider a hamburger or a

~~F~~   those   their
large frosty cone a gourmet lunch. Because ~~them~~ kids are used to cooking on ~~there~~

                                           she
Coleman Keith cooks Dinty Moore Beef Stew better than ~~her~~, but Kim fixes Hormel's

                he
Chili as well as ~~him~~. They assure me that you can eat the way you want to in Yosemite.

              are
      There ~~is~~ few drawbacks to Yosemite as a vacation spot, but preparation, in addition

        helps (20)
to common sense, ~~help~~. Be sure to make reservations well in advance, unless you are a

gambler, if you are, you might find Reno or Tahoe more the spot for you.

Chapter Twelve

NAME: _____ 205

Worksheet 2A: COMMON-WORD
USAGE ERRORS—EXERCISE

DATE: _____

Underline the correct word, the one that is considered standard English usage for each
sentence below.

1. Philip will (accept, except) the prize for his brother.

2. Please (advice, advise) us on the best venture to start for Junior Achievement.

3. The rising cost of a permanent and a hair coloring treatment have had a serious (affect, effect) on my mother's beauty salon business.

4. The Concert Choir members were (all ready, already) to make their first appearance by the end of September.

5. "(All right, Alright)," she responded. "I'm coming as fast as I can."

6. The neighborhood boys worked (all together, altogether) to save money for the go-cart.

7. There are many (allusions, illusions, delusions) to the Bible in literature.

8. Ninety percent of the (alumna, alumnae, alumni) of the women's college are in attendance.

9. Jackie and Barr strolled (among, between) the pigeons at the park.

10. I've never seen Mr. Barsuglia so (angry at, angry with) his supervisors before

11. How do you plan to (affect, effect) any changes in a department with all old employees and no young blood?

12. The first group seems to be (all ready, already) finished with their term projects

13. The steam from the teakettle gave the (allusion, illusion, delusion) that we were at the foggy coast.

14. How much (advice, advise) do you think I need on a job I've already done before?

15. My mother shouted, "This is (all together, altogether) too late to be coming home on a school night!"

16. The two brothers divided the inheritance from their parents equally (among, between) them

---

Chapter Twelve

NAME: _____ 206

Worksheet 2B: COMMON WORD-
USAGE ERRORS—EXERCISE

DATE: _____

17. I have noticed a large (amount, number) of errors in your typing this week.

18. How can you think of (accepting, excepting) Ben from the party and inviting all his best friends?

19. He forced his (allusion, illusion, delusion) of authority upon his co-workers until he was judged incompetent to hold his position.

20. Is that boy an (alumna, alumnae, alumnus) of a community college or a technical school?

Fill in each blank with one of the confusing words from the sentences above

1. No one e **xcept** _____ her high-school friends really knew the kind of person she was.

2. We are a **lready** _____ too late to enter the concert now

3. This touched-up photograph gives my complexion the i **llusion** _____ of being lovely.

4. When I dyed my hair last month, the last e **ffect** _____ I expected was green!

                                            (or alumna)
5. In this company is there not one a **lumnus** _____ of Marina Technical Institute?

6. There was a huge n **umber** _____ of soccer players on the field.

7. I cannot a **ccept** _____ the reward money for doing something I had to do.

8. Mrs. Sorensen wants us to e **ffect** _____ that change in the operating procedure immediately.

9. What e **ffect** _____ can the new foreman possibly have on your raise?

10. My father is a **ltogether** _____ too tense and too much a perfectionist to ever coach a young team.

Chapter Twelve

NAME: _____ 210

Worksheet 4A: COMMON WORD-
USAGE ERRORS—EXERCISE

DATE: _____

Underline the correct word, the one that is considered standard English usage, for each
sentence below.

1. The kitten is sleeping (beside, besides) the basket of pears

2. The baked potato (burst, busted) when we cooked it in the microwave oven

3. The generator in the hydroelectric plant is (broke, broken)

4. Baby Brendan (can hardly, can't hardly) climb up on the couch

5. (Can, May) I invite a guest to your party?

6. He (could of, could've) finished the marathon if he had paced himself better

7. I wish I had (hanged, hung) those pictures by myself.

8. The farmer said his new calf (drownded, drowned) in the flash flood.

9. How dare you (imply, infer) that I cheated?

10. That (broke, broken) old lawn mower is all I have to work with

11. Sharon must (leave, let) home early to take her sisters to day care

12. You certainly (can, may) walk well on those stilts after practicing

13. The teacher (implied, inferred) from the boy's short story that he had a drug problem.

14. Close the gate before you (leave, let) the colt out of the corral.

15. Three men were (hanged, hung) from this tree on April 13, 1880.

Chapter Twelve   NAME: _____ 211

Worksheet 4B: COMMON WORD-   DATE: _____
USAGE ERRORS—EXERCISE

Fill in each blank with one of the confusing words or groups of words from the sentences on the previous page.

1. B**esides** _____ me, there are nineteen girls coming to the slumber party.

2. That Vista Cruiser is b**roken** _____ again; this time it's a head gasket.

3. Don't b**urst** _____ my paper bag; it has my model rocket in it.

4. You m**ay** _____ audition at a convenient time, even if it is not on the regular schedule.

5. The boys c**an** _____ h**ardly** _____ wait until their Uncle Bill arrives from Florida.

6. She c**ould've** _____ swum across Lake Tahoe if she had coated her body with Vaseline for warmth.

7. I could tell right away that my dad h**ung** _____ the new light, because it wasn't centered.

8. How could you i**nfer** _____ such a negative meaning from what your father said?

9. L**eave** _____ me in the movies with my cousins.

10. No Boy Scouts d**rowned** _____ this summer at any of their local summer camps.

11. Come place the baby b**eside** _____ me on the couch

12. You c**an** _____ stay awake until dawn, but do you really want to?

13. Wyoming h**anged** _____ all of its convicted criminals in the old Western days.

14. The newspaper article i**mplied** _____ that Northgate caused the riot at the Ygnacio game.

15. Only those who were at the game could i**nfer** _____ that the newspaper was definitely biased in its coverage of the riot at the ball game.

16. There were f**ewer** _____ kindergarten students last year than this year.

17. Our family used l**ess** _____ gas and electricity this winter because of our wood-burning stove.

Chapter Twelve   NAME: _____ 215

Worksheet 6A: COMMON WORD-   DATE: _____
USAGE ERRORS—EDITING EXERCISE

The following letter contains several common word-usage errors. Some of the words we studied are used correctly. Correct the errors above the words.

June 1, 1987

Dear Brian,

    I ~~can't~~ **can** hardly wait to see you, and it's going to be ~~alright~~ **all right** to stay with your family all summer. I hope ~~your~~ **you're** looking forward to it as much as I am. I'll let you know whether I'm arriving on Saturday or Sunday as soon as I can.

    ~~Who's~~ **Whose** room are we going to sleep in? I don't care as long as I can ~~lay~~ **lie** down and sleep somewhere. ~~Can~~ **May** I borrow your brother's bike, or does he let anyone use it? I feel ~~like~~ **as if** I ~~could of~~ **could've** asked you all this stuff on the phone, but my mother was already angry ~~at~~ **with** me for the ~~to~~ **too** long conversation.

    Do you really think we should take your dad's advice and not go job hunting together? I don't mean to imply that he's not wise, but we've always shared things ~~among~~ **between** just ourselves and I don't think looking for a job together will ~~effect~~ **affect** our chances that much. ~~Alright~~ **All right**, the worst that could happen is that we won't find a job for either of us; but

---

Chapter Twelve   NAME: _____ 216

Worksheet 6B: COMMON WORD-   DATE: _____
USAGE ERRORS—EDITING EXERCISE

we won't be drowned in our sorrow. We'll convince one of ~~them there~~ **those** business owners to hire us, even if it's just to fix equipment that's ~~broke~~ **broken**. Besides, I'm suffering from no delusions about summer work. It is ~~all together~~ **altogether** possible we'll do something we never ever dreamed of; my cousin ~~hanged~~ **hung** wallpaper one summer. And now he's an ~~alumni~~ **alumnus** of Georgia Tech.

    ~~Sit~~ **Set** this letter somewhere you will remember, so you'll answer it.

Your buddy,

Joe

Joe

Chapter Twelve   NAME: _____ 217

Worksheet 7A: COMMON WORD-   DATE: _____
USAGE ERRORS
UNIT QUIZ

Underline the correct choice of the standard English usage in each of the following sentences below.

1. My friend Ed is studying the (affect, <u>effect</u>) of aspirin on the nervous system.

2. (Can, <u>May</u>) we buy our lunch at Lawrence Hall of Science?

3. Shirley doesn't want to (advice, <u>advise</u>) me concerning the separation.

4. I remember the (allusion, <u>illusion</u>, delusion) that the revolving light on the metal Christmas tree produced.

5. One of the graduation speeches really (<u>affected</u>, effected) me

6. There is no one (accept, <u>except</u>) Andrew who would return the empty ice cream carton to the freezer.

7. The mythological (<u>allusions</u>, illusions) in poetry are numerous

8. My aunt is an (<u>alumna</u>, alumnus) of Bryn Mawr.

9. The mirrors were (hanged, <u>hung</u>) on the walls of the living room.

10. The counselor (<u>implied</u>, inferred) that I was not community college material.

11. What could you (imply, <u>infer</u>) from the teacher's notes on your child's behavior?

12. How many outlaws were (<u>hanged</u>, hung) without a trial?

13. His shirt looks (<u>like</u>, as) an old cleaning cloth.

14. Will you (leave, <u>let</u>) me go to Day on the Green?

15. (<u>Let</u>, Leave) go of my kitten now.

16. I shouted (like, <u>as if</u>) my life depended on it

17. I packed the camping equipment (<u>all together</u>, altogether) in the garage.

18. Is it (<u>all right</u>, alright) if I ride to school with Ray tomorrow?

19. The patient had (<u>delusions</u>, illusions) that he would die of germs if someone touched him

314   Practical English: A Complete Course

Worksheet 7B: COMMON WORD-USAGE ERRORS
UNIT QUIZ

DATE: _____

20. The ring bearer should stand (beside, besides) the flower girl.

21. There are (fewer, less) applicants for this position this time.

22. Daniel is an (alumnus, alumni) of two state technical schools.

23. Everyone gave the new boys (advice, advise) on the first day of school.

24. "(Whose, Who's) your new friend?" my father asked.

25. (Among, Between) the two of us, we ought to be able to get the job done.

26. I found the engine for the go-cart (between, among) the many items for sale in the classified section.

27. (Beside, Besides) my brother, there is not one worthwhile mechanic in the class.

28. She (can hardly, can't hardly) get out of bed by 7:30 every morning to get to her 8:00 class.

29. Briana (could have, could of) come to the luncheon if she had wanted to.

30. My mother (drownded, drowned) her sorrows in a cup of coffee.

31. What do you have to say about (this, this here) broken lamp?

32. The birthday boy cried when his balloon (busted, burst).

33. I could (lay, lie) in the sun for hours if you'd leave me alone.

34. Mrs. Erickson didn't know (weather, whether) to believe him or not.

35. How can you (set, sit) here all night and watch television?

36. (Their, They're) the ones I saw entering the building last night.

37, 38. Go (to, too) the doctor's office before it's (to, two, too) late.

39. I know *Annie* was (your, you're) favorite musical play.

40. I don't believe I have a (broke, broken) steering wheel

Worksheet 8A: COMMON WORD-USAGE ERRORS
EDITING TEST

DATE: _____

The following passage contains many common word-usage errors. Some of the words in this unit are used correctly. Correct the errors above the word.

       could
Barbara ~~couldn't~~ hardly wait to attend her ten-year high-school reunion. At first, it
         alumna
was hard for her to accept the fact that she was now an ~~alumnus~~ of ten years. She still
    could've
looked as if she ~~could of~~ graduated just last year. In fact, when people saw her and her
   all together
children ~~altogether~~, they often asked her whose children she was babysitting.

         whether
    She wondered ~~weather~~ the alumni attending would include most of her best friends
Besides
~~Beside~~ Judy, she hadn't been in touch with most of her high-school friends. In fact, those
                    too
letters between Judy and her had had ~~to~~ many months in between this year. She
                   sit
determined not to just let those letters ~~set~~ on her desk anymore. Friends sometimes

became angry with each other over a misunderstanding not cleared up or an

unanswered question. She also wondered about that special guy she didn't marry
                   broken
Would her heart be ~~broke~~ when she saw him with someone else?

         affect
    How would it ~~effect~~ her life to be with all her best friends again? Would being all
             illusion
together present the ~~allusion~~ of being carefree? This ~~here~~ daydreaming would

accomplish nothing, Barbara thought to herself. I'm acting like a teenager, whether I am

one or not

Worksheet 8B: COMMON WORD-USAGE ERRORS
EDITING TEST

DATE: _____

    The Friday night of Reunion Weekend soon arrived, although Barbara thought she
would've burst   **All right**
~~would of busted open~~ if it had taken any longer. "~~Alright~~, everyone, welcome to the Class
              their
Class of '77's ten-year reunion!" greeted ~~there~~ class president, Jim Guenther. "Who's

going to have a good time?" "We are!" yelled almost everyone

All right!   **You're**   **as**
    "~~Alright~~!" responded Jim, "~~Your~~ in for music ~~like~~ you used to know it. I'd advise you

to take advantage of the good weather and swim. I don't want any of my friends
drowned   **you're**
~~drownded~~ at this reunion, so use your good sense and ~~your~~ bound to have a great time! I
    imply   **let**
don't mean to ~~infer~~ that you'd use anything but good sense, of course. Let's just ~~leave~~

each other have a good time, and I won't need to lay down any rules."

                whose   **among**
    "Whew!" said Barbara, ~~who's~~ conversation ~~between~~ her friends Judy, Karen, and

Linda, had been minus illusions and full of friendship renewed. "To think of all those

pictures of Jim I hung on my bedroom wall eleven years ago. I can honestly say now that I
                    couldn't've (or could not have)
made the right decision ten years ago. I ~~could not of~~ been sure unless I'd seen him again!"

Worksheet 10A: ADJECTIVE USAGE
EXERCISE

DATE: _____

Write the comparative and superlative forms of the adjectives given below:

		Comparative	*Superlative*
1.	simple	simpler	simplest
2.	lonely	lonelier	loneliest
3.	short	shorter	shortest
4.	angry	angrier	angriest
5.	calm	calmer	calmest
6.	beautiful	more beautiful	most beautiful
7.	magnificent	more magnificent	most magnificent
8.	awful	more awful	most awful
9.	generous	more generous	most generous
10.	childish	more childish	most childish

Indicate a correctly written sentence with a C and an incorrectly written sentence with an I. Circle the error(s) in the incorrect ones. Write above the sentence any needed word(s).

       can
_I_ 11. Katie (can't) hardly type with that sprained wrist.
       any
_I_ 12. Don't you have (no) time left? (Haven't you any time left?)

_I_ 13. This (here) lunch break is too short

_I_ 14. I asked for that (there) piece of spice cake.

_C_ 15. I will hardly finish before the supervisor checks my progress

_I_ 16. Is working at the bank (more) harder than working for the store?

_C_ 17. Do you like Coke or Pepsi better?
       This   **drives**
_I_ 18. (These) kind of assignment (s) really (drive) me crazy

_C_ 19. Of the two dinner specials, I like the salmon with potatoes and peas better

Chapter Twelve   NAME: _____ 225
Worksheet 10B: ADJECTIVE USAGE DATE: _____
EXPLANATION

__I__ 20.   That is the (most) calmest baby I have ever seen

Underline the correct word in each sentence.

21.   Have you seen (those, them) children?

22.   I wish you'd send (those, them) boys to the office.

23.   Kyle didn't say (anything, nothing) about his surgery.

24.   I (will, won't) hardly make it to work on time.

25.   Of my two cousins, Lynne is the (better, best) swimmer.

26.   (That, That There) book is the one I've been looking for.

27.   (This kind, These kind) of directions is impossible to comprehend

28.   Give me (that, that there, them, those) paychecks.

29.   She swears she told (anyone, no one) the answers.

30.   I didn't see (anyone, no one) come home after 10:00 p.m.

31.   Jackie is the (more athletic, most athletic) of the two sisters.

Chapter Twelve   NAME: _____ 230
Worksheet 12A: ADVERB USAGE DATE: _____
EXERCISE

Write the comparative and superlative forms of the adverbs given below:

		Comparative	*Superlative*
1.	soon	sooner	soonest
2.	late	later	latest
3.	early	earlier	earliest
4.	quickly	more quickly	most quickly
5.	slowly	more slowly	most slowly

Indicate a correctly written sentence with a C and an incorrectly written sentence with
an I Circle the error(s) in the incorrect ones. Write above the error(s) the correct
form(s).

__C__ 6.   Janine looks angry with her mother.

__C__ 7.   Sharon stared jealously at her boyfriend and the strange girl.

__C__ 8.   Those rotten apples smell horrible.

__I__ 9.   My police dog smells so (horrible) *horribly* he can't search for missing people
anymore.

__I__ 10.   My dad barbecues so (good) *well* I entered his name in a chef's contest.

__C__ 11.   I am not feeling very well at the moment

__C__ 12.   She answered the phone so well I thought she was an older person.

__I__ 13.   My brother punts (bad) *badly*

__C__ 14.   Gary passes so badly that the captain changed his position.

__C__ 15.   Mickey is a real friend.

Chapter Twelve   NAME: _____ 231
Worksheet 12B: ADVERB USAGE DATE: _____
EXERCISE

__I__ 16.   I asked Shana to come over because she is (real) *really* nice to me at school.

__C__ 17.   This is a really friendly kitten.

__I__ 18.   She came in last because she ran so (slow) *slowly*

__I__ 19.   We finished that job (easy) *easily* in ten minutes.

__I__ 20.   The garlic smelled so (strong) *strongly* I had to cover my nose.

Indicate whether the adjective or the adverb is the correct choice in the following
sentences. Underline the correct one; then write **ADJ.** or **ADV.** in the blank. Be ready to
explain your choice.

__ADJ__ 21.   Joyce looks (beautiful, beautifully) with her new glasses.

__ADV__ 22.   Your eye is swelling (bad, badly)

__ADV__ 23.   I helped her as (good, well) as I could.

__ADV__ 24.   My grandmother is (real, really) special to me

__ADV__ 25.   Of the two men, John swam (more quickly, most quickly).

Chapter Twelve   NAME: _____ 232
Worksheet 13: ADJECTIVE AND DATE: _____
ADVERB USAGE
EDITING EXERCISE

Make any necessary corrections in the letter that appears below

August 31, 1987

Dear Paul,

really
School is starting real soon, and I just have to tell you about my river rafting trip this
this
summer. Usually these kind of active vacations sound a little too rough for me, but this
here one was perfect
really
You hit the waves and go down real fast, like a roller coaster, and you can't hardly
badly
believe you will live to tell about it! I'd better back up. I want to write it so bad, I'm going
quickly
too quick.

My dad, brother, two uncles, and I rafted down the San Juan River in southeastern

Utah this summer. It was much more scarier than our usual packing through the

mountains vacation, but it wasn't harely any less exhausting or challenging
this
I forgot to mention that one of my uncles is a river guide for these sort of rafting trips.

He'd tell us what to do in rough water, like to paddle left side only or right side only, really
clearly
good directions when you can't think clear and are overwhelmed. Most of the time we
really   *fewer*
were real wet. In fact, there were less dry times than wet times, but the sun dried our
well   *quickly*
clothes out good. When things weren't too rough, we'd jump out quick and go bobbing.
fewer
There were less complaints and less boredom on this trip than ever before.

After we all began to feel less awkward about handling our rafts, we relaxed and

really enjoyed ourselves.

Hope to see you soon.

Your buddy,

Frank

NAME: _____ 233

DATE: _____

Worksheet 14A: ADJECTIVE AND ADVERB USAGE EDITING TEST

Make any necessary corrections in the letter that appears below.

September 15, 1987

Dear Frank,

    I was ~~real~~ *really* excited to hear from you after so long and to read about how ~~good~~ *well* you handled your raft on the San Juan River. I was even more excited because I wanted to go rafting so ~~bad~~ *badly* this summer, but my dad had another vacation in mind that ~~wasn't~~ hardly rafting but was great!

    He had planned a business trip to Australia, and he was really happy when he found out he could take me along. I don't have to tell you I looked eager when he asked me. In fact, I remember I wasn't feeling ~~good~~ *well* that day, but his invitation sounded perfect~~ly~~ to my sluggish body. I perked up ~~real quick~~ *really quickly* and began to ask questions right away. I can't hardly remember whether my dad mentioned exploring the Great Barrier Reef, or whether I did. I do remember that he said if all went ~~good~~ *well* for him on this trip, we'd try to dive at the reef.

    Wow! Of the two of us, I can't say who was the ~~most~~ *more* excited, Dad or I. We talked ~~easy~~ *easily* about the trip, unlike most of our talks lately. This ~~here~~ adventure could do more for me than expand my horizons; I began to think ~~positive~~ *positively* about being with my dad.

NAME: _____ 234

DATE: _____

Worksheet 14A: ADJECTIVE AND ADVERB USAGE EDITING TEST

    There were ~~less~~ *fewer* problems than Dan expected in Sydney, so we left ~~more~~ earlier for the reef than we had planned. I can't barely describe how beautiful the 1,250-mile-long reef is. Of course, I took this trip very ~~serious~~ *seriously* and learned how the little corals are tiny animals, some of which produce a limy substance that forms a skeleton strangely outside their bodies. When the corals die, the skeletons remain and other corals attach naturally to them. It is the most interesting and ~~usefulest~~ *most useful* use of a skeleton you've ever imagined!

    We dove and swam and photographed together, Dad and I, and we understand and respect each other ~~more~~ better than we did before the trip.

Your pal,

Paul

NAME: _____ 235

DATE: _____

Worksheet 15A: COMMON WORD-USAGE ERRORS CUMULATIVE TEST

The following passage contains errors in adjective usage, adverb usage, and confusing word usage. Correct all errors so that the passage is written in standard English.

DAVID FINLEY ~~EXCEPTS~~ *ACCEPTS* WEBELOS LEADERSHIP

MARTINEZ—David Finley, ~~alumni~~ *alumnus* of University of California, Berkeley, has accepted the position of Webelos leader for Den 1 of Martinez. The den includes five Webelos scouts, who will meet ~~altogether~~ *all together* with Finley once a week. The scoutmaster of Pack 12 ~~adviced~~ *advised* the council to approach Finley with the request, as he is ~~all ready~~ *already* serving the pack very ~~good~~ *well* as assistant scoutmaster. "When I was deciding ~~between~~ *among* the four or five available men who are qualified, I ~~could of~~ *could've* asked David right away. But since his son is in a younger den, I didn't know ~~weather~~ *whether* he would ~~except~~ *accept*. Most people wouldn't hardly consider a request to lead a den without ~~there~~ *their* own son in it. Besides, David works ~~like~~ *as* a full-time cubmaster does now. I don't want to ~~infer~~ *imply* that it might be ~~to~~ *too* much for him, but ~~whose~~ *who's* to say? I had to ~~leave~~ *let* him make his own decision. I wanted to influence him ~~real bad~~ *really badly*, but I'm happy to say my wants didn't ~~effect~~ *affect* him in his decision."

    Although David's den is ~~more~~ *fewer* smaller than others in the pack, ~~less~~ boys ~~doesn't~~ *don't* mean the den will have ~~less~~ *fewer* activities. In fact, Finley's ~~illusions~~ *allusions* to past scouting activities that he is planning ~~real~~ *really* soon for this ~~here~~ den led me to an investigation. The scouting office has scrapbooks and records of each local pack and ~~it's~~ *its* achievements, and I found

NAME: _____ 236

DATE: _____

Worksheet 15B: COMMON WORD-USAGE ERRORS CUMULATIVE TEST

David Finley listed as an Eagle Scout. His former scoutmaster had written, "David works ~~real~~ *really* hard and does every job ~~real good~~ *really well*. I've never known a ~~colorfuler~~ *more colorful* scout; he's involved in many activities but he hasn't ~~drownded~~ *drowned* himself with ~~to~~ *too* much." Then I noticed that the offfice had hung pictures and articles of the local Eagle Scouts, and I searched ~~real good~~ *really well* until I found David.

    I guess you folks in Martinez can ~~set~~ *sit* back and relax, knowing that David Finley can do the job with those Webelos. If you find yourself getting a little angry ~~at~~ *with* yourself for not volunteering, contact Finley to find out how you can help

Chapter Thirteen

Worksheet 2A: CAPITALIZATION EXERCISE

NAME: _____ 240
DATE: _____

Copy over the phrases below, adding capitals as needed. Refer to the rules on Worksheet 51 for help with each section.

PROPER NOUNS AND COMMON NOUNS

1. next to st. mark's church — 1. next to St. Mark's Church
2. a baptist church — 2. a Baptist church
3. a big street downtown — 3. a big street downtown
4. the corner of elm street — 4. the corner of Elm Street
5. taft high school and its rivals — 5. Taft High School and its rivals
6. the u.s. senate and the house of representatives — 6. the U.S. Senate and the House of Representatives
7. at the lincoln memorial — 7. at the Lincoln Memorial

ADJECTIVES

8. a panasonic stereo — 8. a Panasonic stereo
9. a toyota pickup — 9. a Toyota pickup
10. her new french sunglasses — 10. her new French sunglasses
11. the new subway line — 11. the new subway line

SCHOOL SUBJECTS

12. my chemistry class — 12. my chemistry class
13. my print shop 3 teacher — 13. my Print Shop 3 teacher
14. his english and math books — 14. his English and math books
15. the history assignment — 15. the history assignment

Chapter Thirteen

Worksheet 2B: CAPITALIZATION EXERCISE

NAME: _____ 241
DATE: _____

TITLES

16. the movie *return of the jedi* — 16. the movie *Return of the Jedi*
17. singing "jingle bells" — 17. singing "Jingle Bells"

SEASONS AND POINTS OF THE COMPASS

18. flying to the south in winter — 18. flying to the South in winter
19. turning east on main street — 19. turning east on Main Street
20. yosemite national park in autumn — 20. Yosemite National Park in autumn
21. going to school in the west — 21. going to school in the West

ADD CAPITALS AS NEEDED IN THESE SENTENCES.

21. His mustang convertible and his apartment on Lake Street are his symbols of independence.

22. She works in the Masterson Building on the street north of the park.

23. While you're at Safeway, get me a loaf of bread, some Wheaties, a quart of nonfat milk, a copy of Good Housekeeping, and a small bottle of Tylenol.

24. This fall my history class is studying the Revolutionary War and the Declaration of Independence

25. Did you know that Reno, Nevada, is actually west of Los Angeles, California?

Chapter Thirteen

Worksheet 3: CAPITALIZATION EDITING EXERCISE

NAME: _____ 242
DATE: _____

The passage below contains many errors in capitalization. Some words that are capitalized should not be, and some words that are not capitalized should be. Correct any errors you find.

When Susan moved to San Jose, California, she faced some real problems getting settled. For a while she lived with her aunt, but since she was allergic to the wool in her aunt's imported Persian carpets, she wanted to get her own place quickly. She bought a copy of the Mercury-News and searched the ads for an inexpensive apartment. The first place she looked at was too far east of town, but the second was conveniently located on Page Boulevard and fully furnished with a General Electric refrigerator, a Tappan gas range, and a wonderful air conditioner. The price was right, so she grabbed the place

Her next task was finding work. She was trained as a computer programmer, and she hoped to find a position in nearby Silicon Valley. Again she scoured the newspaper. She spent days on the phone and driving her Ford Escort to interviews, carefully dressed in her only business suit. Finally she landed a job with Executron Enterprises on Twelfth Street in Santa Clara. It was a growing company that specialized in software for accounting firms. The pay was good, the benefits excellent, and she liked the people she met there, especially one handsome, young vice-president with a Porsche. Things were definitely looking up for Susan.

Chapter Thirteen

Worksheet 4A: CAPITALIZATION UNIT QUIZ

NAME: _____ 243
DATE: _____

Copy over the phrases below, adding capitals as needed.

1. paris in the spring — 1. Paris in the spring
2. winter in florida — 2. winter in Florida
3. the bill of rights — 3. the Bill of Rights
4. driving south on highway 99 — 4. driving south on Highway 99
5. her spanish and science homework — 5. her Spanish and science homework
6. a spielberg film — 6. a Spielberg film
7. next to the supermarket — 7. next to the supermarket
8. where elm street crosses king way — 8. where Elm Street crosses King Way
9. st. mary's catholic church — 9. St. Mary's Catholic Church
10. a cold root beer float — 10. a cold root beer float
11. visiting the american west — 11. visiting the American West
12. a pair of lee's jeans — 12. a pair of Lee's jeans

Add capitals as needed in these sentences

13. She loves to whiz down the freeway in her Porsche convertible with her Blaupunkt stereo blasting

14. My grandmother lives near Kingman, Arizona, not far from the Grand Canyon.

15. I need to make a trip to the hardware store to buy some GE bulbs, a Stanley wrench, some nails, and a can of paint

16. Next spring my biology class is reading A Whale for the Killing.

Worksheet 4B: CAPITALIZATION   DATE: _____
UNIT QUIZ

Correct any capitalization errors you find in the passage below

      Preparing for school by shopping for ~~s~~school ~~s~~supplies is serious business. You'll need the usual notebooks, pencils, and ~~B~~bic pens But it's also important to have new Nike ~~t~~tennis ~~s~~shoes and a couple of pairs of ~~L~~levi's jeans. Stock your kitchen for after-school snacks and late-night study sessions, too. Have a good supply of fruit juice and ~~s~~skippy peanut butter on hand.

Worksheet 6A: ENDMARKS   DATE: _____
EXERCISE

Supply endmarks in the sentences below.

1. Is it time to leave yet ?
2. For the third time in ten minutes the student asked the teacher what time it was .
3. How long can a nuclear submarine remain under water ?
4. A flute is easier for a small child to play than a piano .
5. Her mother asked if a flute would be easier to play than a piano .
6. Watch out for that truck !
7. Although she had a bad start, Julie easily won the race .
8. Is there an easy way to tell the age of a horse ?
9. Ask the guide if the Senate is in session .
10. How dare you say something like that !
11. I've never been so insulted in all my life !
12. Has he finished yet ?
13. Ask him if he has finished yet .
14. Hasn't he finished yet ?
15. Did he say when he would be finished ?

Add periods to the abbreviations below that *always* need them

16. CBS	21. Dr.	26. GM
17. B.C.	22. Ave.	27. Ms.
18. COD	23. Feb.	28. RCA
19. bldg.	24. mph	29. D.C.
20. Ph.D.	25. Jr.	30. J.R. Tompkins

Worksheet 7: ENDMARKS   DATE: _____
EDITING EXERCISE

The passage below contains many errors in the use of endmarks. Sometimes the wrong punctuation marks are used, and sometimes they are omitted, but some sentences are correct. Correct any errors you find.

    Anyone who can drive a car can parallel park. It just requires a little practice, coordination, and a set of eyes in the back of your head.

    Ask someone who has been driving for a while if he or she will come along as a teacher. And ask someone where there is a good place to practice. A quiet street with straight curbs and little traffic is perfect.

    Pick the space you want to park in and pull up to the left of the car in front of the space. Are you two or three feet away? You should be. Are the backs of the two cars even? They should be. Next shift into reverse and swing the back of your car into the space. No, no! That will never do. Turn the steering wheel clockwise, and back in at a forty-five degree angle to the curb. When the right front bumper of your car has passed the left rear bumper of the car ahead, start turning the wheel counterclockwise.

    Doesn't that slip your car neatly into the space and parallel to the curb? If not, ask the teacher you brought along what you did wrong. Ask if you were too close or far from the car next to you when you began. Were the backs of the two cars even? Did you turn clockwise or counterclockwise too soon? Did you turn too far? Perhaps you reversed the way you were turning the wheel too early or too late.

    Keep practicing, and you shouldn't have any problem. In no time you'll be parking like a New York taxi driver.

Worksheet 8: ENDMARKS   DATE: _____
UNIT QUIZ

Supply needed endmark and abbreviation punctuation in the sentences below

1. What a book !
2. What is the name of that book ?
3. I asked her the name of that book.
4. Do you know that England was last successfully invaded in A.D. 1066 ?
5. Athens was a major city long before the birth of Christ .
6. Please explain why Elvis Presley made such good music and such bad films.
7. What a pest she can be !
8. How can I find out whether NBC is a division of RCA ?
9. Boy, did I feel like a jerk !
10. Ask him how long it takes to get a B.A. degree.
11. I have a package for Mr. T.C. Wellington at this address.
12. Is the car ready ?
13. Ask him if the car is ready.
14. Wasn't three P.M. when the car was supposed to be ready ?
15. Look out! You're going to fall!
16. My mother never asked me what grade I received.
17. What is the difference between an L.P. record and a compact disk ?
18. How homely he is !
19. Used car prices have soared since 1980 .
20. Dr. and Mrs. C.M. Antonio cordially invite you to dinner at seven P.M. on Wednesday, January 23. Please R.S.V.P.
21. How long are you willing to put up with this state of affairs ?

Correct any errors in endmark punctuation in the passage below.

    No matter how long you have been in school, the first day in the fall can be full of surprises. It is an obvious chance to size up new teachers. Ask around to find out their reputations. Find out which have a good sense of humor, and which don't. Who are the easiest to talk to? Who are most readily available to give extra help? Study the school class schedule to find out which teachers fit best into your program. Can't good teachers go a long way toward making a good year ?

Worksheet 9A: ENDMARKS
CUMULATIVE TEST
DATE: _____

Correct the capitalization, abbreviation, and endmark errors in the passage below.

What a horrible nightmare! That was what Lulu thought as she left the guidance office. She longed for a class that would help her land a job as a salesclerk at the **S**ummit, the most exclusive boutique at Alpine Valley **M**all. What better way to spend the **S**ummer than surrounded by the latest **f**ashions? And what about that thirty-percent employee discount? Didn't happiness begin with the right clothes? She would return to Alpine **H**igh in the fall as popular as the latest designer labels. How could she know that her dreams of a jammed closet and an endless string of exciting Saturday nights would be so quickly shattered?

She had asked Mr. Tweedy, her counselor, if the school offered classes in **R**etail **S**ales or **S**mall **B**usiness **M**anagement. But there wasn't one. As usual, Lulu was a little late signing up for classes. The only remaining electives were **A**uto **S**hop 2 and ornamental horticulture. Spark plugs and roses were all dear old Valley Union **H**igh **S**chool district had to offer.

How could she face such a drab summer? It was going to be long days in the office of her father's fertilizer plant and long nights with her pet goldfish, Buster Crabbe. She would be lucky if one of her brother's creepy friends asked her out to the **d**rive-**i**n. Ugh!

But as she walked back to her **S**panish class, Lance Steele, the irresistible captain of the **f**ootball team, ran up. Lulu's father had just hired him for the summer as an assistant fertilizer processor. He asked her if she didn't think it would be great to see one another every day? Lulu beamed. Yes, it would be very nice.

As she continued to class, Lulu wondered if Lance had an interest in roses.

Worksheet 11A: COMMA EXERCISE DATE: _____

Add commas to the sentences below according to the rules heading each section. Not all of the sentences require more punctuation.

COMMAS IN COMPOUND SENTENCES
1. Susan tuned the old Chevrolet,but I drove it away afterwards.
2. Either she will be finished,or we'll have to do it for her.
3. I wanted to help Tim with his paper, yet he refused aid from anyone.
4. I searched my route four times,but I still couldn't find my lost ticket.
5. She drove but I flew.

COMMAS IN A SERIES
6. Who is on the committee besides Mr. Thomas,Ms. Meyers,and Mr. Hardy?
7. He gathered his courage,took a deep breath,walked up to the teacher,and asked for his test.
8. A Big Mac hamburger is made with two all-beef patties,special sauce,lettuce,cheese, pickles,onions,and a sesame-seed bun.
9. The huge,craggy,ominous mountain loomed above the climbing party.
10. Mrs. Cookston and the entire class pitched in to clean up the mess.

COMMAS IN ADDRESSES AND DATES
11. She lives at 3224 Walton Circle,Albany,New York.
12. The meeting will be held at the Explorers' Club,9887 Dinston Boulevard,Chicago, Illinois,on Thursday,October 14.
13. Miami,Florida,has been my home since April,1985.

COMMAS SEPARATING NONESSENTIAL PARTS OF SENTENCES
14. Mark,please tell Maria that I'm ready.
15. Dr. Rinaldi,how much longer will it take?
16. To tell the truth,I never dreamed you were wearing that clown costume.
17. This door,on the other hand,has always been stuck.
18. Larry,who always mumbles his words,was elected class president.
19. Teachers who always mumble their words are a real frustration.
20. Oliver,amazed by the cut of her dress,was speechless
21. John,who was sitting in the back seat,escaped unharmed.
22. Sylvia,red-faced and angry,slowly stood up and left the room

---

Worksheet 11B: COMMA EXERCISE DATE: _____

COMMAS IN SENTENCES WITH INTRODUCTORY CLAUSES
23. When I saw Mr. Fletcher,I shouted and waved to him.
24. Before the game the team was confident and optimistic.
25. Before you leave,be sure to check with the boss.
26. Because he has such a reputation,I was careful from the start.
27. Whether you like it or not,Joni will do as she pleases.

Add commas to the sentences below according to all the rules you have studied. Not all of the sentences require additional punctuation.

28. I told her to be on time,Jim,but she just didn't seem to care.
29. We met Nora and Sam,and Fred gave them the assignment
30. Before the prom he'll have to rent a tuxedo.
31. The cruise departs on Sunday,January 13,doesn't it?
32. The boys hid under the garage,under the hedge,and behind the car.
33. The room is always cold early in the day,but it warms up after lunch.
34. Ed raked the leaves,but Edna put them in bags and hauled them away.
35. Edna raked the leaves,put them in bags,and hauled them away.
36. Ed raked the leaves and hauled them away.
37. Her old address was in Rye,but,of course, I don't know her new address.

Worksheet 12: COMMA EDITING
EXERCISE
DATE: _____

The passage below contains many errors in the use of commas. Sometimes they are included where they are not needed, and sometimes they are omitted where they are needed. Correct any errors you find.

The rodent invasion of Craggy Rock High School was no laughing matter,and it was not easily ended. The mice who arrived first stayed well-concealed behind trash and under furniture. They were seldom seen by day,but after dark they emerged from their nests. They nibbled crumbs and made midnight trips to the cafeteria kitchen to feed on stray bits of rubbery spaghetti,wilted salad,and rotting meatloaf

The mice became bolder, gloating over their success. Classes were occasionally interrupted by gray shadows chasing along walls, windowsills, and chalktrays. One English teacher fainted,and several students refused to go into the home economics room. It had become overrun with fat,ugly rodents. Things had gone too far, and the principal called a faculty meeting to discuss the problem,hear suggestions,and take decisive action

Saturday,November 16,1986, spelled doom for the round,happy furballs of Craggy Rock High. Before dawn a five-person team of exterminators,wearing black jumpsuits and carrying frightening machines,descended upon the building. On Monday,of course, there was not a mouse to be seen. The principal,amazed by the efficiency of the deadly team,strutted proudly about the school.

As the week passed,students prepared for a grudge-match football game with the blue-and-gold team from Ziggley Valley High The team practiced with a vengeance,and pep rallies stirred school spirit,but on the morning of the game came the ultimate humiliation. Craggy Rock students were met again by hundreds of tiny "mice"—but this time each one had been dyed blue or gold and placed there as a prank,by their rivals,at Ziggley.

Supply needed comma punctuation in the sentences below

1. His home was burglarized on Thursday, October 24, wasn't it?

2. The restaurant that we ate at last night is open every day

3. The tour departs on July 1, for England, France, and Germany.

4. Chris was so absentminded that someone had to tell him when school was over, where his locker was and how to catch the bus.

5. Nothing is so annoying as a salesperson who is impolite

6. Elaine ran all the way to school, but she was late just the same

7. The man whom you see is really a woman in disguise

8. Beginning Tuesday, July 30, 1985, her new address will be 616 Boynton Way, Salt Lake City, Utah.

9. I walked up to her, smiled irresistibly, and got slapped in the face.

10. It has to be finished and turned in by Tuesday.

11. Whenever Jan is late to class, you are, aren't you?

12. When do you think Jan will finally get here?

13. John, who seldom makes a mistake, failed the test.

14. The stately, elegant, decaying Ambassador Hotel, built before the turn of the century, is to be torn down.

15. Miss Yee, startled by my remark, couldn't think of a reply.

16. When the principal tells Frank, Todd will inform the rest of us.

17. We walked slowly along the winding road to the strange house and carefully entered the yard with its huge oak and brown lawn.

18. The manager came to their table, asked them to leave, and threatened to call the police.

19. Columbus first landed in America on October 12, 1492, didn't he?

20. Mr. Arnold, do you think modern teaching methods include corporal punishment?

21. I left it under the tree last June and never saw it again

22. After the stereo was set up, we started dancing.

Correct any errors in comma punctuation in the passage below.

Because he was the only boy in a home economics class, Scott was shy, nervous, and self-conscious on the first day. Thirty pairs of female eyes, all seemed to be aimed squarely at him and he didn't know what to do. Time passed, and he got to know the girls. They were eager to explain the complicated workings of food processors, microwave ovens, and digital timers. He began to enjoy the class and sometimes even played dumb to get more attention. At semester's end he had learned more than he had ever expected, and that's what school is all about, isn't it?

Correct comma, capitalization, endmark, and abbreviation errors in the passage below.

The V.C.R. will never replace the movie theater. A nineteen-inch television, a tiny speaker, and stale potato chips just aren't the same as a fifty-foot screen, Dolby stereo, and the array of goodies at a snack counter. *Raiders of The Lost Ark* just isn't the same when Indiana Jones is only five inches tall.

And a lively, excited, eager audience adds as much to a movie as a huge screen and monster speakers. Waiting in a line on a cold Winter night and paying for tickets make you even more anxious to see a film. Then you go inside and stock up on popcorn and Coke. As the lights go down and the MGM lion appears, can't you sense the tension? Sometimes people cheer or boo the coming attractions. When the feature begins, a hush falls over the audience. This is what they've waited in line and paid good money to see, isn't it? People laugh at what's funny and scream at what's scary. At the end of the movie you can eavesdrop on other people as they comment on the film. Some people agree with you, and some have no taste at all.

None of this happens at home. You just slap a cassette into the machine, flop down on the couch, and stare. Then the telephone ringing like a fire alarm forces you to stop the action. You have to stop again, you dummy, because you forgot your snacks. You pause again to go to the bathroom. There are even people who stop in the middle of a film. They go to bed and they continue the next day. This completely destroys the pacing of a good film. Why bother watching at all?

So seeing a movie on a V.C.R. is convenient, but it is second-rate. Movie theaters add big screens, big sound, big reactions, and big fun

Each compound sentence below needs either a comma or a semicolon. Supply it.

1. I weeded the garden; my brother mowed the lawn.

2. I weeded the garden, but my brother mowed the lawn.

3. The radio had been left on all day, and the batteries were dead.

4. I didn't care about her problems; I had plenty of my own to keep me busy.

5. You may not fish here with your state license; you need to buy a special permit.

6. I did my best to explain the grade to my parents; they didn't buy it.

7. I went to the store at the address you gave me; if they sell running shoes there, they do it in a vacant gas station.

8. Some people say the old mine is haunted, but most scoff at the idea.

9. He watches the door with one eye; he watches the class with the other.

10. She did all the talking; she was the only one who spoke Spanish.

Add commas and semicolons in the compound sentences and series below.

11. An hour later the roof collapsed; the earthquake had weakened it.

12. The earthquake cracked the foundation, and the roof collapsed.

13. Susan arrived in class soaking wet; she had changed a tire in the rain.

14. The members of the team couldn't stand him; he was always complaining about something.

15. The winning teams were from: Springfield, Ohio; Princeton, Wisconsin; and Bloomingdale, Indiana.

16. Two club members had to leave early; they had paper routes

17. The travel agent advised Stan to take the late plane; it would save him money

Chapter Thirteen
Worksheet 16B: SEMICOLON EXERCISE
NAME: _____ 265
DATE: _____

18 The review committee consists of Mr. Luxley, who is principal; Ms. Shanna, who is a counselor; and Tony Garcia, who is student body president.

19 The Sterns' new house has a family room with a stereo, a fireplace, and a projection T.V.; a kitchen with a built-in food processor, a microwave oven, and two dishwashers; and a back yard equipped with a swimming pool, a tennis court, and a hot tub.

20 Laurel was expected to answer the phone for Mr. Post, Mr. Lowrey, and the rest of the sales staff; take dictation for Mrs. Isaacson; and do typing, bookkeeping, and payroll for the entire office.

On the lines below write a compound sentence requiring a semicolon.

21 (Answers will vary) _____

_____

On the lines below write a sentence with a series requiring semicolons.

22 (Answers will vary) _____

_____

Chapter Thirteen
Worksheet 17: SEMICOLON EDITING EXERCISE
NAME: _____ 266
DATE: _____

The passage below contains many errors in the use of commas and semicolons. Sometimes the wrong punctuation marks are used, and sometimes they are omitted. Some sentences are correct. Correct any errors you find.

Disneyland has a private face in addition to the public one; its millions of visitors have seen. Disneylanders, which is what park employees are called, see a side to the Magic Kingdom hidden from the view of visitors from St. Louis, Missouri; London, England; and Canton, China.

Workers pass daily through locker rooms where mountain climbers, astronauts, and turn-of-the-century popcorn boys suit up side by side. They even catch occasional glimpses of a Mickey, Goofy, or Donald without a rubber head.

The park itself is wonderfully quiet before the public gates open. Gardeners put finishing touches on flowerbeds; ride operators run the Matterhorn bobsled safety check; and fry cooks ride the raft to Tom Sawyer's Island to deliver the day's supply of hot dogs.

Then thousands of tourists descend upon the place, but employees are provided with restful break areas away from the crowds that they must serve with unvarying safety, courtesy, and speed. Behind Main Street, where visitors shop for souvenirs; adjacent to Adventureland, where steamers challenge jungle rivers; and near Autopia, where youngsters develop driving habits they will later perfect on California freeways; employees sip Cokes away from the noise, crowds, and heat.

Many say Disneyland is prettiest at night, but its prettiest time of night is when it is empty. When workers wander out of the park, the recorded music still plays, and the lights still twinkle, reflected now on freshly washed sidewalks.

Chapter Thirteen
Worksheet 18A: SEMICOLON UNIT QUIZ
NAME: _____ 267
DATE: _____

Supply needed comma and semicolon punctuation in the sentences below.

1. The subway was slow, but Mr. Kimura made his appointment on time.

2. The plane was delayed; she missed her connection.

3. The three members of the committee were Mrs. Reynolds, the principal; Mr. De Rue, the vice principal; and Mrs. Elmore, the chairperson of the English department.

4. A century ago most Americans worked on farms; today most live and work in cities.

5. Our neighborhood basketball team consists of Jerry, the center; Bob and Rick, the forwards; and Sue and Elizabeth, the guards.

6. From now on there will be no more monkey business; today begins a new regime.

7. The South High *Tiger* specializes in stories on student activities, school sports, and administrative foul-ups.

8. We got to the dock at dawn, but we waited until nine o'clock before the wind, tide, and weather permitted us to sail.

9. What small colleges lack in reputation they often make up for in instructor-student ratio.

10. Our English teacher always allows us time to think, plan, write, and revise before we turn in our papers.

11. During the week I'm usually in bed by ten; on weekends I stay up much later.

12. Would you rather spend a winter vacation in Miami, Florida; Phoenix, Arizona; or Honolulu, Hawaii?

13. I remember where I read the article; it was in *Time* last spring.

14. Thick gloves are a help for any heavy work.

15. Kitty had lost her engagement ring, and immediately everyone started furiously searching the furniture, floor, and wastebaskets.

Chapter Thirteen
Worksheet 18B: SEMICOLON UNIT QUIZ
NAME: _____ 268
DATE: _____

Correct any errors in comma or semicolon punctuation in the passage below

The substitute's arrival was very exciting; it meant Mr. Tremble's wife had had her baby. The students immediately wanted to know the sex, size, and time of delivery, but the poor substitute knew nothing. She had received a brief phone call from the school; a substitute was required; there was no other word. The class settled down to work. Halfway through the period Mr. Tremble entered the room, smiled, sat down, and announced the birth of triplets. There was Michael, weighing five pounds; James, weighing five and a half; and William, weighing four and three-quarters. His wife was very tired.

Worksheet 19: SEMICOLON CUMULATIVE TEST

NAME: _____ 269
DATE: _____

Correct semicolon, comma, endmark, capitalization, and abbreviation errors in the passage below.

Spending summers as a cook in a fast-food restaurant can be hard work. The heat is high; the pressure is high, and the wages are usually low.

Few things are hotter than a hamburger grill in August. Hour after hour you lay rows of patties on the blackened steel, wait for them to fry, and flip them over. The only real entertainment is asking yourself how many need cheese. An occasional Dr. Pepper helps avoid dehydration, but soon your head, arms, and back are soaked with sweat, and a film of hamburger grease.

At breakfast, which comes between seven and ten; lunch, which comes between noon and three; and dinner, which comes between six and eight, the pressure is on. Waitresses scream for orders; food flies in all directions; and, of course, the manager supervises your every move, and tries to spot any inefficiency. If anyone fails to do his or her part, there could be a disaster. It is possible to run out of ice, hot fries, or even thawed patties. What if a soft drink machine breaks down? That means unhappy customers, lower sales, and an angry boss.

And what do you get paid for this agony? To tell the truth, you get minimum wage, and rarely do you get more. Tips are unheard of in fast-food chains. If you don't like the pay, scores of other unemployed teenagers are waiting to take your job.

Don't you think it's a tough way to make money? If you can't stand the heat you should stay out of the kitchen.

Worksheet 21A: APOSTROPHE EXERCISE

NAME: _____ 272
DATE: _____

The underlined item in each of the following groups tells what is owned. The second item (the possessive noun) tells the name of the owner or owners. To the right of each set of words, write the correct form of possessive noun followed by the name of the thing owned.

Example: clock Kelly   Kelly's clock

1. house the dog   1. the dog's house
2. house the dogs   2. the dogs' house
3. department the girls   3. the girls' department
4. department the men   4. the men's department
5. purse the lady   5. the lady's purse
6. purses the ladies   6. the ladies' purses
7. turn Sam Jones   7. Sam Jones' turn
8. pickup the Joneses   8. the Joneses' pickup
9. tools the repairmen   9. the repairmen's tools
10. gifts his friends   10. his friends' gifts
11. conference the teachers   11. the teachers' conference
12. visit my brother-in-law   12. my brother-in-law's visit
13. kids my brothers-in-law   13. my brothers-in-law's kids
14. hats the team   14. the team's hats

Write the contracted form of the words below.

15. it is   it's   19. shall not   shan't
16. they are   they're   20. who is   who's
17. will not   won't   21. Tom is   Tom's
18. you are   you're   22. must have   must've

Worksheet 21B: APOSTROPHE EXERCISE

NAME: _____ 273
DATE: _____

Supply apostrophes as needed in the sentences below

23. It's under John's geometry textbook
24. Bob's going, but he shouldn't.
25. It's the Millers' fence that's too high.
26. That lady's dog's collar isn't too uncomfortable, is it?
27. There were seven 2's on the home team's scoreboard
28. Didn't Phil say he'd wait until ten o'clock?
29. You shouldn't interrupt him when he's talking

Worksheet 22: APOSTROPHE EDITING EXERCISE

NAME: _____ 274
DATE: _____

The passage below contains many errors in the use of apostrophes. Sometimes apostrophes are included where they are not needed, and sometimes they are omitted. Some sentences are correct. Correct any errors you find.

Some days you just shouldn't get out of bed. Last Wednesday was a day like that for Jim Taylor. The more the day wore on, the worse it got.

Days start early for Jim. The alarm's buzz jarred him out of bed before seven. He was able to shower, grab a bite, and be to school in time to do some last minute homework before classes began. First period he faced a metal shop quiz; second it was a biology lab with a partner whose idea of helping was minding his own P's and Q's, and third it was a lesson on apostrophes. Lunch should've been a pleasant break, but it wasn't. Jim waited in line twenty minutes for a chance to battle other students for the cafeteria's lousy food The cook's idea of a hamburger was a chewy bit of ground crud on a stale bun. Jim's lunch conversation with two friends was the highlight of the day. They talked about cars, records, and last Saturday's basketball game. Then it was back to class. Mr. Thomas' surprise fourth period was the announcement of a math exam later in the week. Fifth period Jim got the sad results of last week's business test, and sixth period there was no hot water in the gym's showers.

Now you'd think he'd have a chance to go home and enjoy a nice snack of his mom's cooking, but the minute he walked in the door, his boss called for him to come down to the gas station. One of Jim's co-worker's had called in sick. When he got back home, it was after ten. There was just enough time to study and fall into bed.

As he was dropping off to sleep, Jim remembered his father's words. "Jim," he had said, "these are the best years of your life."

Chapter Thirteen   NAME: _____ 275
Worksheet 23: APOSTROPHE   DATE: _____
UNIT QUIZ

Supply needed apostrophes in the sentences below.

1. Didn't Shannon say she'd wait at Tess' house?

2. Who's been fooling around with whose camera equipment?

3. He told me you'd find it in the men's and boys' department.

4. My mother-in-law's luggage is still at the station, isn't it?

5. The Wongs' front yard is always the neighborhood's pride.

6. Mr. Langly's ties are always so colorful!

7. That lady's packages fell all over the hallway. Help her, won't you?

8. Let's put Ruth's books, folders, and binder in Elaine's locker.

9. The freshmen's float didn't win, but it showed lots of hard work.

10. That's the girl whose notes I borrowed.

11. It's hers and Joanna's, not theirs.

12. The odometer on the Johnsons' car is all 2's.

13. Eisenhower's administration was in power during the 1950s.

14. They're over there with your costume.

15. Don't forget to cross your t's and dot your i's.

Correct any errors in apostrophe punctuation in the passage below.

A computer's keyboard is much like one for a typewriter, but it's important to keep a few things in mind. You mustn't use capital O's instead of zeros, and don't confuse i's and l's; the differences are important to a computer. There are also some computer keys that you'll never see on a typewriter. The one's marked "control" and "esc" are used with other keys to make the computer do some of its tricks. Don't touch them unless you know what ~~your~~ **you're** doing. But don't be afraid of a computer keyboard either. It's impossible to damage the machine by pushing any of the key's.

Chapter Thirteen   NAME: _____ 276
Worksheet 24: APOSTROPHE   DATE: _____
CUMULATIVE TEST

Correct the apostrophe, semicolon, comma, endmark, capitalization, and abbreviation errors in the passage below.

When school's out and summer's here, meals around our house become very informal. Other things are more important than eating during hot July weather, and Mom or Dad's cooking is usually light, fast, and easy to fix. ~~Whose~~ **Who's** in the mood for more?

My summer breakfasts are usually hurried. I roll out of bed late, and ready to get going, and I don't like to fool around with a nutritionist's idea of a well-balanced breakfast. I swallow some Cheerios, fruit, orange juice, and coffee, and I'm on my way. Lunch can be even more hurried; sometimes I skip it altogether. Occasionally I'll have one of my mother's bag lunches, but a cheeseburger, some fries, and a diet cola from the Burger King are all I usually need to keep going through the afternoon. When dinner comes, the family tries to eat together, but ~~it is~~ **it's** hard to get someone to cook on hot days. Dad, who is a Mexican-food fan; Mom, who always wants salad; and my sister, who loves fried chicken, have great debates about where to go for some fast food. I usually win by asking who'd like pizza.

One thing we'll always agree on is that the best summer meals are cooked and served outdoors. Our backyard barbecue won't produce gourmet French cuisine, but it treats good beef better than anything we can think of. Dad's favorite is rare steak, Mom's is fresh corn on the cob, and I go for potatoes baked on the coals. These are the only really big meals we eat all summer. Can you think of a better way to spend a warm summer evening?

Chapter Thirteen   NAME: _____ 279
Worksheet 26A: QUOTATION   DATE: _____
MARKS—EXERCISES

Some of the sentences below contain direct quotations and some contain indirect quotations. Put quotation marks where they are needed in the direct quotations and leave the indirect quotations unchanged.

1. "I didn't touch your motorcycle," said Don.

2. Don said that he hadn't touched my motorcycle.

3. Penny explained that she couldn't stand anchovies on her pizza.

4. "I can't stand anchovies on my pizza," Penny explained.

5. "Do you have a pencil?" Frank asked.

6. Frank asked if I had a pencil.

Supply needed quotation marks and underlining in the sentences below.

7. "I have no intention of staying," he announced.

8. She told me she had just replaced her lost copy of Moby Dick.

9. "Hamlet is the only play by Shakespeare I've seen," she said.

10. Bob told me that The Lottery is a frightening short story.

11. The best article in this issue of Rolling Stone is "John Lennon: The Myth and the Man."

12. "Whenever he walks into the room," she explained, "I get nervous."

13. "Why did you invite him? He's such a bore," moaned Ron.

14. "He's home sick with the flu," explained his mother.

15. "I know which one is the center," said Paul, "but which is the quarterback?"

16. "No seat-saving allowed!" screamed the angry bus driver.

17. Then she said that she wanted us all off the bus immediately.

18. The Chronicle is a good newspaper, but I get most of my current events from Newsweek.

19. "When this ordeal is over," she sighed, "I'm going to sleep for a week."

Chapter Thirteen   NAME: _____ 280
Worksheet 26B: QUOTATION   DATE: _____
MARKS—EXERCISES

20. They say that the smell from the dump is overpowering.

21. Robert Redford's best film was Butch Cassidy and the Sundance Kid.

22. Ellen thinks that Robert Redford's best film was Butch Cassidy and the Sundance Kid.

23. Ellen said, "Robert Redford's best film was Butch Cassidy and the Sundance Kid."

24. "Do you know I'm leaving soon?" he asked.

25. "No, I don't. Hum a few notes and I'll fake it," she replied, sitting down at the piano

Copy the passage below. Provide missing quotation marks and paragraphing.

¶ "Well, I finally made it, didn't I?" Diane announced as she entered the room. ¶ "You're half an hour late," David answered. "What kept you?" ¶ "Oh," she said, "my car's battery went dead on me again." ¶ "What a nuisance," replied David. "Don't you have jumper cables?" ¶ "Yes, I do," she sighed, "but they don't do any good if they're home in the garage!" ¶ "Too bad. You should keep them in your trunk," he said. ¶ "I've learned my lesson," Diane replied. "I'll never leave home without them again."

Correct the passage below. Add or remove quotation marks and underlining as needed, and mark new paragraphs with a P

P   "Well, how was your weekend?," Dave asked Jerry as he slumped into his desk. Mr. Madonwald was late to class, as was usual on Mondays, and it was a good time to talk over the weekend. Jerry looked up and replied, "Don't even ask!" "I worked all day Saturday and when I got home the only thing on T.V. was an old movie called Gold Diggers of 1933." "But you must have seen the Dolphins' game on Sunday afternoon," said Dave. That pass that won the game was incredible." "I'm sure it was, but I didn't see it," sighed Jerry. "Sunday morning our television went on the blink while I was reading an article about the game in the Times." Just then Mr. Macdonwald arrived. "Good morning, people, he said cheerfully. "Isn't it splendid to be starting a new week together?" The class groaned in unison; it was the old joke every Monday morning. "Open your books to act two of Macbeth," he said. Jerry, will you read the part of Banquo?" "Mr. Macdonwald, I'm not feeling very well," said Jerry. "Couldn't you get someone else?" Jerry thought to himself that the last thing he needed was fifty minutes of reading Elizabethan drama. He asked himself why he had taken this class. Christopher, the class eager-beaver, saved him. His hand shot into the air. "I'll be happy to read, if Gerald is feeling under the weather, Mr. Macdonwald," he said. "I love this play!" Jerry relaxed and slouched into his seat. "Shakespeare's not as bad as I thought it would be," Jerry whispered to Dave, "but I'm just not in the mood." "I'm never in the mood for anything on Monday morning," Dave replied. "Only five days till Friday," Jerry muttered.

Supply needed quotation marks and underlining in the sentences below.

1   She told me yesterday that she lost her latest issue of Time.

2   Why are you shouting? asked the coach.

3   Have you ever read Gone with the Wind? Mrs. Jenkins asked.

4   When he leaves the room, we'll sneak out, suggested Timothy.

5   My favorite musical is Cats, but I also really liked A Chorus Line

6   I just finished an excellent Reader's Digest article called Ten Ways to Have a Good Marriage.

7   Sit down, Kate, George said. Don't move until I return

8   I want to go! shrieked Sarah's little brother. Give me one good reason why I can't.

9   I asked him why he liked Star Wars so very much.

10 Terri moved close to Scott and whispered, Did you hear a noise?

11 Grady asked if I had an extra copy of the geometry book.

12 It's just not fair, whined Bob. You always single me out.

13 Talking to your father, complained Grandpa, is like shouting down a well.

14 The zookeeper shouted, Look out! A rabid gerbil has escaped!

15 Unquestionably the Beatles most innovative album was Sargeant Pepper's Lonely Hearts Club Band, he stated gravely.

Correct the following passage, which is adapted from Lewis Carroll's Alice's Adventures in Wonderland. Supply quotation marks as needed and mark places where new paragraphing should occur with a P.

P Suppose we change the subject, the March Hare interrupted. I vote that young lady tells us a story. I'm afraid I don't know one, said Alice. Then the Dormouse shall, said the March Hare. Wake up, Dormouse! I wasn't asleep, said the Dormouse. I heard every word you said. Tell us a story, said the March Hare. Yes, please do! pleaded Alice, and the Mad Hatter added that he should be quick about it.

Correct underlining, quotation mark, apostrophe, semicolon, comma, endmark, capitalization, and paragraphing errors in the passage below.
      From the day she entered Colter high as a freshman on September 8, 1986, Loni wanted to play basketball for the school. She loved to play the game and she loved to watch it on television. She was a sophomore now, she was eligible for the varsity squad the following year. She talked things over with her mother.

      "Well," her mom said, "I'm not happy with your grade in Spanish. "I know Mom," Loni replied, "but I know I can keep it up. You saw how well I did last quarter." "And you know I need help at home," her mother sighed. "It hasn't been easy since I started work when your father and I separated."

      "But, Mom." Loni pleaded. "Don't I always do my chores?"

      "O.K." her mother said. "Give it a try if it's really what you want."

      And she did try. She borrowed her cousin's sweatsuit and her boyfriend's basketball, and she headed for tryouts. She really gave it her all; that's the way to win, isn't it? She never missed practice, practiced additional hours at home, and even checked a book titled Advanced Basketball Technique out of the library. The chapter on free throws, called Advantage Under Pressure, was particularly helpful. But the day of the final cut came closer, and she wavered. She asked herself whether she was really good enough. Did she have the timing Did she have the drive?

      Before the final selections were made, she was depressed. She wasn't at all sure she'd made it. But the new team for next year was posted during her gym class, and she let out a squeal of joy. Her work had paid off.

Supply colons, if needed, in the sentences below.

1. It's certainly a beautiful day: bright sun, blue skies, and crisp autumn air.

2. His beautiful home was full of pests: ants, termites, and his little sister.

3. The train leaves at either 6:30 or 6:40. I'm not sure which time.

4. Job 3:4 is always an inspiration to me.

5. Don excelled in basketball, geometry, and chess.

6. Three members of the team deserve special credit for the victory: the quarterback, the center, and the manager.

7. There's a special schedule tomorrow, and I'm not sure if school is out at 3:00 or 3:30

8. Day after day he wore the same ridiculous outfit: faded jeans, a Save-the-Chocolate-Mousse T-shirt, and green sneakers.

9. Every employee has a responsibility to take short breaks, obey every company rule, and be loyal to the boss.

10. Carrie has the qualitites that make for corporate success: a driving ambition, endless energy, and the ability to play scratch golf.

Some of the sentences below require a colon before their quotations; some require a comma, and some are indirect quotations that require neither. Supply what is needed

11. The speaker quoted from Poor Richard's Almanac: "A penny saved is a penny earned."

12. My mother said with a smile, "A penny saved is a penny earned."

13. My uncle always says that a penny saved is a penny earned.

14. Mr. Van Loon opened his daily television commentary with a thought-provoking statement: "Television is a bore."

15. Lenny walked into the classroom, took his seat, and announced, "I'm dropping this class."

16. One film critic wrote the following after viewing the film: "In the future Miss La Rue's attempts to act should be confined to the privacy of her own home."

Chapter Thirteen NAME: _____ 287
Worksheet 31B: COLON AND DATE: _____
PARENTHESES—EXERCISES

17. Coming out of the theater, Bill said,"I certainly don't go to Lora La Rue films because I like her acting."

18. Ralph said excitedly that there was food available at the snack bar around the corner.

19. The warning on the container stated:"Danger! Do not take internally."

20. James walked up to Mr. Langston and casually asked,"When will you be giving the next surprise quiz?"

Supply necessary parentheses in the following sentences.

21. Tanzania(formerly Tanganyika)is located in East Africa.

22. The Grand Tetons(a French name)are an inspiring mountain range.

23. *Leave It to Beaver*(Why did it ever go off the air?)was an early television show that extolled the virtues of the American family.

24. I knew Kim had the money for a ticket(She saved it by skipping lunches)but I don't know how Sally bought hers.

25. The chart on(page 251)shows the decline in unemployment.

Chapter Thirteen NAME: _____ 288
Worksheet 32A: COLON AND DATE: _____
PARENTHESES—EDITING EXERCISE

The passage below contains many errors in the use of colons and parentheses. Correct any errors you find.

Good morning, class. Let's begin our review of punctuation (Where are my notes?) with endmarks: periods, question marks, and exclamation marks. The endmark you use depends on your purpose: a period to make a statement, a question mark to ask a question, and an exclamation mark to show great feeling.

Next let me quote from your explanation sheet on commas: "The most common comma errors are made in: compound sentences, in series, in addresses and dates, and in separating nonessential elements of sentences." Be sure to look over these rules carefully: (Remember that a test is approaching): they can be complicated.

The semicolon has: only two: uses: in a compound sentence, where it replaces a comma and a conjunction, and in a series with elements that contain commas. Master these two rules.

Apostrophes are used to form plurals of: numbers, letters, and symbols, but they are usually used in contractions (They replace missing letters): and in possessives. Three steps form the possessive of any noun: first, write the noun; second, add an apostropohe; and third, add an *s* if the word doesn't already end in one.

Chapter Thirteen NAME: _____ 289
Worksheet 32B: COLON AND DATE: _____
PARENTHESES—EDITING EXERCISE

Quotation marks are used around the titles of short works like stories, articles, poems, and songs. They are also used in direct quotations, but there are five rules (see Worksheet 25) to keep in mind.

That just leaves: colons and parentheses. The colon has four uses: in formal quotations, in lists preceded by nouns, in expressions of time between the hour and minute, and in references to the Bible between numbers for chapters and verse. Parentheses (Use them sparingly) keep any extra words of explanation you add from standing out strongly.

Chapter Thirteen NAME: _____ 290
Worksheet 33A: COLON AND DATE: _____
PARENTHESES—UNIT QUIZ

Supply colons and parentheses, if needed, in the sentences below.

1. I love everything about her sports car: its chic styling, its good acceleration, its low gas mileage, and its owner.

2. Her new sports car has chic styling, good acceleration, and low gas mileage.

3. Two graduating seniors(Max Canfield and Roy Gold)are planning on spending the summer in Hawaii.

4. Two graduating seniors will be spending the summer after graduation in Hawaii: Max Canfield and Roy Gold.

5. Kate ran into the room and shouted, "We've won the championship again!"

6. The man behind the counter told us at 8:30 that the 7:10 flight from Chicago wouldn't arrive before 2:00 a.m.

7. My father likes to say that kids today have it easy.

8. She quoted Song of Solomon 4:9: "Thou hast ravished my heart my sister, my spouse! How much better is thy love than wine!"

9. The new president of the class(We hope it's Connie, but who knows?)will have fund-raising as first priority.

10. Study the diagram(figure B)to understand the relationship between supply and demand.

11. The mayor's press representative made the following announcement at 2:00 p.m.: "Due to unforseen circumstances the press conference has been cancelled."

12. The senator(think what you want of her politics)certainly uses television effectively.

13. Mrs. Lazzoli(How rude!)asked him how much his new house cost him.

14. Maria has unusual talents in three areas: drafting, sailing, and baking chocolate-chip cookies.

15. From the back of the hall it was impossible to hear what Sam had to say, but I heard your remarks from the audience loudly and clearly.

16. He has high grades, but they're the result of good concentration, hard work, and a little luck.

326   Practical English: A Complete Course

17 Her hard work paid off in two ways, a check from her boss and a tidy sum from tips.

18 Julie shouted furiously, "The last person who did that was sorry she lived to tell about it!"

19 The lead sentence of the newspaper article was, "A fire, believed to have been set by an arsonist, swept through Taylor's Hardware Store last night, doing $400,000 damage."

20 The girl in the shadows (See her next to the oak tree?) is the same girl I met last week at Claire's party.

21 From early in the morning until late at night I had only two things in mind: staying warm and finding my way home.

22 Cragmont State Beach offers balmy temperatures, clear water, and beautiful white sand.

23 Our poetry unit covered the following concepts: metaphor, simile, rhyme scheme, meter, and personification.

24 That huge guy in the third row (They call him Monster Malone) is the center on their team.

25 Those two teachers (the ones who leave together each day at 4:00) are the most helpful in the school.

In the letter below correct errors in the use of colons, parentheses, apostrophes, semicolons, commas, endmarks, quotations marks, abbreviations, and paragraphing

May 14, 1987

Dear Louise,

I'm really in a fix. Do you believe (I certainly can't!) I actually have three dates for the junior prom? It's next Friday, May 20, at 9:00 pm, so I need advice fast. Here's a description of the three guys: Larry, my cousin whom I asked to take me two months ago; Tom, an absolute hunk who asked me last month; and Jason, a very sweet boy I'd really like to go with but who didn't get up the courage to ask me until two weeks ago. It sounds like a soap opera, doesn't it?

I just don't know how I ever said, "Yes, that would be wonderful!" to all three boys. My cousin is really no problem, and I can call him and explain; he's always been close, understanding, and willing to help me out of a jam. Tom's not so easy. All my friends' advice is to go with him because he's so cute and has a Nissan sports car. But I really think he's stuck on himself, to tell you the truth. And, of course, I really like Jason. You should've see how shy he was when he asked me (I just fell in love) and he has the greatest eyes.

I asked Mom (It took guts, believe me!) what to do.

"Squeekie, how do you get into these things?" she asked. "Just lucky, I guess," I answered. "Well, don't expect to use your dad's charge account to buy a formal until you straighten things out," she said, and that was that.

Louise, please give me some advice. Meantime I'll just remember my favorite Scarlet O'Hara quote: "I'll think of it tomorrow."

Love,

Squeekie

Copy the phrases below, adding capitals as needed.

1. a sony television   1. A Sony television
2. gone with the wind   2. Gone with the Wind
3. a west turn on elm street 3. a west turn on Elm Street
4. yellowstone park in spring 4. Yellowstone Park in spring
5. a school in the south   5. a school in the South

Supply endmarks in the sentences below.

6   Again he asked the boss what time it was .
7   Hasn't he finished the assignment yet ?
8   Ask if he has finished the assignment yet .
9   Watch out for that falling piano !
10 Checkers is easier to learn than chess .

Add periods to the abbreviations below that always need them.

11. NBC   12. Ave.   13. RCA   14. H.T. Stevens   15. bldg.

The underlined item in each of the following groups tells what is owned. The second item (the possessive noun) tells the name of the owner or owners. To the right of each set of words, write the correct form of the possessive noun followed by the name of the thing owned.

16. locker room the boys   16. the boys' locker room
17. compliments his friends   17. his friends' compliments
18. car my sister-in-law   18. my sister-in-law's car
19. uniforms the team   19. the team's uniform
20. lawn the Thomases   20. the Thomases' lawn

Chapter Thirteen   NAME: _____ 295

Worksheet 35B: PUNCTUATION   DATE: _____
UNIT TEST

21 it is   _it's_   24 shall not   _shan't_

22 you are   _you're_   25 Leo is   _Leo's_

23 who is   _who's_   26 should have   _should've_

Supply apostrophes as needed in the sentences below.

27 Its' hidden behind Kerry's bicycle.

28 You're your own worst enemy.

29 Its speedometer is its problem.

30 My social security number has five I's in it. Theirs have none.

31 Whose books are in rooms 103 and 105? Yours.

Chapter Thirteen   NAME: _____ 296

Worksheet 35C: PUNCTUATION   DATE: _____
UNIT TEST

Correct the punctuation errors in the following passage.

Entering Smiling Sam's used-car lot, Joni remembered her conversation with her father

"Owning a car is your first real financial responsibility," he had said. "You know you'll have to take care of your own gasoline, repairs, and insurance."

"I know, Dad," she had replied, "And I'm sure I can handle it."

She opened the door of the red Volkswagen convertible, slipped onto the seat, and gripped the steering wheel. This moment (she would always remember Thursday, April 6, 1987) fulfilled years of working, planning, and dreaming. The car was perfectly equipped with an automatic transmission; soft, black vinyl seats; and a stereo with F.M., a cassette deck, and four powerful speakers. Her head filled with plans: trips to football games with her girlfriends, shopping sprees whenever she wanted, and quiet drives on warm summer evenings.

But there were also misgivings. She asked herself how much it would cost to support the car. How many evenings a week would she have to work at the Empire Theater? And what would happen to her grades in English, Biology 2, and History?

She remembered the hours she had spent poring over "Consumer Reports" and "Car and Driver". One night she had stayed up so late reading (almost 2:00 a.m.) that her mother grew concerned. This was the car she wanted; she was certain.

She stepped out of the car and headed for the sales office to make the purchase.